Street-Smart Advice

to Christian College Students

Street-Smart
ADVICE
to Christian College Students

From a Professor's Point *of* View

Michael J. Bozack, Ph.D

VMI Publishers • Sisters, Oregon

Published 2008

Published by
VMI Publishers
Sisters, Oregon
www.vmipublishers.com

ISBN 13: 9781933204796
ISBN: 1933204796
Library of Congress: 2008942262

Printed In the USA

Cover design by Joe Bailen

This book is dedicated
to the students of Auburn University.
War Eagle.

TABLE OF CONTENTS

Why I Wrote This Book

Are you a prospective Christian college student who:

- Is anxious about attending college?
- Wants a high GPA?
- Is undecided about what college to attend?
- Wonders whether you can cut it academically?
- Is clueless about what to do with your life?
- Is unsure about living in a secular college environment?
- Worries that you will abandon Christian values in college?
- Is already in college but barely making it?

If you answered yes to any of these questions, this book is for you. My audience is primarily prospective and current Christian college students and the people who mentor them. I'm betting that your parents will spend a few dollars for a book written by a seasoned college professor who knows the ropes to success. My unique selling proposition is that, if Christian students in the target market read this book, then they will find invaluable information about the following:

- Reasons why most high school students aren't ready for college prime time

- Characteristics of the current generation of college students
- The unique situation of Christian college students in a secular university
- Seven effective strategies for guaranteed academic success
- The most common bad habits and mistakes made by college students
- What major college professors do besides teach college students
- How to manage student life outside the college classroom
- How to effectively live the Christian life as a college student in a major university

A secondary audience for the book includes parents, ministers, education professionals, and a host of affinity groups who care about education and its direction in our nation. We seek to help (1) parents understand what factors are affecting their children's education, (2) secondary educators who seek to prepare their students for college, (3) youth ministers and pastors who deal with teenagers, and (4) employers who are trying to understand today's new college graduates.

One of the handicaps to success in college is that there are few books, owner's manuals, or sympathetic professors to help guide you. You go to the local Christian book store to find a book on the subject and find blank shelves. True, there are many fine advice and devotional guides for college students written by such popular writers as Chuck Swindoll, Rick Warren, and John Maxwell, but nothing really cuts to the chase of the problems faced by Christian students who attend major universities. Most are after-the-fact books and none are written by college professors. Even the broader secular book market offers little help for college students. *Street-Smart Advice to Christian College Students* is the book I looked for but never found when I was a Christian student at a large secular university.

ACKNOWLEDGEMENTS

God has led me on an amazing journey through life.

Many fond memories of my undergrad years at Michigan State (MSU) came by Dr. Sherwood K. Haynes, past president of the American Association of Physics Teachers (AAPT). Dr. Haynes taught me to be a physics teacher who cared and was effective in communication. Thanks also to the faculty at MSU's National Superconducting Cyclotron Laboratory (NSCL), who showed me what stepping up the plate of big-league physics research was all about.

During my graduate studies at the Oregon Health and Science University (OHSU), I worked in the surface physics laboratory of Dr. Lynwood W. Swanson. It was wonderful to have a Christian mentor during my Ph.D. studies. Our work on liquid metal ion sources and the status of this group nationally led to a postdoctoral research position with Dr. John T. Yates of the Surface Science Center at the University of Pittsburgh. Working with Dr. Yates was the surface science equivalent of working for a rock star. The association opened many doors and led to my current position at Auburn University.

Two years at Western Conservative Baptist Seminary (WCBS) pursuing an M.A. in systematic theology gave me a good academic background in the Scriptures. Dr. Earl D. Radmacher, editor-in-chief of the *Nelson Study Bible,* was my mentor. WCBS taught me to eat humble pie, as I went from one of the largest universities in the nation to a campus that was so small you could toss a Frisbee across it. I nearly choked in amazement when I first drove up to the campus in Portland, Oregon and remarked "This can't be all of it."

Three years as chief surface scientist with Intel Corporation during the heyday of the early Pentium microprocessors (then called the 486) afforded me a chance to work with some of the top electrical engineers in the world during an exciting period of growth in Silicon Valley. The early workers at Intel changed the world by making the computer an affordable and ubiquitous part of world culture. It's sobering to think that something you worked on has had such a profound effect on mankind. The experience also showed me that money isn't everything, although I admit I had to find this out for myself. More on this later.

Then, thank you to several of my faithful pastors. I became a Christian in college under the late Dr. Howard F. Sudgen of South Baptist Church in Lansing, Michigan. Dr. Sudgen was a pastor's pastor and one of the best expository preachers to come from the Creator. He helped me immensely during the start of my Christian life and his enormous library and long-time association with Dr. Warren W. Wiersbe, then pastor of Moody Church in Chicago, gave me a thirst for Bible study and the courage to risk going to seminary.

After moving to the Southeast, I taught a large singles Sunday school class at First Baptist Church, Atlanta, home of *In Touch Ministries* and Dr. Charles F. Stanley. Dr. Stanley taught me how to live the Christian life, and it was the gracious hand of God who led me there during difficult times at the church. My present station is with Dr. Bill Purvis of Cascade Hills Church in Columbus, Georgia, where I teach a weekly Bible study class. Brother Bill, as we lovingly call him, is currently seen nationally on his *Real Time* program. We knew this day would come, when each of us would finally get some time to start writing Christian books. Thank you, Bill, for your friendship and support.

Last, I am grateful to the Department of Physics and the College of Sciences and Mathematics at Auburn University and want to thank Bill Carmichael and Lacey Hanes Ogle at VMI Publishers for taking a chance on a novice Christian writer whose resume looked more like a nerdy book report than one for a promising book author.

ONE

Introduction

THE NATIONAL DOWNWARD TREND IN AMERICAN EDUCATION

It's important for students to see at the outset why they are frustrated and unsuccessful with the high school–to–college transition. There are several contributing factors. Let me begin with the current educational environment in our nation.

The problems with secondary and early college education in our nation are well-documented. While our university graduate-level system remains the envy of the world and our universities attract brilliant students from all over the world who seek masters or doctorate degrees, something goes tragically wrong with our teenagers.

The best way to illustrate is to examine the impressions of an outstanding veteran high school teacher. In the March 8, 2007 issue of *USA Today*,[1] Patrick Welsh, an English teacher at T.C. Williams High School in Alexandria, Virginia and a member of *USA Today's* board of contributors, wrote an article that had classroom educators nodding with high-fives. The piece made such pointed observations on today's students that it's a good way to start this book. As a Christian student, what do you think? Is he right or wrong? Does the article make your blood boil or is Welsh off his rocker? Is it largely the rant of a burned-out high school teacher or an accurate depiction of what's going on in American schools? Does it apply only to public school students? Does it describe you? Here are excerpts from the article.

> Last month, as I averaged the second-quarter grades for my senior English classes at T.C. Williams High School in Alexandria, VA, the same familiar pattern leapt out at me. Kids who had emigrated from foreign countries—such as Shewit Giovanni from Ethiopia, Farah Ali from Guyana, and Edgar Awumey from Ghana—often aced every test, while many of their U.S.-born classmates from upper-class homes with highly educated parents had a string of C's and D's. As one would expect, the middle-class American kids usually had higher SAT verbal scores than did their immigrant classmates, many of whom had only been speaking English for a few years. What many of the American kids I taught did not have was the motivation, self-discipline or work ethic of the foreign-born kids. Politicians and education bureaucrats can talk all they want about reform, but until the work ethic of U.S. students' changes, until they are willing to put in the time and effort to master their subjects, little will change.
>
> …a study released in December by University of Pennsylvania researchers Angela Duckworth and Martin Seligman suggests that the reason so many U.S. students are "falling short of their intellectual potential" is not "inadequate teachers, boring textbooks and large class sizes" and the rest of the usual litany cited by the so-called reformers—but "their failure to exercise self-discipline." The sad fact is that in the USA, hard work on the part of students is no longer seen as a key factor in academic success.
>
> …when asked to identify the most important factors in their performance in math, the percentage of Japanese and Taiwanese students who answered "studying hard" was twice that of American students. American students named native intelligence, and some said the home environment. But a clear majority of U.S. students put the responsibility on their teachers. A good teacher, they said, was the determining factor in how well they did in math.

"Kids have convinced parents that it is the teacher or the system that is the problem, not their own lack of effort," says Dave Roscher, a chemistry teacher at T.C. Williams in this Washington suburb. "In my day, parents didn't listen when kids complained about teachers. We are supposed to miraculously make kids learn even though they are not working." As my colleague Ed Cannon puts it, "Today, the teacher is supposed to be responsible for motivating the kid. If they don't learn it is supposed to be our problem, not theirs." And, of course, busy parents guilt-ridden over the little time they spend with their kids are big subscribers to this theory.

Maybe every generation of kids has wanted to take it easy, but until the past few decades students were not allowed to get away with it. "Nowadays, it's the kids who have the power. When they don't do the work and get lower grades, they scream and yell. Parents side with the kids who pressure teachers to lower standards," says Joel Kaplan, another chemistry teacher at T.C. Williams. Every year, I have had parents come in to argue about the grades I have given in my AP English classes. To me, my grades are far too generous; to middle-class parents, they are often an affront to their sense of entitlement. If their kids do a modicum of work, many parents expect them to get at least a B. When I have given C's or D's to bright middle-class kids who have done poor or mediocre work, some parents have accused me of destroying their children's futures.

It is not only the parents, however, who are siding with students in their attempts to get out of hard work. Blame schools too. "Schools play into it," says psychiatrist Lawrence Brain, who counsels kids in public schools to manipulate guidance counselors to get them out of classes they don't like. "They have been sent a message that they don't have to struggle to achieve if things are not perfect." Neither the high-stakes state exams, such as Virginia's Standards of Learning, nor the requirements of the No Child Left Behind Act have succeeded in changing that message;

both have turned into minimum-competency requirements aimed at the lowest in our school.

As a teacher, I don't object to the heightened standards required of educators in the No Child Left Behind law. Who among us would say we couldn't do a little better? Nonetheless, teachers have no control over student motivation and ambition, which have to come from the home—and from within each student. Perhaps the best lesson I can pass along to my upper- and middle-class students is to merely point them in the direction of their foreign-born classmates, who can remind us all that education in America is still more a privilege than a right.

Take a breath. Reread the article. Chill for a minute. It's difficult to say this, but whether or not you agree with Welsh, the facts surrounding the demise of American students are indisputable. Nearly every academic study and the collective experience of thousands of teachers for over two decades have fired warning shots across the bow of the American education system. Report after report has warned that high school seniors aren't ready for college. Report after report has cautioned that something has to change or the rest of the world will eat our academic lunch. The real question is not with the evidence, which is overwhelming, but whether you as a prospective or current college student will embrace the facts and then determine to do something about it.

When asked what he would like to see changed about K–12 education in America, Craig Barrett, CEO of Intel Corporation, one of the world's leading technology companies, answered "If we could capture 1% of the hot air that has gone out on this topic and turn it into results, it would be wonderful. The results are how our kids compare to their international counterparts, particularly in math and science. The longer kids stay in the system, the worse they do compared to their international counterparts. In fourth grade, our kids are roughly comparable. By eighth grade, they are behind. By the 12th grade, they are substantially behind other industrialized nations."[2]

When I worked at Intel, Barrett was head of the vaunted Technology

Development Group, whose charter was to come up with the next-generation, miles-ahead, whiz-bang computers that we have today. He served on a national education commission that studied how to improve math and science education in K–12. In interviews, Barrett implies that few of his commission's recommendations have been taken seriously and he reminds anyone who will listen that there is more at stake that you can imagine. He's right. The stakes are huge, not only for our nation but for you personally as a college student.

Getting off to the right foot in college will take some of the effort that Welsh says you don't have—effort that will define and direct the rest of your life. But you first must gulp hard and see how you size up. How do sociologists see your generation, called the millennial generation, those born after 1978? Are you smarter, bolder, cleverer, more talented, and more affluent than your peers in other nations? Are you willing to go where previous generations haven't? Or are you more boorish, arrogant, self-indulged, pampered, and over rated? How you see yourself and your generation goes a long way toward determining your success or failure in college. Most of the news, as you will see below, is bad, but unless you realistically assess your background and abilities up through high school, you won't be able to embrace the advice offered in this book. Consider some of the research data Barrett and his commission examined.

- The Manhattan Institute (2005) reports that only 32% of high school seniors graduate with the skills they need to succeed in college.[3]
- David Spence, California's chief academic officer, reports that about 60% of freshmen in the California State University system need remedial help in math or English.[4]
- *Achieve, Inc,* a school reform group led by business leaders, found that more than 70% of high school seniors end up taking remedial English or math courses in college.[5]
- According to an analysis of students who took the 2005 ACT college admissions test, only 51% of high school seniors are ready for college reading demands.[6]

- The American Institutes for Research (AIR)[7] found that many college students don't possess sufficient knowledge to accomplish necessary everyday tasks. The AIR study showed that ~ 20% of students in college have only "basic" quantitative skills which are those necessary to compare ticket prices or calculate the cost of food.

There's more, especially in the area of science and math education. According to a National Academy of Sciences (NAS) report, *Rising Above the Gathering Storm*,[8]

- Last year, China graduated five hundred thousand engineers; India, two hundred thousand; and North America, seventy thousand.
- The U.S. trade balance in high technology goods fell from $33 billion in the black in 1990 to $24 billion in the red in 2004.
- Leadership in high energy physics, a U.S. franchise since the Manhattan Project built the atomic bomb, is shifting overseas. Beginning in 2007, the most powerful particle accelerator on earth will be outside the USA for the first time in decades (Europe's CERN lab in Switzerland). The world's largest nuclear fusion facility (ITER) is currently being built in France.
- Cost and talent advantages continue to drive businesses to pursue talent across borders. Intel announced recently it would invest $1 billion in India over five years for a research and development center. Microsoft said it would invest $1.7 billion in India.
- Despite having a sixth of the U.S. population, South Korea graduates just as many engineers.
- More than half the students attending the top U.S. engineering schools are foreign-born.

The NAS report notes that "Many adults with whom students come in contact seemingly take pride in 'never understanding' or 'never liking math.'" This is underscored by a Raytheon Corporation survey of 1,000 eleven- to thirteen-year-olds released in January 2006, which found that 84% said they would "rather clean their room, eat their vegetables, go to the dentist or take out the garbage than learn math or science."[9] Finally, a 2006 National Geographic Literacy Study[10] found that only 37% of Americans ages eighteen to twenty-four could correctly locate Iraq on a world map, 37% could find Saudi Arabia, 26% could find Iran, and only 25% could locate Israel. You read that correctly. How can students go through elementary school, junior high, high school, and college and not be able to locate Israel? Stephen Prothero, chairman of the Boston University's Department of Religion, wrote a book called *Religious Literacy: What Every American Needs to Know—and Doesn't.*[11] He found that 60% of Americans can't name five of the Ten Commandments and 50% of high school seniors think Sodom and Gomorrah were married. What happened during those fifteen years of education? Is it really cute to be dumber than a fifth grader?

Your reaction? Do you believe the studies? Can it really be that bad? Do they suffer from bias? Flawed methods? Were they performed by organizations with a vested interest in attacking the competence of American students? Are you mad? Embarrassed? Could you care less? When I share some of the data with my freshman college students, they shake their heads in near-universal disbelief. "How can those studies be right when most of the students I know, myself included, have nearly straight-A averages coming out of high school?" is a common response.

One of my goals in citing the educational research is to pry you away from your belief that you are ready for college. Yes, the studies address small cross sections of students. Secular students. Yes, many of you were educated in private Christian schools or home-school situations where the educational standards may have been higher than many public and secular schools. You don't think the studies really apply to you. You can't believe you compare so unfavorably to the rest of the world's students. But it also could be that you've been insulated from knowing your true academic prowess and you're not as ready for college as you believe.

Let me tell you what I see. After a year of college, many of my students are disenchanted with their high school education. They're angry and frustrated over not being prepared for college. After slugging it out with the core curriculum in the freshman year, most students are ready to quit, switch majors, call the whole thing off, and hunker down with their teddy bears. As the C's and D's pile up, they wonder what went wrong. As a professor, I'm tired of the drama and feel bad for my students. That's why I wrote this book—to spare you that sinking, sickening feeling of being so far behind the academic ball that you'll never be able to recover.

Christian students are not inoculated from the problems encountered by college freshmen. Hate to say it, but I find few differences academically between secular and Christian students. The first point is that most Christian students in large secular universities are not from small private Christian high schools. This means they receive the same secular, public education in high school that everyone else does. The second point is that Christian students, although devoted to issues of faith, are still members of the millennial generation, those born after 1978. You can't help but adopt some of the characteristics of that generation, which I describe in the next chapter. The third point is that secular high schools often do a better, not a worse, job of preparing students in some subject areas than home and Christian schools. This is especially true in technical subjects such as chemistry and physics, where expensive laboratory equipment is needed to teach inquiry-based science. It behooves you to understand how the secular world has affected your performance in college.

MONETARY AND SOCIETAL VALUE OF BEING A GOOD STUDENT

Studies clearly show that college educated people make more money over their lifetimes than people without a college education. The disparity is about a million dollars. While money is not the major motivating force for Christian students, you should nevertheless be aware of some of the economics involved with college education.

- Census Bureau data[12] shows that a bachelor's degree is currently worth about $23,000 a year, which is the average yearly gap in adult earning between a high school diploma and a bachelor's degree.
- In terms of percentages, in 1970, workers with bachelor's degrees

earned 36% more money than employees with only high school diplomas. Now that gap is 76%. When accrued over an average lifetime working span of forty years the differential results is ~ $1 million more in earnings.

- Using 2004 data, college graduates made an average of $51,554 compared to $28,645 for adults with a high school diploma.
- High school dropouts earned an average of $19,169 and those with graduate degrees (masters and doctorate) made an average of $78,093.

Despite the dollar disparities all is not lost if you're not a college graduate. The job outlook for people without a bachelor's degree is fairly optimistic. That is good news for those not planning to get a college degree. Millions of job openings are projected for high school graduates over the decade 2004–2014 according to U.S. Bureau of Labor Statistics.[13] The number expected is roughly forty million, divided into one group (twenty-five million) who possess a high school diploma and another group (fifteen million) that has some college or tech school education. That's a lot of jobs and more than twice the number of openings for college graduates. The hitch is that many of these job openings will be in occupations that require some kind of training after high school, either on-the-job training, taking a few college or vocational classes at a technical school, or some kind of apprenticeship program. Later in the book, I will make the case that not everyone is suited for college. Why waste four good years of your life if you're happy doing work in an industry that doesn't require a college or advanced degree? There are highly successful people in all walks of society who didn't go to college. But be aware of the salary differential over the course of a lifetime.

Dollars aside, there are other, more intangible benefits that accrue to a college education. Here is a list of some that have been important to me:

THE BACHELORS DEGREE BADGE

Around the middle of the last century, a high school diploma was sufficient to open the doors to professional society. Not any more. Now you need a college degree. A bachelor's degree is society's badge of accomplishment, the needed key for entry into many of the highest paying and most responsible vocations.

One good thing about a college education is that, once you have a bachelor's degree, nobody can take it away from you. It represents a quantifiable and universally recognized standard of achievement. It opens the door to parts of society that are shut to those who stop at a high school diploma. It broadens your possibilities, the places you can work, the vocations you can pursue, and the opportunities that await you. You always have it in your hip pocket and never have to worry about going back to school to get it. To realize the significance of your college diploma, you only need to peruse monster.com or other job postings sites to see how many times the words "college diploma required" are cited. In many cases, it doesn't matter what sort of bachelor's degree you have, just so you have one. It's a minimum prerequisite for entry into many of the more desirable jobs today.

SATISFACTION OF ACHIEVEMENT

Not everyone can get a college degree. It takes time and effort. There is a level of satisfaction that accrues to earning a college degree that gets sweeter with time. You appreciate the fact that not everyone can do it. To those who get good grades in college, you will appreciate the fact that not everyone can graduate summa or magna cum laude. A college degree is like the stripes and bars solders wear on their uniforms. It's a lifelong source of pride and satisfaction.

I've had heated debates with friends with high school diplomas who bemoan the fact that college graduates get paid more than they do just because they are college graduates. The pay differential is especially hard to defend when it's clear that a high school graduate can do the same job at least as good as a college graduate. While it's true that some college graduates can graduate with little common sense and even less street smarts when it comes to the practical world, it's also true that a college graduate spends four extra years in the salt mines of academia than high school graduates, losing four years of wage earnings in the process. If you were given the assignment to come up with a list of appropriate criteria to determine an employee's starting pay, you would be forced to conclude that the extra four years of work and study should be worth something in the paycheck. It may not be fair, but a degree is at least an objective measurement of achievement that can be pegged to salary. You want objective and not subjective criteria when it comes to judging your job performance. It's difficult to assign point values to effort and good intentions.

SATISFACTION FROM AN ENLARGED VIEW OF THE WORLD

Most college students won't appreciate this until later in life, but a liberal-arts college education opens your soul to the vast array of esthetic and cultural nuances in the world. Without a college education, it's doubtful I would have much appreciation for the great masterpieces of Michelangelo, the artistic brilliance of Mozart and Bach, the mathematical genius of Einstein, or the literary talents of Wordsworth and Coleridge. Without history courses, it would be difficult to appreciate the aesthetics of the gothic cathedrals of Europe, the Renaissance, the mistakes and contributions of Western Civilization, and the influence and role of Christianity in world history. Without science courses, it would be impossible for our leaders to make educated choices when it comes to medical treatments, global warming, and how to fight the war on terror by using our technology advantage. It's impossible to put a price tag on the enlarged view of our world offered by a college degree. It may not be this year, or next year, but someday you will thank your college or university for making you take courses spanning the broad liberal-arts spectrum in order to make you a well-rounded citizen and not merely a job seeker.

SHOULD EVERYONE GO TO COLLEGE?

It's a given today that children must go to college. I'm not convinced. Every year, perfectly good time and money is wasted by students who aren't ready for college prime time. I talk to students nearly every month who say they hate college and don't want to be there in the first place. If it was up to them, they would work for a couple of years and find out who they are and what they want in life. A good way to answer these questions is by observing how the real world works outside the protected walls of a university. It's not enough for students to attend college merely to please mommy and daddy. College is not for everyone. You should be aware of the important issues involving your college decision.

First, it may be that you are just not ready for a major college. In particular, many students from the State of Alabama are better suited to a junior college before jumping into Auburn or Alabama. The transition from a small rural high school to a major college is simply too radical for many students; they are better served by smaller classes and a home-town environment similar to high school. If a junior college has adequate college prep courses that seamlessly transfer to major colleges, community colleges offer a viable option. According to the American Association of Community Colleges,[14] about 46% of all undergraduates are community college students (eleven million in 1,202 institutions). Junior college students have lots of company. The downside is that some junior colleges are little more than glorified high schools and have weak academic standards. Such a situation only postpones the inevitable shock to major college standards. If you plan to use the junior college option as a stepping stone to a major college, carefully examine the reputation and quality of their college prep course offerings.

Second, it may be that you just want to learn a trade. The Bureau of Labor Statistics predicts huge numbers of jobs in the service, education, and health care segments of the future U.S. economy.[15] It's expected that the United States will add over ten million new jobs over the next decade that will span fields from science and technology to entrepreneurship to arts and entertainment to finance, law, and health care. Everybody is not suited for the high demand computer and engineering jobs. If you know that you're interested in say, cosmetology, auto repair, computer repair, radiation therapy, dental assistant, or any of the scores of professions that require certification or an associate's degree, then don't waste time attending a four-year college. Nearly every year, for example, I have female students that are interested in fashion merchandising. While AU has an excellent program in fashion, there are several two-year, specialty institutions that would be better choices for certain students. Search yourself, and see if you are better suited for a trade school. Most trades have outstanding job prospects and exceptional job flexibility, meaning you can work anywhere in the country. You don't need a bachelor's degree to be an outstanding chef; better to go to a cooking school and intern at a restaurant under an established chef.

Third, there is the disparity in lifetime wealth to consider. As we showed above, college graduates, on average, make considerably more money in a lifetime than their non-college peers. You will find, however, that it's not the money you make, but the satisfaction you receive, that makes the difference in life. Money can't buy happiness and shouldn't be a major part of the career decision for Christians. There is joy in seeing how God provides your needs; if you make an obscene amount of money, it's easy to rely on the money and not on God for your happiness. Many filthy rich people are miserable and unhappy. Don't buy the lie Hollywood tries to sell you that you have to make a lot of money to be happy and successful. Jesus was pretty successful and he died without a dime.

Fourth, it's best to get your college degree earlier than later. While a year or two of work experience will help many students determine if they want to attend college, it's possible to wait too long. Ask any older, re-entrant student, or single mom who returns to college after being away to raise their children. It's not a cakewalk. While the number of returning students I teach increases every year, you are surrounded by eighteen- to twenty-year-olds who make you feel ancient. Returning students need to have a strong self-image and high motivation to get back to the classroom. After being out of school for a few years, the transition back to the demands of studying is difficult. You're not used to the hectic schedule and having your nights taken up by concentrated effort. The upside to postponing college is that older students usually love learning and have a wholly different appreciation of it. Instead of playing the game of school, returning students want to learn and enjoy it.

WHAT ABOUT ADVANCED PLACEMENT (AP) COURSES?

Years of educational research have shown that the best predictor of success in college is the rigor of a student's high school courses. Enter Advanced

Placement (AP) courses. Parents and students alike ask me about AP. It's a program that allows bright secondary students to get a jump start on college by taking college-level courses while still in high school. After the course, a student takes the AP subject exam, a national standardized test administered by the College Board. Currently, AP offers courses in thirty-seven subject areas, the most popular being history, English, biology, and calculus. In 2006, 15% of all students passed at least one AP exam.[16] Sounds great, right? But the question is whether AP courses are really substantive, difficult, and college preparatory. It depends on who you ask. AP is a step in the right direction, meaning any attempt to promote rigor in high school is welcome, but not all of us are convinced AP courses measure up to actual college-level courses. Many college professors view them with suspicion. More show than go. To show you what I'm talking about, almost no institution in the SEC accepts AP physics credit.

The current mad rush to pile students into AP courses reminds me of keeping up with the Joneses. Loading up on academic materialism. An AP arms race. In 2006, more than 1.2 million students took 2.1 million AP exams, twice the number eleven years ago.[17] Nearly fourteen thousand graduating seniors had amassed nine or more AP exams during high school, a 743% increase over a decade ago.[18]

The AP arms race traces largely to the high-stakes college admission process. Simply stated, AP courses pad the resume of incoming students. Students taking AP courses are often given extra weight when high schools and colleges calculate incoming GPAs since AP offerings are perceived to be the most rigorous courses. Some students even attempt to scam the system by taking easy online AP courses from other schools. But for my money, the best summary of how many of us in the college ranks view AP courses is given by Joe Britt, eighteen, a senior at Fairfax (Virginia) High School: "You're not trying to be educated; you're trying to look good to colleges, everyone is fighting for these few slots."[19] Thank you, Joe, for being honest. Edith Waldstein, vice-president for enrollment management at Wartburg College in Waverly, Iowa, observes that admitted students who brag about how many AP courses they completed "really weren't in many ways ready for the rigor of our college curriculum."[20] That's also my experience. Many AP courses seem to be good mostly for impressing parents and college admissions committees. They make money for the AP test generators ($82 per test) and let parents bulge their chests when talking about their brilliant kids. But as far as substituting for an actual college course such as physics, calculus, or chemistry, it's not clear at all that AP courses measure up. My advice on AP courses? Patrick Welsh, our favorite English teacher at T.C. Williams High School in Alexandria, Virginia, and whose article appeared at the beginning of this book, says it best: "Don't believe the labels in a school curriculum guide. Check out who's teaching the courses, not just whether they have an AP moniker. It's better for a child to have a great teacher in a regular course than a poor teacher in an AP course. Most of all, don't believe the propaganda coming from all sides about AP. In the year of its 50th anniversary, the Advanced Placement program should not be reduced to a fad."[21]

TWO

The Students of Today

THE MILLENNIAL GENERATION

Students benefit by understanding their generation. The current generation of college students is called millennials by sociologists. If you were born between 1978 and 2000, you're a millennial (sometimes called Gen Y). A 2007 estimate[22] showed that millennials make up 26% (seventy million) of the overall U.S. population. Many of the sociological characteristics of millennials allow me to trace the trials and tribulations of college achievement to your prior experiences and education. There is a cause and effect relationship, even for Christian students. Sociologists have identified several characteristics that impact how you view the world and affect your past and present education. As you read this section, ask yourself if the traits of the millennial generation apply to you.

HELICOPTER PARENTS

Neil Howe and William Strauss in their book *Millennials Rising*[23] characterize millennials as America's most protected and watched-over generation. The people who are watching them are helicopter parents, defined as parents who hover, take care of millennials, fight their battles, address their needs, and micromanage their lives. Helicopter parents regard their kids as delicate wallflowers that should be protected from anything resembling failure; a child's self-esteem depends on never having the slightest setback, upset, or adversity. Helicopter parents are determined to do anything they can to make life better for their children and work unceasingly to create a perfect childhood for their kids. On the surface, you may wonder what the problem is. Helicopter parents seem to be doing what parents of all generations have tried to do—they want to make their kids' lives better than their own.

Trouble is, when helicopter parents create an artificial, dependent, and utopian environment for their children, their good intentions end up hurting the very children they seek to protect. Millennial children eventually go out into the big bad world and face stressful situations, failures, and assaults to their perfect bubble. One of those stresses is college. Psychologists long ago discovered that children need to face adversity, challenge, and competition to grow into adulthood. Did you read that? You need challenge and competition. This should be no surprise to Christians. The Bible affirms that trials and valleys in our life make us stronger and force us to live closer to Christ. Ask yourself where David or Joseph or Abraham or Moses or the apostles or anyone of stature in the Bible would be without adversity. Adversity makes us like Christ.

Helicopter values seep into the educational establishment in subtle ways. Take the recent national movement against playground games. Playground games, goes the argument, are too competitive and might harm the delicate egos of children who are not athletically inclined. Some kid might strike out, throw a wild ball, make an error, fumble the football, come in last place in a race, or fail to do as many pull-ups as more muscular peers. But the experts say that protecting children from playing dodge ball because Johnny's self-esteem might blow a tire if he gets hit early and has to leave the game, does Johnny few favors. Anthony Pellegrini, professor of early childhood education at the University of Minnesota, says the arguments against playground games are "ridiculous…even squirrels play chase."[24] When helicopter parents swoop in, students can't practice finding their own answers. Laura Berk, professor of psychology at Illinois State University and author of *Awakening Children's Minds*[25] claims "Parents who overdo may have a child who doesn't engage in the thinking process." Matt Thornhill of the Boomer Project, a marketing firm specializing in generational research, traces the roots of helicopter parents to soccer moms. "They [millennials] are used to constant feedback because every accomplishment was cherished, honored, and discussed," Thornhill says. "That included trophies to every soccer player on every team."[26]

GROWING UP AT LIGHT SPEED

Ask any adult over forty what they think about their children and they will marvel at how fast they are growing up. Millennial kids are bigger, stronger, and smarter than any previous generation. Visit any Little League baseball game and you will find twelve-year-olds who are over six feet tall with size fourteen shoes. Visit the Biltmore Mansion in North Carolina, constructed for a wealthy family who lived in the early twentieth century, and you will find adult beds that are so small that only ten-year-olds could fit into them today. It's not just size that is different about millennials. Millennials also have more exposure to and experimentation with adult behavior than any previous generation. Puberty begins at around age ten. Sex education starts during elementary school. Movies, TV, mass media, and changing social norms bombard students with mature topics far in advance of when they're ready to hear it. Millennial college students describe the high school–to–college transition, not in terms of the new freedoms it brings, but rather more of the same, because they have already been partying and drinking in high school.

Millennials are the most informed generation to have lived on planet earth, but critical life management skills such as discipline, work ethic, deferred gratification, and staying on task lag far behind the sheer volume of information. As a result, millennial students frequently lack the ability to explore a topic in depth, and college professors have found that our students lack systematic methods for managing their life, their studies, their time, their money, and their personal life and health. While college students have always lived by the seat of their pants, today there is less hands-on mentoring by parents, teachers, and pastors on what is acceptable behavior. Most of the ethical behaviors learned by students are gleaned by the culture and peer groups instead of the family, church, or synagogue.

Fed High on the Self-Esteem Hog

Millennials raised by helicopter parents are led to believe they can do anything. Nothing is criticized, everyone gets a trophy, and critiques are relative. The chief goal is to preserve self-esteem, even if it comes at the expense of truth. Now, there's nothing wrong with imparting to young minds a healthy self-confidence and fearless pursuit of life. Confidence is a chief ingredient for success. But the question concerns how accurate and balanced the message is. Time for a reality check. Students can't nurture their soul or feel good about their performance if parents and teachers feed them a steady diet of junk praise that inflates the ego and leaves them yearning for true self-assessment. The evidence is strong that undeserved praise can do more harm than good, especially when dispensed thoughtlessly to impressionable teenagers. What's more, with problem-solving parents constantly engineering their kids' life, the kids don't develop the resolve to address the problems all students face in college. This is especially true for Christian students who should be learning to depend on God for wisdom and guidance.

Rejection Not in the Vocabulary

Millennial students have high career aspirations but unrealistic expectations about what it takes to reach them. Nobody has told them the truth about how they match up against their peers in other parts of the world. Nobody has given them the real facts on how difficult it is to be successful. Nobody has told them that most of the MTV world of fame, fortune, and celebrity is just an illusion. Nobody has told them how worthless their high school grades are at showing what they really know. But the real world, starting with college, is different. Everyone gets rejected. Few glide through with a 4.0 GPA. But many of my incoming freshmen prefer to think that if they align themselves with the right peer group, the right professors, the right sororities, and let their folks fight their battles when they get into trouble, that they'll be impervious to heartache. I can't count the times I've heard high school athletes brag about how they are going to make the pros and how AP students are going to breeze through college, though only a tiny fraction actually do.

Nothing wrong with being a supportive parent, but when it goes over to coddling, stroking, housing, and waiting on children well into their twenties, then parental concern becomes codependent enabling that defers adulthood and the march to maturity. The problem with trying to be perfect is that nobody is. Both teachers and parents need to call a spade a spade and, if a child's performance on a math test is terrible, then they need to truthfully know it. If all content is open to interpretation and evaluation is subjective, then what can students believe?

DEFERRED ADULTHOOD

Millennials as a group grow up faster but leave the nest slower than previous generations. Past generations were concerned about the number of "boomerang" children who moved back home after college and stayed well into their twenties; but millennials, by comparison, have deferred adulthood in a number of other measures of adulthood. A study in *Contexts*[27] (2004), a journal of the American Sociological Society, compared young people now with those who lived forty years ago. They found that by age thirty, only 46% of millennial women and 31% of millennial men had finished school, left home, got married, had a child, or reached financial independence. In 1960, by contrast, 77% of women and 65% of men had reached the same mile-markers of adulthood. Analysts estimate that roughly eighteen million adults between the ages of twenty to thirty-four live with their parents, which amounts to about a third of that age group. The book, *Mom, Can I Move Back in With You?*[28] observes that "The parents of the 39 million twenty-somethings in the United States face the unprecedented challenge of their children's prolonged adolescence." It's not that multigenerational households are inherently destructive, because extended families have lived under the same roof throughout history, but when living with mom and dad becomes a license for mooching off them for a few more years while you find yourself, it's a problem.

FAME AND FORTUNE INFATUATION

Ask the average young person on the street to list the top goals of his generation, and it's likely that they want to be rich and famous. Celebrity is about money, fame, and power. Teen-centered networks such as MTV and E! air programs about the lifestyles of the rich and famous and their $7 million castles in Beverly Hills. Paparazzi feed us pictures of Paris, Britney, and the Hollywood bad girls. Supermarket tabloids are chock full of the latest news on Brad and Angelina. There is little doubt that Gen Y relates to loaded and spoiled celebrities. The infatuation was illustrated recently while I was waiting for a movie at the local Carmike Theater. During the movie promos, Carmen Electra was quoted as saying "Life is not worth living unless there is a camera around." Secular students aren't the only ones who suck off our infatuation with celebrity role models; Christian students can be equally guilty.

A Pew Research Center survey[29] (2007) found that Gen Y's top life goals are to be rich (81%) and famous (51%). The percentages are breathtaking. Money and fame. That's the ticket of choice for most Gen Y students in my freshman classes. Everyone wants to be glamorous, to be in front of a camera, and to have a top-of-the-line Lexus. Gen Y loves to revel in attention having been showered with prizes and acclaim for years. When I see college students obsessing on dollars, I'm reminded of Allan Bloom's classic book *The Closing of the American Mind*,[30] which held that the academic crisis in colleges is, fundamentally, a spiritual crisis brought on by the cultural decadence of an affluent consumer society.

That money is driving the bus for Gen Y was also found in an annual survey (2005) of college freshman by the Higher Education Research Institute at UCLA.[31] To be "very well off financially" was cited to be "essential" or "very important" by 74.5% of the respondents, up from 41.9% in 1967. Contrastingly, "developing a meaningful philosophy of life" dropped in importance from 85.8% (1967) to 45% (2005). To see the importance of money to millennial students, walk over to the average freshman designer dorm room. A National Retail Federation (NRF) survey[32] of 6,141 people (2005) found that the average college freshman spends $1,152 during their off-to-college shopping spree. Parents can expect to spend anywhere from a few hundred to thousands of dollars on dorm-room décor, electronics, furniture, clothes, banners, microwaves, blow dryers, and so on. The number can easily balloon up to $5–7K. You ought to see the cardboard mountain of trash each fall at the AU Quad Dorms as freshmen move in with their new goodies. AU even offers a Move-in-Mania service during welcome week with on-call guys that help coeds carry all their stuff to the dorm rooms. A small army is needed. Millennial students view their dorm rooms as a fashion statement. They want decorator dorm rooms. The NRF reported that parents and their college kids spent $3.6 billion in 2006 to decorate their dorm rooms and apartments, second only to Christmas seasonal sales. J.C. Penny's even has a back-to-school Website to help you spend your money. Good golly molly.

SOCIALLY, ETHNICALLY, AND CULTURALLY TOLERANT

Millennials have grown up with terms like multiculturalism and diversity rammed down their throats. They are more tolerant of a variety of ethnic and cultural viewpoints and lifestyles than previous generations. Even in the heart of Dixie it's no longer surprising to observe mixed-ethnic dating couples on college campuses. Studies by the Gallup Poll[33] (2006) showed that 60% of eighteen- to twenty-nine-year-olds have dated someone of a different race. Teenage Research Unlimited[34] has found that 60% of teenagers say they have friends from diverse ethnic backgrounds.

Social connections in prior generations revolved around close relationships with a few good friends or a single, exclusive significant other. Millennials are less likely to be paired off in couple relationships and are more likely to engage in group activities with brief intimate encounters. Bisexual, gay, and multiracial relationships are not off the table. Sorry to tell you this parents, but shacking up, a term used to denote the freedom to experiment with overnight intimacies with a relative stranger, are commonplace among millennial college students.

LOW REGARD FOR CONVENTIONAL SOCIAL NORMS

Millennials as a group toss traditional social norms and standards of behavior to the wind and prefer to live by their own rules. You might remember the widely-circulated photograph of the Northwestern University women's lacrosse team that visited President Bush in July, 2005. Most of the athletes wore flip-flops, a previously unheard-of dress code for a White House event. Jean Twenge, associate professor of psychology at San Diego State and the author of *Generation Me*, [35] finds that "It goes beyond etiquette. It's not just about manners. It's more obliviousness that characterizes it—just not thinking about what other people think and other people's feelings." Studies reveal that millennials display low concern about making a good impression or showing courtesy. Remember the dress for success idea? Forget it. Visit the average college classroom and you'll find students who look like they just rolled out of bed and threw on a dirty tee shirt and sweatpants. Malcolm Henderson, a freshman at James Madison University, says that "The only time I'd say people worry about what they look like is when they go to a party or social event…there's no real need to impress a professor"[36] Apparently, there's no need to impress a client either, given the culture war going on between employers and millennial employees who insist on wearing whatever they want to at work. The Marlowe Crowne Social Desirability Scale[37] finds that 62% of millennial college students say they pay little attention to social conventions. This compares to 50% in 1958. AP–Ipsos polling data (2005) concluded that 70% of U.S. adults believe people are ruder now than twenty years ago and 93% blamed parents for failing to teach manners. Public Agenda (2002)[38] found that only 9% of adults thought kids they see in public are respectful toward adults. Twenge traces the collapse of manners to society's focus on individual rights in recent decades. I attribute it to rudeness and self-centered, me-first, attitudes. Thankfully, not all millennial students think rudeness is cool; I have scores of students in my classes who are respectful and a joy to teach.

GROWING GENDER GAP IN ACADEMIC PERFORMANCE

Millennial boys are falling behind girls in terms of high school and college academic performance. Take their sheer numbers alone. At the University of North Carolina, for example, the current freshman class is 60% female.[39] A study in Maine showed that women compose 63% of the public college population.[40] College graduation rates show that 133 women (57%) graduate for every 100 men.[41] Department of Education data shows that women earn nearly three-fifths of the bachelor's degrees. The disparity is not due to the ratio of boys and girls in society; Census Bureau data (2004) shows that there are more men than women in the age group eighteen to twenty-four (15 million vs 14.2 million).[42]

The reason for female dominance is not difficult to understand. Millennial girls take tougher courses in high school, they get better grades, they have better work habits, and they generally take school more seriously. This is readily observed in my physics courses each year. While physics is traditionally viewed as a "guy course" it's nearly clockwork that seven out of ten of the top students in my classes are women. Many of the guys are unmotivated, with terrible study habits and poor reading skills. The numbers will continue to tilt toward women unless we change something fundamental in the way boys view and pursue education.

DIGITAL NATIVES

Technology pervades millennial lifestyles. You know that technology is important to millennial college students when iPods are ranked higher than drinking beer in a 2006 *Lifestyle and Media Study* by the Student Monitor.[43] Technology is used not only at school but to maintain relationships. Digital native is a term used to describe millennials as the first generation who grew up in a world saturated by computers, cable TV, cell phones, IM, text messaging, iPods, and social networking Websites such as Facebook. Millennials are the first wireless sociologically-connected group of humans on earth.

Most millennials get heavy with technology starting in middle school. A study of eighteen- to twenty-four-year-olds by Greenberg

Quinlan Rosner, an international consulting firm, found that the average age for first Internet use was twelve years and three months.[44] Roughly 24% of the 1,021 youngsters they surveyed said their first exposure to the Internet was before they were ten years old. The average amount of time spent online each week was 21.3 hours. A related survey of twenty-eight thousand students at ninety-six colleges and universities performed by Richard Katz of the nonprofit organization Educause showed that some students are spending "literally 10, 12, 14, 16 hours **a day** online."[45] A study by the American College Health Association showed that 18.5% of college students at Michigan State attributed low grades or dropping a class to the amount of time spent on the web surfing or playing computer games.[46] The effect was found to be twice as great for men as women. Michael Bugeja, author of *Interpersonal Divide: The Search for Community in a Technological Age,* questions whether this is a good thing. "Not only are the students addicted—the institutions of learning are addicted," he says, and no one seems to be studying its impact on learning; rather, "We're still operating as if access is going to improve learning."[47] Most of my college students can relate to Ball State junior Ben Mangona, who admits "There's times when I should be doing homework and instead am on MySpace and Facebook or instant messenger. It happens to a lot of us. It's there at our fingertips and…sometimes it pulls us away from things we need to do."[48] Clearly, millennials are shaped by technology. Electronics even exists to help college students wash clothes and order food. A service called E-Suds allows students to determine which washers are available in their dorms. An email, phone call, or PDA announces when the wash cycle is completed. A new service called DCsnacks.com allows students at George Washington and Georgetown to order ice cream, pizza, condoms, and other common late-night commodities with a mouse click. Campusfood.com provides menus from local restaurants for over three hundred campuses around the country where students can order food for delivery.

Gen Y's thirst for digital electronics rears its most ubiquitous head in entertainment; specifically, too much of it. Students will cut classes, postpone graduation, fail to study for tests, and skip class projects if it interferes with Desperate Housewives, Dancing with the Stars, or any number of game shows, movies, and concerts. One student I knew took an extra half year to graduate because she refused to take a required night lab because it was scheduled on American Idol night. The availability of entertainment and media are serious threats to the current generation of students. A recent article in the *Chicago Tribune* highlights the issue with a headline "Media Options Swamp Nation."[49] The piece showed that the average American spends 9.6 hours a day consuming media—watching television, surfing the Internet, and going to the movies. Two months of the year are spent watching TV. Teenagers today are the most entertained children who have ever lived on planet earth. As a result, it's no coincidence that college students are also some of the most academically derelict in history. Nielsen Media Research (2004–05)[50] concluded that the average college student watches more than twenty-four hours of TV a week, which is nearly double the amount of time most students spend in class (twelve to eighteen hours). That is a day of TV watching each week. According to Vicki Courtney, author of the book *Logged On and Tuned Out*, the average teenager spends seventy-two hours per week using electronic media.[51] That's three days.

Millennial students might ask, "What's the problem? What's wrong with entertainment? What's wrong with having fun and enjoying yourself?" For one thing, it seduces you away from reality. The cushy world of entertainment promotes couch-potato attitudes toward life. Students hooked on media substitute watching for doing and morph you into a mindless spectator programmed by media executives to contribute to their Nielsen ratings. For every hour you watch TV, you could have spent that hour studying, participating in productive activities, church events, helping people, writing papers, and a host of various and sundry creative activities. Nothing wrong with entertainment, we all need it; we all have stresses in life that call for relief, but when entertainment becomes the prime directive to which you ascribe, you are succumbing to second-rate citizenship in the real world. The very people you respect on television, in the movies, and on the Internet didn't get where they are by spending a majority of their lives numbing down on entertainment.

To show you how bad it can get, a couple of weeks ago, a parent called me with a question about his eighth grader. His boy's grades had taken a dive over the last school year. We chatted about the usual possibilities—drugs, laziness, stress at home, boredom, hormones, girlfriend problems, learning disabilities, too many extracurricular activities, too many hours of TV, and so on. None seemed to account for the poor grades. Then it dawned on me to ask if his boy was text messaging on his cell phone. A look at the phone bill turned up 19,300 text messages in the previous month. We couldn't believe it. How can you do nineteen thousand of anything during a month and expect to get anything done? That averages out to be about 27 messages per hour assuming you never sleep. No way can anybody be productive when you're gabbing that much over the course of a month.

RIDING THE CREST OF GRADE INFLATION

Any book on student performance needs to talk about grade inflation. Here are some observations on grade inflation and how it affects the high school–to–college transition.

DEPENDENCE ON GRADE INFLATION TO MIMIC TRUE PERFORMANCE

Grade inflation is a major problem in education. It's rampant in secondary schools and is starting to rear its ugly head in colleges. Consider for a minute what inflation means. In economics, when money is inflated it means it becomes less valuable. If the economy is inflated, a dollar buys fewer goods and services than when the economy is flat; there are too many less valuable greenbacks in circulation during inflationary periods. Gasoline is a good example. Many baby-boomers remember when the cost of gas was about fifty cents per gallon. It's currently much higher. The quality and quantity of the gas hasn't changed, but the cost of it has increased. A dollar clearly does not buy the same amount of gas today as it did years ago. You get less for your money.

The same is true of grades. Grade inflation means it's no longer the case that an A means excellent, a B means good, a C means average, a D means poor, and an F means failure. Inflated grades are devalued because teachers are assigning too many A's and B's to students who haven't earned them. When everyone gets A's and B's, it's difficult to know who is outstanding, who is average, and who should flunk. Think of the scoring system used for Olympic figure skaters. When the scores are all 9.5 or better, it's difficult to discriminate a good performance from a bad performance. Standards erode. You can't tell who is good at something and who is bad at something. When grades inflate, brainiacs in calculus get the same grade as slackers who can't do a simple derivative. There are too many A's in B's in academic circulation and not enough D's and F's. When too many dollars are in circulation, money becomes too common and loses its value. Grade inflation follows similar laws.

That grades are inflating isn't just my imagination. Out of 47,317 applications received by UCLA in 2006, nearly twenty-one thousand had GPAs of 4.0 and above.[52] That's an incredible 44%. Nationally, the UCLA Higher Education Research Institute found that almost 23% of incoming college freshman in 2005 had a GPA of A (in 1975, the percentage was about half that).[53] How is this possible given the current deplorable performance of secondary students on standardized achievement tests? The answer is grade inflation. Jess Lord, dean of admissions at Haverford College in Pennsylvania notes that "We're seeing 30, 40 valedictorians at a high school because they don't want to make those distinctions between students."[54] In 2004, more than eight hundred high school valedictorians applied to Notre Dame (three hundred were rejected).[55] According to federal studies, the average GPA in high school has increased from 2.68 to 2.94 between 1990 and 2000. SchoolMatch, an educational audit company, found that more than 70% of the schools and districts studied had average GPAs significantly higher than they should have been, based on standardized test scores.[56] Colleges are also beginning to see grade creep. *Declining by Degrees,*[57] a PBS documentary, recently reported on professors in research-oriented universities who make few demands on students in large lecture sections and hand out inflated grades.

College professors who spend time in the front lines of teaching can readily see how grade inflation arises. There are three major factors.

SPINELESS ADMINISTRATORS, EGO, POWER, AND POMPOSITY

Principals and school administrators who don't support their teachers' decisions in the classroom open a wide door to grade inflation. Here's a typical scenario. A spoiled student who is unhappy with a low grade on an assignment returns home and blasts the teacher, throwing a major temper tantrum for the parents. Helicopter parents, who are used to spoiling their kids, can't accept that their kids are getting low grades. It's too bruising to their fragile egos. No way is their kid at fault. So they call the school principal and complain up one side and down the other about how their kids have never received less than a B on an assignment. Since it can't possibly be Little Johnny's fault, there must be something lacking, incompetent, unfair, or stupid with the teacher.

Parents who can't stand that their kid comes in second place are a major contributor to grade inflation. Arkansas has a high school Smart Core curriculum that parents can choose for their kids that offers a heavy dose of science and mathematics. But nearly one in ten parents chose the easier Common Core program, opting for the easier curriculum.[58] When parents can't accept the fact of their kid getting less an A, the tactics they employ to intimidate teachers, principals, coaches, and other educational professionals shoots the entire educational system in the foot. You only need to go the nearby Little League baseball game in your neighborhood to see what I mean. Parents are getting thrown out of the ballpark more than their kids. An umpire who calls Little Johnny out at the plate is subjected to a verbal assault of four letter words. Sons and daughters who see this learn to defer to mommy and daddy to bail them out and fight their battles. It breeds lower standards due to the constant and incessant criticism of honorable teachers who only wish to step up and make a difference. Eventually, it's not worth it.

When teachers sense their competence and job security is in jeopardy due to administrators who tolerate unacceptable behavior from students and parents, there is ambiguity on who is really in control. Who is the dog, and who is the tail? If principals allow aggressive parents to dictate policy and interfere with a healthy educational environment, teachers find little support for excellence. The tail (the parents) begins to wag the dog (the educational professionals) and the educational environment succumbs to amateurs calling the shots. Eventually, teachers are worn down and give up to the prevailing system of mediocrity. You can't fight city hall forever. Easier to just give Little Johnny an A to shut him and his parents up and spend more time on students who really appreciate the help with learning.

SLIPPERY SLOPE OF GENERATIONAL ACHIEVEMENT

A second factor in grade inflation involves progressively lower standards of expected achievement. Take the current textbooks for the standard freshman physics course. Pedagogically, the textbooks are better than ever; color graphics, beautiful photography, tons of illustrations, chapter objectives, glossaries, ancillaries, Websites, computer simulations, study guides, workbooks, and sample test questions. You couldn't ask for more study helps. But the textbooks are also watered down from textbooks produced a generation ago. The material is less rigorous, there is less mathematics, and the coverage is gauged at a lower level than textbooks of my generation. It's not necessarily bad; I'm merely noting a trend.

Then take the amount of material professors are covering in a semester. It's nowhere near the quantity of information covered fifteen years ago. When I go back and review my course outlines, I was able to get through almost double the material in a semester compared to now. It's becoming harder and harder to reach my coverage goals in a course. Not that quantity is the important metric in college courses, because many college courses push so hard to complete a set amount of chapters that students do well just to hang on throughout the course. But professors have to proceed at a reasonable pace in order to provide comprehensive coverage of the subject matter, especially when there are subsequent courses which need the material as prerequisites. What is slowing us up? Are we talking slower with age? No, our students are slowing us up. The students of today are unable to keep up with a reasonable course speed because they lack the prerequisite skills that should have been learned in previous courses; and worse, they quit on courses if the rate is too high. They refuse to put in the work necessary to keep up. A professor either has to slow down to match their pace, flunk half the class, or admit that very few students are going to learn anything. It's a balancing act for me every semester. If I go too fast, students tune out and quit. If I go too slowly, well, I can't really go too slowly. When textbooks are dumbed down and students can't keep up with a reasonable course rate, the average performance level slides downward and grade inflation results.

THE FEEL-GOOD EDUCATIONAL CULTURE

The consequences of the feel-good educational culture have dramatic effects on grade inflation. The logic is simple. If grades are based on anything other than actual student achievement, then there is an inevitable erosion of objective criteria by which to evaluate performance. Feel-good schemes offer all manner of strange ideas on how to evaluate students. College professors see them every day in the variety of things students tell us should matter regarding their grades. Let me give you three of the feel-good schemes students tell us we should consider when grading.

- **EFFORT.** Students believe that grades should depend on how hard they try in our courses. They could learn nothing, hand in careless projects, turn in confused and poorly written essays, do homework incorrectly, and yet expect we should reward the amount of time they spend on poor work. This idea originates from secondary schools and teachers who don't want to hurt their students' feelings. Apparently, rewarding something is more important than actual achievement. The problem, however, is that effort is not the same as achievement.
- **ATTENDANCE.** Students often think they should be rewarded in some tangible way if they come to class. This is ridiculous. The reward for attendance is built into courses. Come to class and do well; cut courses and do poorly. No artificially imposed gold star for attendance is necessary. Enough said.
- **BUSYWORK.** The third common feel-good criterion is the idea of working for your grade. Professors see this when students who do poorly on tests beg us to give them extra work to improve their

grade. Extra work usually refers to easy, mindless, comforting, and busywork exercises students are familiar with from high school. One student in my physics course asked me if she could earn extra credit if she sat down and wrote out all the chapter answers that were given to her at the back of the book. Nothing about actually doing the problems; she just wanted to copy the answers. Other students ask if they can do extra reading, write a report, make flash cards for key terminology, or do extra math problems. Not all of the suggested exercises are useless, but their dodging of real learning reduces the effort to busywork.

PLAYING THE NUMBERS GAME

One of the impediments to high performance in college is surviving the freshman year. The first year is critical in setting the tone for your entire college experience. Get off to a bad start, and it makes everything more difficult; get off to a good start, and it makes everything easier. Surviving the freshman year is like scoring in the first quarter of a football game. You get some positive momentum and take control of the game rather than letting the game control you. Doing well in your freshman year takes the pressure off and allows you to cruise later as a junior or senior. It's a work first, play later strategy. Nobody wants to play catch-up. Better to get out of the blocks quickly and get down the track.

Upcoming sections offer guidelines to get your college career off to a good start. Here I focus on the importance of your freshman GPA. The best strategy for college academic success is to work hard in your freshman year and get your GPA up as high as possible. I can't emphasize this enough. If you start your college life with a high GPA in your freshman and sophomore years, it's difficult to knock it down during your junior and senior years. Correspondingly, starting as a freshman in a GPA hole makes it difficult if not impossible to build it back to acceptability during the remainder of your college years.

It's largely a numbers game, the numbers being those used in the GPA calculation. There's just not enough time in a college career to improve your GPA if you start out in the hole. Say you blow off your freshman year and end up with a 1.5 GPA at the start of your sophomore year. This means only six chances remain to improve your GPA—two semesters in each of your sophomore, junior, and senior years. The numbers are brutal under those circumstances. As applied to college GPA calculations, the numbers are not in your favor unless you start fast with a high GPA. Not even close. Here is how the GPA numbers game works out for a few examples.

Take the student who gets off to a bad start and ends up with an overall GPA of 1.5 at the end of his freshman year. Before you say this would never happen to you, this is not an unreasonable freshman GPA; the overall average freshman GPA at AU is ~ 2.5 and lower in some universities. Now assume our hypothetical student takes a standard credit load of 30 semester hours per year. Question: If his target graduating GPA is 3.5, what does it take to get there by graduation day? Take a look at the table below.

Possibilities for Obtaining a Target GPA=3.5 at Graduation		
Sophomore Starting GPA		
1.5	2.0	2.5
600 hrs with 3.6 GPA	450 hrs with 3.6 GPA	300 hrs with 3.6 GPA
300 hrs with 3.7 GPA	225 hrs with 3.7 GPA	150 hrs with 3.7 GPA
200 hrs with 3.8 GPA	150 hrs with 3.8 GPA	100 hrs with 3.8 GPA
150 hrs with 3.9 GPA	112 hrs with 3.9 GPA	75 hrs with 3.9 GPA
120 hrs (4 yrs) with 4.0 GPA	90 hrs (3 yrs) with 4.0 GPA	60 hrs (2 yrs) with 4.0 GPA

This is all bad news. It means that a student ending up with a 1.5 after his freshman year needs to get a 4.0 in 120 semester hours of remaining course credits to achieve a 3.5 GPA upon graduation. Since there are 120 semester hours in a four-year college career, you'll never make it. It's impossible to get an overall graduating GPA of 3.5 if you end your freshman year with a 1.5. You would have to spend four years after your freshman year and you only have three years. Worse, you would have to get a 4.0 in all the rest of your courses. Fat chance.

Let's try a more optimistic example. Say you started with a 2.0 GPA at the end of your freshman year. This is better but still mostly more bad news. It means that a student ending up with a 2.0 after his freshman year would need to get a 4.0 in 90 semester hours of course credits to achieve a 3.5 GPA upon graduation. Since there are 120 semester hours in a four-year college career, you have to get a 4.0 in all the rest of your college courses. Not very realistic.

One more. The overall average GPA for freshman students at AU during the Fall 2006 semester was 2.45 (males) and 2.68 (females). Let's call it 2.5 for simplicity. The data shows that it's getting more reasonable, but still highly unrealistic. The average sophomore student at AU would need 60 hours of course credits with a 4.0 to achieve a 3.5 GPA at graduation. This is two years worth of credit, meaning all your junior and senior courses would require a 4.0.

Analyses of this sort show why the national average graduating GPA of undergraduate students is about 2.9, nowhere near 3.5 or above. The lesson is obvious. It's nearly impossible to graduate summa cum laude if you get off to a slow academic start in your freshman year.

SURVIVING THE DREADED FRESHMAN YEAR

Now that we've looked at the numbers game, let me offer some advice to survive the dreaded freshman year. Consider these the top things you can do to insure a successful high school–to–college transition. The details are fleshed out in upcoming sections.

CHOOSE EXCELLENCE AND AVOID MEDIOCRITY

College students spend too much time on the politics of getting through instead of enjoying the ride and doing a good job at it. I often hear students saying "I got A's in high school without studying, so why should I study here?" The simple answer is because it won't work. High school was high school. This is college. A college education is determinative of the rest of your life. The stakes are much higher. What worked for you in high school is not going to work in college unless you are majoring in basket weaving. College professors are less sympathetic with mediocrity. If students want to choose mediocrity, fine, but get out of our way because other, more talented students will want to learn and rise to take your place. You will get rudely left behind. Forgive my blunt language, but most professors won't adjust to you but expect you to adjust to them. They don't know and don't care to know the rap artists, the rock stars, the MTV celebrities, and the role models you hold dear. They have a different set of role models for their lives consisting of brilliant and talented intellectuals throughout history. That's why they are academics. The mediocrity of high school doesn't fly in college if you want to be a person of excellence. It's not cute to be dumb in college.

GET OFF THE MARK QUICKLY

Imagine spotting your competition twenty-five yards out in the hundred yard dash. It's unlikely you will win the race. Yet that is standard fare for many freshmen students. Too many freshmen wait for the professor to tell them everything. My freshman students sit and wait for me to tell them when to study, what to study, and how to study. In the meantime, you are getting eaten alive by more experienced upperclassmen. Professors at large universities won't hold your hand. They think you should know how to study. They treat you as an adult learner. You've been in school for twelve years, and professors expect you to know something about the craft of learning. They're not helicopter parents, and they're not going to baby you; they frequently won't reteach you things you should have learned already. They won't wait for you to come up to speed. You have to stay up with them and not vice versa. They establish the standard for performance and set the bar for what is required to get a bachelor's degree. This will be one of your first huge shocks as a freshman student. In some courses you will get more work, more reading assignments, and more homework problems in one week than you got during months of high school.

ORGANIZE A REASONABLE FRESHMAN SCHEDULE

Counseling is problematic at large universities. You would think that, because students are our main customers, that counseling would hold a lofty place in the pecking order of a university. Not so. Counseling is a thankless activity lacking tangible rewards. It gets buried near the bottom of the priority list at most large institutions. The reason is that universities are driven largely by financial interests and less by student services. Services at universities are often viewed as financial liabilities; entities that suck up money rather than generating money. The result is that pitifully few qualified academic counselors are in the loop to help students set up a reasonable schedule and program of courses for your freshman year. Counseling can consist of little more than a professor who reads the college bulletin with you about what is required in your freshman year. While colleges are developing better schemes at advising new students, still there is a lack of qualified personnel who know their way around the course requirements.

It's not just colleges who lack counselors. There's also low numbers of college counselors working in high schools. According to a study[59] by the National Association for College Admission Counseling, in the largest high schools, there's only one college advisor for every 654 students. For private high schools, the ratio is one per fifty. It's estimated that only 66% of American high schools have a full-time college counselor. What this means is that the bad or negligent advice given to high school seniors gets translated into wasted time and efforts during the high school–to–college transition. The shortage of college counselors has spawned a cottage industry of private counselors that few blue-collar students can afford.

Since quality college counseling is sporadic, it's useful for new students to attend the freshman orientation programs run by nearly all universities. In the case of AU, our orientation program is called Camp War Eagle (CWE), one of the premiere orientation programs in the country. CWE occurs in the summer before your freshman year and gives incoming students an introduction to the University and signs you up for courses. There are parallel working groups for the parents of college students to educate them on what their sons and daughters will be facing in college. Professors have mixed feelings about the value of most orientation programs. Some of us think that the orientation programs are little more than pricey rah-rah sessions similar to pep rallies, lacking useful content about how to be successful in college. While this is probably true, the upside is that you get signed up for classes, receive practical knowledge about college life, and you get one up on the power curve of freshman life.

Two Words: Time Management

You have enough time in college to do all the things you need to do, but you must manage yourself wisely. Decide on what four to five things are important and stick with them. There's little time for much else. Freshman students in particular are often locked into particular schedules because they are low on the enrollment pecking order. High enrollment courses fill up quickly with upperclassmen and there is little or no space for adding courses at convenient times. Freshman students are forced to take what they can get. There is a concerted push on most campuses to cater to student schedules by adding courses or opening more sections of a popular course; that being said, it's best for students to organize their courses, as much as possible, around blocks of time, usually in the morning. To be specific, it's best to take three to four courses one after another than to spread them out over the day. Yes, you will be brain dead after, say, four straight hours of lectures, but you will appreciate the uninterrupted time in the afternoon to study or schedule labs. If you have an hour here and an hour there between classes, it's unlikely you will use the time wisely. Too easy to stop at Starbucks for coffee, surf the Internet in a campus computer lab, text message your friends, or watch TV in the student union.

Don't Avoid Hard Work

Do an experiment. Choose five people you know who have been successful in life and ask them what made the difference. Every single person will say something about hard work. Every successful person I know got there with toil and sweat. You have to earn most of what you get in life. Your daddy can't study for you, can't take your tests, and can't go to class for you. Learn to work hard rather than switch majors when the going gets tough. For Christian students reading this book, I have a section later that shows you the high value that God places on work. In the Bible, work is viewed as a blessing and a gift, not as a necessary evil. Adam had to work in the Garden; he didn't just sit and twiddle his thumbs enjoying the flowers. If he had to work in Paradise, the most perfect environment, then God must view work as a necessary and valuable part of humanity, worthy of our effort and time. Work was one of the first things mandated by the Creator. Christian students, if necessary, should change their attitude about work to be successful in college.

GO TO YOUR INSTRUCTORS AS A FIRST RESORT, NOT A LAST RESORT

When the going gets tough, it's amazing how many students turn to everything and everyone except their college professors. Sometimes it's because students are so far behind the pace of the course that they don't want to let the teacher know it. Sometimes it's due to a bad experience with a professor. Sometimes it's because professors are not always adept at helping students. But I am finding more and more students who don't ask for help because they don't want to make the effort to ask for help. Asking for help takes courage. It takes time and effort. But the reward is great. I encourage my students to ask for help early in the semester, usually by my saying "Why hire a tutor or get a roommate to help when you have an expert in the field who you've already paid for? Use me!" It's true without exception that when a student gets in early and lets me help him, the one-on-one interaction turns an F on the first test into an A or B before the course ends. I'm always amazed that more students don't take me up on my offer.

DEVELOP DISCIPLINE AND EFFECTIVE STUDY HABITS

Few students have good study habits when they enter college. They either come from high schools where high grades could be achieved by not studying or they were never taught how to study without memorizing everything in sight. Effective study habits in college, however, require practice, work, and discipline.

Think again about the most successful people in society. Do you think they got there by being lucky, politically connected, or by working the system? Very few. Most successful people arrived where they are by hard work. I will have more to say on this subject later, but for now I want to encourage you that it's possible for you to work hard in college and feel good about it. Studying is largely a matter of practice and discipline, like any learned behavior. It will take practice and behavioral changes, but it's one of the constants of success. The earlier in your freshman year you get yourself alone in a library and begin to study, the better you will do in college. Say you have a job while you're a student, maybe flipping burgers at McDonald's. What would be expected of you? At the minimum, your boss would require you to be on time for work, to do your job competently, to be professional, and to be accountable. Why not treat being a student just like you have a job? Why would you do less as a student, where there is much more at stake than cooking burgers? Why would you be on time for a job, but then cut your classes? Why would you work to be competent on a job, but then turn in sloppy, careless homework in college? Why would you be a professional at work but an amateur at school? You wouldn't. If you treat being a student with the same loyalty and respect as you treat a job, you will make fewer of the common college rookie mistakes and feel much better about your college experience.

Understand Grading Systems

Students save enormous amounts of time and energy by understanding grading systems used by professors in college. Most of us employ either an absolute or a relative system, commonly called a curved grading scheme. Students seem to understand absolute systems because they were used by teachers in high school, but most of my students taking introductory physics do not understand how curved systems work. I will talk later about how to interpret grading systems; for now, recognize that when you don't understand how you're graded you place yourself in jeopardy by putting your effort where it's minimally effective. Don't shoot yourself in the foot by misplaced effort. Effort is costly and should be placed where it matters.

Whatever Happened to Curiosity?

One of the things I find seriously lacking in our college students today is curiosity. Curiosity may be defined as a meddling desire to learn something even though it may not directly impact your daily life. When you are curious, you want to know, say, how a tornado spins up, or what makes the Sun emit energy for millions of years, or what happens in your brain when you learn a new fact. It's a drive to figure out how things work and discover the broad principles that govern the universe. For the Christian, it's to wonder what God is like, how He works, how He thinks, and what is important to Him.

Professors see the lack of curiosity in several ways. For one, students rarely ask questions during a lecture. We can be covering the most fascinating, awe-inspiring material, facts involving the mysteries of the universe, the incredible human body, the history of the world, the beauty of literature, art and music, and yet no questions. There are some legitimate reasons for not asking questions in college. Many students are shy and do not want to interrupt a large lecture class with what might be perceived as a dumb question. Some students don't ask questions because they are behind in the course and don't want to embarrass themselves. Others don't know what to ask and would prefer not to show their ignorance.

But much of the silence originates from a simple lack of curiosity. In my Dave Letterman physics course, for example, I have a week of lectures on "The Great Inventions of Mankind." I usually introduce each invention with a question such as "have you ever wondered how a radio works" or "what makes the picture on your television set?" or "do you know how a car engine works?" During my car engine lecture, I sometimes ask how many students have ever looked under the hood of their car. Nearly ~ 40% of the class answers yes. This means that ~ 60% of my students have lived roughly twenty years but haven't been curious enough to wonder what makes a car operate. It's just not on the average millennial student's radar scope and the numbers are trending in the wrong direction with time.

Never looked under the hood of a car? Are you serious? When I was a child, I remember taking apart everything and driving my mom crazy. If you've ever observed a baby for any length of time, their whole life is about curiosity. They are forever touching things, evaluating colors and shapes, getting into trouble, and wandering away from their mothers. They are fascinated at their surroundings. That was me. And I never outgrew it. I wanted to know how everything worked. Yet, when I inquire about curiosity in my students over a wide range of subjects, I get things like "my daddy does all of that" or "it doesn't concern me" or "that's for someone else to worry about" or "that thought never entered my mind."

What's causing the curiosity void? There are several factors, but it surely involves something that happens after elementary school. I know that much because whenever I visit elementary schools to do science demonstrations, I get bombarded with questions. Good questions. Elementary students ask better questions than college students. Two of the important factors are pop culture and that millennials have been spoon-fed for so long that they find it difficult to think outside the box. The spoons are not only parents and teachers, who have done too much for you and made your life easy, but also television, the Internet, video games, MTV, cell phones, all things that are wonderful inventions, but also things that do your thinking for you. Things that numb your mind. Things that entertain but discourage curiosity. Things that are mesmerizing and help pass the time but offer little to make you think independently and nurture curiosity.

Christians have few excuses for being low on the curiosity scale. How can any Christian not find fascination in the things of our Creator? How can we possibly look up at the heavens on a star-filled evening and not marvel at the mysteries of the physical universe? How can we not ponder in amazement at how two microscopic entities merge in a woman's body and yield a fully-functioning human being nine months later who will live forever? How can we consider the billions of times our heart beats in a lifetime and not be astonished at how reliable our biological machinery is when compared to anything mankind can fashion? How can we not wonder about the awe-inspiring diversity of fish, birds, animals, plants, micro-organisms, weather, people, and climates on the Planet? How can we not ask how anyone but God could create things as original as turtles, electric eels, fireflies, butterflies, dinosaurs, bats, and babies? We of all people should be curious, and you as Christian college students should be the first to wonder about God, His creation, and His ways.

THE NUMBERS AND NERDS HARDSHIP

The numbers and nerds hardship, as I call it, is a major show-stopper for college students. It refers to the inability of college students to do mathematics. This is unfortunate for their lives and a loss to American technological society. I hate to see a student who is truly interested in engineering;

for example, opt out of it because they can't handle the mathematics. Even courses in business, economics, psychology, and other traditionally liberal arts courses require some competency in mathematics. A college student who is handicapped by poor math skills ends up bouncing from major to major to avoid it. What a tragic waste of time.

The problem is simply that many American students never learned mathematics in the first place. They didn't learn what math was good for, where it's used, why it's used, and they've never seriously pondered how math works or the logic behind it. They just memorized the rote steps necessary to survive a math class. Teachers know that students can survive courses involving math by plugging and chugging until they get the answer in the back of the book. But that's not education. That's a waste of nearly a dozen years of your life. When students who plug and chug are thrown into the deep end of college education they quickly drown. How can students who take some kind of math nearly every week of every year of their lives come out nearly mathematically illiterate?

It doesn't take a long journey into night for a physics professor to see the numbers and nerds hardship. Try the first week of the course. What to do about it? When the prerequisite math skills are not learned in the first place, there are few easy answers. You either have to play catch-up, switch majors away from disciplines involving mathematics, or retake courses containing material you should have learned earlier. To avoid these options, I try to help my students with their deficiencies by reteaching the relevant mathematics during the course, but most professors are not so sympathetic. They expect you to be ready for their courses. Another suggestion is to spend some time at the start of your courses reviewing the mathematics appendices added to most textbooks. Almost no students bother but the appendices are there specifically for students who are rusty at their math skills and need to improve and be ready for mathematical prime-time.

THREE

Distinctives of Christian Students

CHRISTIAN AND SECULAR STUDENTS

There are many similarities between Christian and secular students during their college career. You face the same pressures, the same need to study, and the same time constraints. You enroll in the same courses and sit under the same professors. You dump and get dumped by girlfriends and boyfriends. You feel the same guilt over parents and grandparents you neglect during your busy week. You pull all-nighters. You long to fit in and struggle to find yourself.

On the other hand, there are significant differences between Christian and secular college students. In this chapter we examine some of the distinctive issues faced by a Christian student at a large university. Looking solely at academics, being a Christian doesn't necessarily give you an edge over your secular counterparts and, in some cases, Christianity can conflict with the highest levels of expected performance in college. Some of the comparisons and contrasts:

DIVIDED LOYALTIES

Christian college students face divided loyalties about who is on the throne of their lives. You struggle to balance your life in Christ and your life as a college student. You desire and need an intimate relationship with the Savior, but you also have to study. Divided loyalties result because a relationship with God takes time, energy, and commitment—time that could be spent studying or living the college life. In my case, for example, the last thing I wanted to do after a long day at the library poring over books was to go home and pore over another book called the Bible. You are tired of concentrating, tired of reading, tired of books, and tired of discipline. Worse, it's a zero-sum game. For every hour you spend with devotions, with prayer, or with your church group, you have one less hour to spend with the books. Christian students have a vital, added priority in your life. Secular students, with no interest in the Lord, have no equivalent divided loyalties. Or so you think.

Truth be told, secular and Christian students both face a zero-sum game. True, secular students don't have God in their lives, but they do have things, important to them, that clamor for attention, such as partying, working, socializing, going out, fraternity activities, and game-day celebrating. They also have choices to make about their time. Rather than thinking you're at a disadvantage because of the time you "have" to spend with God, it's better to recognize that everyone in college sets priorities and has conflicts of interest. The difference between Christian and secular students is not that secular students have less things that demand their attention, but rather what is demanding their attention.

How you handle the divided loyalties is important. First, recognize that all college students struggle with divided loyalties. You're all in the same boat. Don't think that because you're a Christian you have more balls in the air than your secular friends. Second, it's beneficial to prioritize your loyalties. People disagree on which prioritization strategy is best. Many pastors advocate rank-order prioritizing, which means to sequentially order what is important in your life, usually God first, family second, work third, and so on. I find ordered prioritization too simplistic and unrealistic for a college student. We discuss this further below, but better to develop a short list of important loyalties in your life and view all of them as equally important. The trick is to choose a limited set. You don't have time to do everything, and it's better to do a few things well than a bunch of things poorly.

Here's what not to do with divided loyalties—use them as an excuse for mediocre performance or special treatment. My Christian students sometimes tell me, for example, that they are unable to hand in an assignment due Thursday because they were participating in their church group on Wednesday night. Would God buy that reasoning? I don't think so. God would tell you to honor your commitments. God would tell you to get your act together and not use Him as your excuse for poor time management. Just the other day one of my female Christian students emailed me after the fact and asked me when she could schedule a makeup test for the one she missed while attending a Beth Moore conference. Nothing wrong with Beth Moore, she is wonderful, but I didn't buy it. Ask me to take a test early but not late. I have a hundred students in a class, and professors can't dispense special treatment to every student who asks for exemptions. All my student had to do is plan ahead instead of putting me in the position of denying her request; she should have sought permission instead of forgiveness. From an instructor's viewpoint, how is attending a Beth Moore conference different from a secular student who tells me that he needs another day to complete his assignment because he was out partying? Or going to a basketball game instead of taking a test? Or going to a Sara Evans concert? None are acceptable excuses.

Turmoil over Ethically Challenging Situations

Christian students at secular universities face a series of questionable situations that demand a high level of reasoned thought about whether you should participate. This is different from secular students who lack a consistent ethical system which helps them decide what to do and not do. Secular students will try most everything; in fact, trying everything is a rite of passage in college.

Say you are invited to a party where you know there will be a keg. Secular students would jump at the opportunity; the question for them is not whether they will show up but "When does the keg arrive?" Christian students, by contrast, are wise to stop and reflect whether this is something they should attend and, if they do, what it says about their Christianity. This means a Christian student has to decide what they think about drinking. Is all drinking sinful? Is beer okay? What about a Margarita? How about going to a party but not drinking? Should you even have college friends who invite you to keg parties? Decisions involving ethical situations are difficult for Christians as we ponder the best and most godly course of action.

Try this one. Say you are a male Christian student in an anthropology class and sit beside a beautiful coed who seems to be a good person but you know she's not a Christian. You are attracted to her and ponder whether to ask her out. Should you? Is it wise for a Christian to date a non-Christian? After all, while the Bible says not to become unequally yoked with an unbeliever, you're not talking about marriage, just a few dates. Further, it may be the case that you are the one God sends to lead her to Christ. What to do? There are arguments on both sides. But what first seemed to be a simple act of asking someone out now turns into a major values dilemma. As a Christian student, you face ethical quandaries every month of your life at a secular university that your unbelieving friends avoid because ethical questions have less importance to them. Your counterparts at Christian colleges don't have the same problem because Christian colleges have largely Christian students in a Christian environment. Life is harder at a secular university.

Ah, but this is why I love the secular college environment. It forces Christians to evaluate our value systems and see whether our Christianity is legitimate or borrowed. It provides an acid test of whether we believe what God says or what the world says. It challenges us to see whether we have the courage to follow our convictions. It makes us stronger because we have to critically assess what we believe and what principles determine our actions. Do you have a live or a Memorex brand of Christianity? As Christian students, you have to get into the Scriptures, study, ponder, and decide how to evaluate the ethical situations that arise in college. It's good practice for when you graduate and move into the real world.

Notice that I didn't tell you what you should do as the college male in the anthropology class. I didn't give you the answer. There are no "odd" answers in the back of that book. Everyone has to decide for themselves, as the Bible offers principles on how to live but doesn't consider every specific situation that students confront in college. This means that the struggle is what is important; the quest to find out the best answer per the available Scriptural principles. But that is how you grow as a Christian. God doesn't want spoon-fed Christians but believers who slug it out with the moral questions posed by our culture. While students at Christian colleges are not immune from weighing the pros and cons of ethical situations, there is not the same worldly laboratory available to rub the rubber against the road. You get a different education in the real world outside the bubble of Christian colleges, Bible institutes, and seminaries.

Some advice. To help with ethical situations in college, Christian college students should make sustained progress in their personal, daily Bible devotions. The more you learn about the Scriptures, the more the Holy Spirit can work in your life when a values question arises. It's difficult to hear the Spirit when you neglect your Christian life. Further, it's beneficial to have some older saints in your life, either at your home or college church. We all need spiritual mentors. The best counselors are your parents, but college students are usually not comfortable talking to their parents about personal, college-level subjects. When I was a college student, I was well served by adopted parents in college, college ministers, coaches, and pastors at churches in my college towns. In some cases, my Christian friends and girlfriends have helped me work through the tougher ethical cases. Personally, while it's rare, I enjoy it immensely when my Christian students at AU show the daring to knock on my door and ask for guidance on ethical issues. The goal is to develop relationships with mature, seasoned Christian mentors who can help guide you through the treacherous paths in secular college environments.

The Value of Secular Higher Education

Christian parents frequently ask me about the potential negative effects of a secular college education on their children. They worry that secular higher education will corrupt a young, naïve college student—with godless ideas. There are a number of points on this issue that both students and parents should consider.

MUCH OF THE DAMAGE WILL HAVE ALREADY BEEN DONE

College students have already been exposed to a stiff drink of worldly culture before ever darkening the doors of a secular college classroom. They have been bombarded with the secular value system for eighteen years of life. If you're a parent reading this, you'd have to be living in a quarantine bubble to shield your kids completely from the effects of mainstream culture. Even if parents have been moderately successful at deflecting the seamier elements of society, total isolation from the world has its own risks. There are too many unstoppable inputs from secular media that interact with the life of a teenager. If a college student is going to be corrupted by humanistic values, it would have begun years before.

One way for Christian students to avert humanistic influences during college is by developing a realistic view of their professors. Here's what not to do. When I was a student, I nearly worshipped the ground my professors walked on. They were brilliant and seemed to know everything. They graduated from Ivy League crème-of-the-crop schools such as Cal Tech, MIT, Yale, Columbia, Johns Hopkins, and Cal–Berkeley. They headed national scientific committees and were called to testify before Congress on technology issues. They could calculate the most amazing things and were totally out-of-the-box thinkers; wild-brained revolutionaries cut in the mold of Cal Tech physics professor and Nobel laureate Richard Feynman. Some of my older professors in college worked on the atom bomb in the Manhattan Project during World War II. One of my professors was a thesis student of Albert Einstein. The war generation of physicists saved the world, stopped the Nazi advance, won the war, and were the Olympic gold medalists of science during the heyday of physics. Students were in awe of their intellect.

But what I later found was that the further you go in the academic world the more you realize that not all ideas are equal even when developed by brilliant minds. Everyone is colored by nature, nurture, strongly-held beliefs, and agendas. Hitler was not a stupid man. Look how he deceived what was clearly the most educated nation at that time. We were lucky to defeat the Germans during the war. The Apostle Paul was brilliant, educated in the Harvard University of religious studies at the time, yet his early ideas were completely reversed during his road to Damascus experience. The Sanhedrin was composed of academics that were completely wrong about Jesus. Solomon was the wisest person on earth but chose to take hundreds of women as wives and set up altars to their gods. Anyone who has been married knows that's not too smart.

Brilliant professors are no exception. They might be brilliant but they can be brilliantly wrong. They might be exceptional logical thinkers but start from dubious presuppositions. They might derive results based on unsupported starting assumptions. Their objective analyses can be tainted by their point of view. They can massage the data to support what they thought all along. They suffer from parochialism, jealousy, herd mentality, and envy. Many are arrogant and think they are better than everyone else. They have bad hair days if they have hair at all. They watch their backs around their peers and are fiercely competitive. The bottom line for Christian students is to look at your professors as real people and not as academic gods. Doing so will divert a young student's hero worship to a more realistic appraisal of who professors are and what they know. Here's what I tell my students: "The real difference between us is age and experience—not brains—so continue to study and you will be as brilliant as you think I am."

CHRISTIANITY TRUMPS THE TEST OF SECULAR INQUIRY

Christianity is tough; it can stand on its own. The incessant barrage of attacks on Christianity throughout history has only made the Christian message stronger. Let the godless write their books. Let the humanistic professors rant. Since the French Enlightenment, the death of God has been confidently proclaimed throughout the humanistic world. Religion, they say, has been rendered obsolete by science, technology, and industrialism. Yet, Christian arguments still carry the day, and the Christian world view is favorably received by millions of critical thinkers over the wide spectrum of alternative religious systems vying for adoption.

The superiority of Christianity is especially evident when you consider what a world without God would look like. Without Christianity, morality as a normative guide to behavior completely loses its meaning. Laws involving morality become difficult if not impossible. The Ten Commandments are morphed into ten suggestions. Ego becomes the driving force in the universe as people see choices in terms of what promotes individual preferences. What's to stop someone from killing off children with congenital defects? What code of ethics argues against a suicide bomber blowing himself up to kill innocent civilians? One only needs to replay the video clips of the mass looting in New Orleans after Hurricane Katrina to see what the world would look like without a police force guided by morally-based laws. Affirmations of God lead to the great moral and ethical documents of history while godless doctrine leads to puffed-up ego stroking and dead-end streets of anarchy. There are few secular counterparts to Mother Theresa, Pope John Paul, Billy Graham, and Martin Luther King. The most heinous horrors of history such as the Holocaust were carried out with the approval of godless political creeds. Christianity is a brute in the world of ethical ideas. Don't be swayed by professors who ridicule Christianity. There is a vast army of intelligent people who think otherwise.

A Secular University Education is Not the Problem

There is another side to this discussion. Christians overgeneralize when they bad-mouth all secular ideas as morally bankrupt. This assumes guilt by association and throws the baby out with the bath water. Without twenty-first century secular universities, students would have fewer opportunities to learn about foreign cultures, foreign languages, mathematics, philosophy, anthropology, sociology, medicine, geography, geology, astronomy, chemistry, the environment, and healthy living. Should a truly educated person know nothing about Shakespeare, Edgar Allen Poe, the classics of literature, and the great music compositions of Mozart and Bach? I think not. Should we ignore the sweep of human history just because it isn't taught with a Christian slant? Are Christian ideas so weak that alternative ethical, religious, and political systems threaten our viewpoint of God? The top people across a broad range of the human sphere were educated in secular universities. No matter how you cut it, most of our leaders, Christian and otherwise, benefited from a secular university education.

A secular university education isn't the problem. Alternative ideas are never the problem. The real problem is to be able to think through the arguments—the ability to critically assess, compare, and contrast what Christianity offers compared to what secular humanism offers. Not all Christians are up to the task. The word is apologetics. Christians young and old lack the mental acuity to defend our faith. We either don't know much about what we believe or what we do believe isn't deep enough to withstand critical assessments from the humanistic gun ships. This gets back to Christian education. Students who come to college from stable homes where Christian education was fostered early will have little trouble separating Christian fact from humanistic fiction in the classroom. They're not going to get knocked off their Christian game by liberal professors having godless world views. But Christian students who enter college with weak Christian backgrounds are asking for trouble and can easily succumb to leftist ideas. My advice to parents who are worried about their kids in college is that, if they have trained them properly at home or at church, then their children will be able to survive the secular college culture. Even better than that, they will become the light to bring other students to a critical examination of Christianity and see firsthand in the messed-up lives of unbelieving students how good it is to be a Christian.

Take the case of Shadrach, Meshach, and Abednego (Dan. 3:1–30). They were surrounded by a thoroughly secular culture in Babylon yet strong enough in their beliefs to face up to King Nebuchadnezzar. Or how about Joseph? He was educated in the top secular schools of Egypt. He had near zero in terms of formal Christian education and, in fact, had all kinds of reasons to turn his back on God. But Joseph held deep Christian convictions that were unmoved by his secular education. In contrast, the children of Israel at Mt. Sinai succumbed within a week to Moses' absence while he was receiving the Ten Commandments. The Bible says to build our lives on the Solid Rock and not on the shifting sands. It recommends we govern our lives by convictions and not by opinion polls.

Thus, it's an individual matter as to whether a Christian college student is ready for secular university prime time. Every student and parent should weigh the risks and benefits.

CHRISTIAN COLLEGE OR SECULAR UNIVERSITY?

Is it better to attend a Christian college or secular university? There is no one-fit best answer. It depends on the following:

- Who you are
- How strong you are spiritually
- What you want to do with your life
- What your academic background has been
- How much money you want to spend
- What you see as your final career goal

Ultimately, you should choose where God leads you. We offer some general advice for students on what genre of college to choose. There are two common mistakes.

NAÏVE IDEAS OF COLLEGE BRANDS

There is something wrong when the dinner table conversation of third graders involves what college they will attend. The commercialization of college culture has perpetuated the myth that only the Ivy League and a few other college "brands" are good enough for Little Johnny. But this view is naïve, uniformed, and reflects Madison Avenue's attempt to influence common sense. Top students today start getting recruiting materials, phone calls, and recruiting brochures in their junior year of high school. There's a mountain of material to evaluate and major ego stroking by colleges to get your education dollar. Huge money is at stake; last year (2006), the average cost of four years of college (tuition, fees, and room and board) reached $51,184 at a public college and $121,468 at a private school. This is too much money to fall prey to platitudes about how wonderful it is to attend a particular college. You have to go beyond the marketing, do your homework, and examine a broad range of facts about your short list of universities, and it's not necessarily easy, as there are real problems in finding credible information that allows the educational consumer to compare colleges. There are currently 2,582 four-year colleges and 1,694 two-year colleges in the United States. Given the abilities of the Internet, you would think there would be a database to allow side-by-side comparisons of colleges, but there currently is not, unless you want to buy into the rankings of publications such as *US News and World Report*. Professors are generally suspicious of ranking lists, recognizing that the standings are usually dominated by entrenched impressions of Ivy League institutions with their huge endowments, prestige, and famous faculty and alumni.

NAÏVE IDEAS OF PERSONAL SIGNIFICANCE

Seems everyone millennial with over a 3.5 GPA aims to attend Harvard, Yale, Vanderbilt, and Duke with little knowledge of just how difficult it is to get into those institutions. Nothing wrong with shooting high in your college choice, but your claims of academic prowess need to be grounded in fact. When you consider that the desirable institutions are private, low in enrollment, highly expensive, highly competitive, and dependent on political and alumni connections, it's unrealistic to believe they are viable choices for most students. In the case of physics, for example, several of us at AU are either graduates or have connections to places like MIT, Cal Tech, Yale, University of Chicago, Cal–Berkeley, Carnegie-Mellon, and so on. But many of us rarely recommend that even the best high school students go to these schools as a physics undergraduate. True, there are few substitutes for holding the prized Harvard badge, but at what price? Many of us believe you get just as good and, in many cases, a better education at a state university, with its much smaller price tag and emphasis on undergraduate education.

The elite universities are tilted toward graduate studies. Undergraduates are often taught by teaching assistants and not the professors you thought you were paying the big dollars for, who instead are out building their reputations on the lecture and speaking circuit. The competition is fierce. You have to have a thick hide to survive as an undergraduate in the Ivy League. Then there is the narrower range of social experiences at small, elite institutions compared to what exists at a Big-Ten, Pac-Ten, or SEC school. When is the last time Harvard, for example, had a sports team of any kind in the top ten nationally? The top schools are think tanks that nurture the mind but often lack the diversity of social and athletics experiences you get at larger state universities.

My standard advice to high school students who think they can't live without Harvard is to stop for a minute, breathe, and at least consider a state university near your home. Good students from most of the major universities can later transfer and do graduate work at the top-rated private schools. The Ivy League and other top-tier schools are unsurpassed at graduate and professional education due to the huge endowments, famous faculty, and worldwide reputation.

Now back to the choice of Christian colleges vs. secular universities. Step back philosophically for a minute. Believers have varying views on the value of a Christian education. The arguments are similar to whether Christian parents should homeschool their children or send them to public school. One side argues that public schools are cesspools of godless teaching and worldly bad habits. Who would ever send their children into that? The other side questions whether isolating children in home-schooling environments causes more problems than it solves. Eventually, a home-schooled student has to go out into the big bad secular world. Advocates say it's cruel not to prepare your child for the rude awakening.

It's best to avoid the extreme positions. There are few dogmatic answers to choosing a college because it depends on how God leads you and what you want from a college education. There are students who do great at either Christian or secular addresses. Take the case of Rachel Friesen. Rachel was on schedule to graduate debt free from the University of Colorado. In her junior year, she opted to transfer to Azusa Pacific University, an evangelical Christian college near Los Angeles, a decision that would run up a debt of roughly $40K. Listen to the reasons for her decision. "At a large university, it's easy to go through your college experience knowing a lot of people but not having deep, meaningful relationships. I've been able to have deep relationships, and those are the ones you keep."[60] Friesen is among many students who choose to study among like-minded believers in Christian colleges. Data from the 105 evangelical schools belonging to the Council of Christian Colleges and Universities (CCCU) shows that enrollment has increased 71% since 1990, while, over the same period, enrollments at all public and private colleges increased by 13% and 28% respectively.[61] Naomi Schaefer Riley, deputy editor of the Wall Street Journal and author of *God on the Quad: How Religious Colleges and the Missionary Generation are Changing America,*[62] finds that faith-based students want to study where their beliefs are respected rather than ridiculed, which is often the case on secular campuses.

Prospective college students should look beyond the colorful brochures and try to visit the campuses on your short list. Adam Owings of Marymount University, during a call to USA Today's College Admission and Financial Aid Hot Line said, "A campus visit and conversations with faculty and other students is the best way to tell whether a college's program is right for you."[63] Sandy Ware of Texas Christian University remarks "The Internet seems to be decreasing the reliance on the campus visit. A visit is essential to experience the culture and community of a campus. And the culture and community are absolutely essential to academic success."[64] Surveys show that the vast majority of students who transfer after their first year of college did not bother with a campus visit before they enrolled. Truth be told, a campus visit is one of the few ways to get reliable data on the campus atmosphere. While it's difficult for many students to shell out the time and money to take a college tour during a summer break, if you can, there's no better way to choose a college that fits you, whether secular or Christian. We're always visiting with prospective high school students and their parents at AU, and I'm brutally honest about the pros and cons of our university and its programs. There's too much at stake in a student's life for me to give them a snow job. If you can't visit a campus, at least seek out advice from people who have insider knowledge about your Christian colleges of choice, such as your pastor, alumni, or friends who have attended the colleges on your list. Look for the faculty commitment to the Word of God and whether there is a vibrant spiritual life at the school.

So much for what not to do when selecting a college. Here are specifics for students debating whether a Christian or secular college is best for them.

How Much Money?

It's undeniable that in today's market, cost plays a major role in school choice. Had I won the lottery in high school, I might have opted for Duke University for my undergraduate studies. But no way was I going to Duke without divine intervention since Duke is one of the most expensive institutions in America. Many students believe that small colleges are cheaper than state universities. It's really just the opposite. Think $30K as compared to $13K per year for an order-of-magnitude tuition comparison. The reasons for the cost differential are important to understand when deciding where to attend college. It's not that Christian schools are trying to soak your parents, merely that they have limited sources of income.

Christian colleges are private institutions. They receive little or no operational money from the state or federal government. By contrast, the State of Alabama supports a public institution like AU through a negotiated, budgeted, line item in the yearly state educational budget that runs into millions of dollars. We also receive funding from the federal government through contracts and grants, pork-barrel money, and key senators and representatives on appropriations committees in Congress who channel money back to their districts. Money is also donated by grateful, wealthy alumni who wish to leave a legacy with the school that started them off in life; that's why so many buildings on large campuses are inscribed with the names of donors.

Few similar funding mechanisms exist for Christian colleges. Federal funds often come with legal and sociological strings not acceptable to Christian schools. Christian colleges have a larger fraction of alumni in lower-paying Christian ministries compared to more lucrative employment in the secular world. Christian colleges can't compete with secular universities for research dollars and grants, which require expensive state-of-the-art laboratories and professors who are established leaders in their fields. The financial situation at many Christian colleges is faith based and tuition driven. Many a Christian college president has spent time on his knees to stay afloat. The financial situation was especially bad in the 1960s and '70s when religious colleges struggled to attract enough students. According to data collected by historian Ray Brown[65] at Westminster College in Fulton, Missouri, about 120 religious colleges closed between 1960 and 1979, largely due to a lack of operating money. There has been a recent resurgence in Christian colleges since the '70s, but financial life can be tough on a small private college. Given the financial realities, Christian colleges must charge more for tuition than secular colleges.

THE SPIRITUAL ENVIRONMENT AT CHRISTIAN COLLEGES

It's difficult to beat the warm spiritual atmosphere at a Christian college. No way can most secular universities compete with the small classes, intimate setting, caring professors, and spiritually-nurturing environment of a dynamic Christian college. One of my girlfriends in college was a graduate of Word of Life Bible Institute (WOLBI) in Schroon Lake, New York. She loved the Bible emphasis, the professors, the Word of Life family, the opportunities for ministry, and the WOLBI summer camp program. She loved upstate New York and the Adirondacks. She loved the founders of Word of Life, Jack Wyrtzen and Harry Bollback. It would have been torture for her to attend a Big-Ten factory with the thousands of students and impersonal environment. So, if being in a Christian environment is primary for you, or if you don't think you're ready enough or strong enough for a secular university, then a small Christian college is the obvious choice.

IS RESEARCH INFRASTRUCTURE IMPORTANT?

Say your career goal is to become a professional scientist. There are clear advantages in choosing a secular university over a Christian college. This is because Christian colleges lack the research infrastructure needed to expose you to state-of-the-art scientific research early in your career. Small institutions, even if they are state supported, lack the financial horsepower to generate and support the expensive laboratories required for big-league science. The situation is similar to athletics at the two types of institutions. A Christian school such as Wheaton College, for example, is not going to have a ninety thousand seat football stadium necessary for a successful NCAA Division-I program. Please don't send me nasty emails if your dad is a Wheaton graduate, but you simply get a different education in football if you play in the SEC, say, compared to playing at Wheaton College. The same is true in other highly professional, expensive academic disciplines. If you want to go into a profession where the vast infrastructure of a secular university is necessary, the choice is obvious. You wouldn't choose a Christian college.

IS A WIDE RANGE OF FACULTY IMPORTANT?

Small Christian colleges don't possess the range of faculty offered at say, an Indiana University or a University of Georgia. Michigan State had something like eighty faculty members in the Department of Physics. We had faculty who were experts in astrophysics, condensed matter physics, nuclear physics, high-energy physics, physics education, and a broad range of theoretical physics. In a small Christian college, you may have one or two faculty members who teach all the undergraduate physics courses assuming they have physics in the curriculum. While they may be great instructors, you will not be able to hang out around a laboratory that is doing forefront physics research, which increases your exposure to a broader range of physics than you could ever get at a small college. Christian colleges lack the breadth of faculty in many disciplines to compete with secular universities.

IS STRENGTH OF UNDERGRADUATE CURRICULUM IMPORTANT?

Christian colleges have become more academically rigorous in recent years, but the strength of the undergraduate curriculum can be vastly different between Christian colleges and secular universities. Professors at large universities lead nationally-recognized programs, and the courses they teach are typically presented at a higher level compared to the more relaxed pace at a small Christian college. We see this difference at AU for students we accept into graduate school from small institutions. They often struggle with the pace and depth of our graduate courses and we usually advise taking some of our senior-level physics courses to smooth the transition. There is a difference in the level of performance expected from most programs in major universities, again similar to the difference experienced by athletes who transfer from a Division-III school to a Division-I school. The athletes are bigger, the competition is tougher, and the academic standards are generally higher.

IS A WIDE RANGE OF SOCIAL ACTIVITIES IMPORTANT?

Recently, I was trying to help a female student determine her best course of action in fashion merchandising. She wanted a hands-on program that was well connected to the fashion industry to help her get a job at one of the leading retailers such as Neiman-Marcus. Her choice came down to whether she would choose a two-year professional fashion school in Atlanta or the more traditional, four-year fashion merchandising program at AU. Her decision came down to the importance of social activities.

At a large institution there are nearly uncountable social events. There are scores of clubs, fraternity and sorority activities, free movies, concerts, travelogues, plays, not to mention a multitude of sports programs. Have you ever found an equestrian program at a small college? At Michigan State, we had a fencing program. That is sword fighting, in case you've never heard of Zorro. Once you experience tailgating during football Saturday at a Big-Ten, Pac-Ten, or SEC school, it's addictive and you don't want to miss it. Once I began to describe what social activities my student would miss if she chose the two-year school in Atlanta, she decided that the range of social activities available at AU were a vital part of her college experience, and that tipped her decision. But other students who could care less about sports, sororities, and so on, and who just want to get on with the job program, might opt instead for the smaller, focused, professional or Christian school.

IS LIVING YOUR CHRISTIAN LIFE
IN A SECULAR ENVIRONMENT IMPORTANT?

Students often ask me why I opted to work at a large secular university instead of a Christian college. There was a time in my early college career when a small, four-year liberal arts Christian college was my ultimate professional goal, but my feelings changed the longer I stayed in graduate school. As I worked for more eminent physicists, my confidence increased, and I grew hungrier to work at the highest levels. In my case, the short answer was that God kept aiming me toward the university. But allow me to share some thoughts on the issue.

Strange as it sounds, when it comes to my job, I am more comfortable as a Christian in the secular world than I am as a Christian in the Christian world. One reason for this quirk is that I became a Christian relatively late in life, during my sophomore year in college. I remember my life before becoming a Christian; what I was thinking, what was motivating me, and what was important to me. While my Christian conversion changed all that, it didn't change me so much that I wanted to leave the secular world completely. And you shouldn't either. Ask yourself why Christ came in the first place. It was to set the captives free, and many of the captives are in the secular world. The same is still true today.

God gave me the ability to feel comfortable in either the secular or Christian world. I feel strongly that one of the reasons He chose to save me at such a relatively late time in my life was so I would have an inner pull to remain in a secular environment. He needed a Christian scientist to work in a secular environment, to give Christian students a role model, and to show the world that you can be successful as both a scientist and as a Christian. I enjoy living out my Christian life in the secular world; it's a passion for me. I would be much less effective for the Lord at a Christian college. The same may be true of you. If your gut tells you that you have a passion for unsaved souls who live in the secular world, it may be the Lord telling you that you should choose a secular over a Christian college.

Let me underscore, however, that there is no blanket answer. My professor colleagues at Christian colleges feel as strongly about their position in the Body as I do in my position in the Body. Many Christian college students love their schools and swear that the warm Christian fellowship is essential to their lives. They can't imagine themselves happy anywhere else. And that's the way it should be when you're in the will of God. The important thing is to serve the Lord where He plants you, because where He plants you is the best place you can be.

Is Exposure to a Large Number
of Potential Employers Important?

Placement services are an overlooked factor when considering a college. For students who are keen on getting a job after graduation, matching students with employers is important when securing a job after four years of hard labor. Getting a good job is a large part of why you go to college in the first place.

There are several ways of getting a job after graduation. Most involve marketing yourself. There are a multitude of strategies involving the Internet, friends, and teachers to get your name recognized. Many students send letters of introduction and resumes to prospective employers. A method less known to many college students is to use the placement services at your college. Problem is, few small schools have a placement center.

Michigan State had the largest placement center in the nation when I was there. It was wonderful. It was a convenient magnet for corporate recruiters from around the country and had all manner of services to help you land a job. Placement services offer mock interviews to sharpen your interviewing skills and experts who critique your resume. They have brochures and information on a huge variety of potential employers. They do studies on what jobs are hot and how to find them. The best part is that they set up interviews for students with corporate recruiters. Rather than having to drive or fly to visit a potential company—which takes a huge investment of time, effort, and money during your senior year—the employer comes to you at the placement center.

Once when I was sampling the job market after my B.S., the placement center at MSU arranged an interview with the Shell Oil Company in New Orleans. Shell was looking for geophysicists to search for oil in the Gulf of Mexico. I wasn't seriously interested, but Shell was recruiting so hard at the time that they were willing to fly me to the Big Easy, set me up in a fancy hotel near Bourbon Street, shower me with expensive dinners, and give me a personal limo tour of the city to convince me to join them. Not too shabby, and all arranged through placement services.

Networking is a common way to find a job. Networking means using your contacts, friends, teachers, and associates; it's usually more effective than sending out a large number of letters to human resource divisions at companies that end up in the circular file. When it comes to networking, Christian colleges often have the edge because with secular universities it's difficult to get to know your professors since we can have hundreds of students in a given year. Nevertheless, scores of students each year ask me to write them a letter of recommendation for a job, students who are not physics majors but former students who had me for physics. While I am always happy to help a student get a job, I find it sad that students from outside physics are asking me for a letter. It means that they don't know professors in their own major very well. So I write a dutiful, generic, and well-intentioned letter, but it lacks the punch of a recommendation letter written by a professor who is more intimately associated with you.

In a small Christian college, you live and move and breathe in an intimate, warm family environment. Your professors know you, and you know them. Since many students at a Christian college eventually seek a job in a Christian environment, your professors, who are well connected to the Christian world, can work the phones and help you find a job. Secular universities can't do much for a student who wants a Christian job. Even the best secular placement center wouldn't know what to do to help a Christian Education student, for example, land a job at a church. On the other hand, a Christian college would be straining to help you find a job at, say, a secular corporation such as Merrill Lynch.

IS A NURTURING CHRISTIAN ENVIRONMENT IMPORTANT?

Finally, one of the biggest advantages of a Christian college is the nurturing, supportive environment. Christian colleges have an atmosphere similar to a good church. You get the academics found at any college, but everything is filtered with the Bible and Christian perspectives. Many Christian colleges, for example, have a chapel where Christian speakers are invited to speak on Christ-centered topics. Your professors are committed believers who love the Lord and are dedicated to watering your spirit as well as your mind. They get close to their students and want to mentor you. Not to say that societal problems such as drugs, booze, and other vices are completely absent in a Christian college, but it is nothing like you find in a secular university. The other side is that, while it's tough to beat the nurturing, accepting environment of most Christian colleges; many secular universities, particularly in the South, have incredible, often overlooked, resources to help a student grow in the Christian life.

THE CHRISTIAN WORK ETHIC

College students have trouble developing a healthy view of work. College success rises or falls on your work ethic; your Christian life depends on your work ethic; everything depends on your work ethic. Work is important to God. It's His gift to mankind and one of the ways He molds us and makes us. You read that correctly. Work is a gift. Through work we become more like Christ and develop the important character traits of persistence, responsibility, and discipline—qualities that God highly esteems. Through work we stay out of trouble and help God with His program on earth. Through work, our mind stays occupied on meaningful tasks instead on negative thinking, such as what is wrong with us, what we should have done differently, and whatever worries us about our past and future. Ask any retiree what they miss the most about working and they will mention feeling useful and productive in life.

In contrast, God hates waste, sloth, and laziness. God did not hand Joshua the Promised Land; he had to work for it and there was a steep price to pay. Through numerous conflicts and wars, Joshua experienced countless nights of sleeping in foxholes, fighting in blinding sandstorms, and enduring separation from family and creature comforts. He saw fellow warriors fall brutally to the enemy. Then take the Apostle Paul; he did not have a cakewalk either. He was beaten, stoned, imprisoned, ostracized, isolated, chained, abused, and left for dead. The missionary journeys did not happen by osmosis; Paul had to walk, sail on uncomfortable ships, ride on wagons without shock absorbers, and around every turn there were bandits waiting to attack him and his entourage.

If a Christian college student studies how God views work, it will dispel the notion that work is for other people. It's especially important for millennial students who have been smothered by well-meaning helicopter parents who tend to do your work for you. Several passages in the Bible assert the positive value of work in the life of a Christian. The nature of work is not evil but good. Work was given before the Fall, not after it. Work is not a result of the curse, and God's perspective on work remains positive after the Fall. God makes His first appearance in Scripture as a worker; He is found creating the heavens and the earth in Genesis 1:1. Genesis 2:2 calls this activity work. The same Hebrew word is also used for man's work in the fourth commandment (Exod. 20:8). Since the time of creation, God continues to work. It's true that, after completing the creation, God "rested" from His work, but God didn't rest because of fatigue (Isa. 40:28–29) but because He was finished. Jesus declared to the Pharisees "My Father is always at his work to this very day, and I, too, am working" (John 5:17). God continues to work today. He upholds the creation (Col. 1:16–17), meets the broad range of needs of His creatures (Ps. 104:10–30), works out His purposes in history (Deut. 11:1–7), and accomplishes the work of atonement at the Cross (John 4:34; Ps. 111).

God created man in His image as a worker (Gen. 1:26, 28–29). The concept of mankind ruling over the other creatures and subduing the creation all point to man as a worker. Ecclesiastes 3:13 calls work a gift of God: "That everyone may eat and drink, and find satisfaction in all his toil—this is the gift of God." Exodus 35:30 describes the blending of various artistic and construction skills in the building of the tabernacle. Good workers take pride in the quality and beauty of their work. God is concerned with the excellence of what you do. Whether you are a CEO of a Fortune 500 company or a part-time burger flipper, your work should reflect the creative abilities God has given you. Whatever major God has designed for you, ask Him to make you skillful as you represent Him in college. Our service should be for the Lord, not only for man (Luke 19:11–27). This applies to your work as a college student.

What Should Motivate Students?

Imagine getting a call saying you just won a new pickup truck for having near-perfect attendance in high school. It happened to Kaytie Christopherson,[66] a sixteen-year-old student in the Casper, Wyoming school district. And it was no ordinary truck. It was a red $28,000 Chevrolet Colorado crew cab with an MP3 player. Would this motivate you to show up to high school every day for three years? Would paying you to go to school motivate you?

Apparently school districts around the country are betting on it, because many are regularly plying students with free iPods, computers, clothing, shopping sprees, movie tickets, gift cards, food, cars, and trucks. Several school districts (Yuma, Arizona; South Lake Tahoe, California; Pueblo, Colorado; Hartford, Connecticut) are currently giving away vehicles for attendance. Others are offering cash for good grades.[67] In New York City, several thousand fourth and seventh grade students can win up to $500 for improving their scores on math and English tests. The Baltimore school district offers up to $110 to high school students to improve their scores on state graduation exams. In 2007, seven states (Alabama, Arkansas, Connecticut, Kentucky, Massachusetts, Virginia, and Washington) participated in a program funded by Exxon Mobil to pay students $100 for each passing grade on the AP exam.

Why are educators trying to bribe students to attend school? Does it really work? While the evidence is not clear-cut, some people in the school districts think that freebees boost attendance. Gary Somerville, district attendance officer in the Casper district, says giving away cars helps reduce the 29% dropout rate, which he blames on Wyoming's gas and oil industry. By dropping out of school, students can make $17 an hour swinging a hammer in an oil field. Jack Stafford, associate principal at South Tahoe High, remarks that changing times call for unusual incentives.[68] Changing times? A whopping $17 per hour swinging a hammer? Where is the parental control in all of this? What parent in their right mind would allow their kids to drop out of school to pursue a few short-lived pieces of silver? It's a sad day when we have to bribe students to do the things that ensure success in life.

What should motivate college students? Why should you study hard? Why should you commit to deferred rewards? What's in it for you? Here are some hints of the correct answer. It's not the freebees, not the graduation car from your daddy, not the guaranteed stipend for clothes each month, not the breast implants, and not the $1K for each A. If it takes money and prizes to motivate you to do well in college, you are in danger of being bought off by a secular, false, and materialistic society that seeks to chew you up, take your money, rob you of your dignity, and leave you for dead after it has sucked you dry. Strong words but I'm just being honest. Talk about losing control of your life. Let me give you some of the healthier, longer-term, motivations that I discovered during my years as a college student. They need little explanation:

- A passion to please God
- A desire for excellence
- A fear of failure
- A desire to be successful
- A desire to find the profession God has made you for
- A desire to go farther than your parents
- A desire to honor your family
- A desire to become a productive member of society and the Body of Christ

What would God say to a Christian student who needs freebees to motivate him in college? He would say that the natural man has taken you over and that you should get a real instead of a fake Christian life. If you need a stocking stuffer to make you work then you have missed the whole point. Consider why you are on the Planet in the first place. What is the first goal of man? It's to love, obey, and serve the Lord (Eccles. 12). He created you for fellowship, for relationship, and for His pleasure. He has a plan for your life. He desires the best for you and wants an intimate relationship with you. Part of the plan is to develop you into a mature Christian person who becomes more Christ-like with the passing years. Christ would not approve of a Christian student who needs material incentives to perform. If you find that you are relying on cars and money more than Christ as your motivation, then you should take a hard look at your life and ask yourself why. A Christian college student should seek to do well in college because he wants to please God and live for Him. It's that simple.

FOUR

Strategies for Academic Success

Meaningful pursuits in life are best accomplished by following established principles and strategies that determine success. The strategies for academic success refer to those values, behaviors, skills, and activities that are crucial for high achievement in college. They are the core doctrines that determine success. Master them and you thrive; neglect them and you struggle.

The word strategy originates from two Greek words that together mean "to lead an army." Etymologically, strategy refers to the art of planning and conducting military operations. It requires savvy, bravery, planning, creativity, and knowledge of what you're trying to conquer. The same is true of success strategies in college. The strategies identified below are the critical skills needed for high performance in college work. When students come to college, oblivious to the rules of engagement, it's no wonder they struggle or get killed off.

The academic success strategies aren't matters of special talent. They don't require that you are brilliant or gifted. Anyone can learn them. They are largely the nuts and bolts of how you manage your academic life. Hundreds of my former students will testify that, if you faithfully apply the strategies below, there is a high probability your GPA will soar and your level of satisfaction in college will increase.

THE LEARNING ONION

It's useful first to put the process of education into a broad context. Consider what steps are necessary to learn something. Think first about simple tasks such as tying your shoes, learning to tell time, or how to cook a meal. Ponder for a minute how you learned to complete those tasks. Then advance to more abstract concepts such as the first time you learned about jealousy, lust, or greed. What is common to these learning experiences?

When I'm working with college students, it has been useful to identify five steps to learning that I collectively refer to as the learning onion. When you break each learning experience into five steps, it becomes easier to identify what is happening when you fail to learn an important idea or concept in your college courses. You get a useful gauge on how far you've progressed in your understanding. The learning onion, as I call it, tells me if my students are actually learning something in my courses. The successive peels of the onion are as follows:

- Hearing
- Listening
- Understanding
- Application
- Wisdom

Say I am teaching my students about gravity. Students are aware that gravity operates on Earth because they observe that objects always fall downward. But do they really understand it? Here are my steps to teaching, modeled after the learning onion.

- **Hearing.** Hearing is the input step in education. Your five senses detect information. The hearing step begins by attending your course lectures, reading the textbook, doing the laboratory exercises on gravity, and attending the recitation portion of the course. You observe that objects always fall toward the ground. The sensory data you have gathered over the course of your life on gravity goes into the hearing step. It's possible to hear something but not listen.

- **Listening.** Listening is the processing step in education. You make sense of the words, process the thoughts, and begin to cognitively react to the sensory information. Listening is more than the words hitting your hear drums; it's when you assimilate the message and begin to think about it. This relates to vocabulary, jargon, and terminology. If I say that gravity is a force, you have to know what force means. What is being forced? Why is it being forced? The words you hear, the words you read, the ideas and laws governing gravity have to be grasped and comprehended. It's possible to listen but not understand.

- **Understanding.** Understanding occurs when you begin to fit the new information about gravity into a broad framework. You ask yourself what is the difference between gravity and mass. You recognize that the universal law of gravity $F = Gm_1m_2/r^2$ correlates a wide variety of physical phenomena. You wonder if gravity is different on other planets. You begin to calculate the effects of gravity on other objects in the universe. You see that gravity not only applies to objects near the Earth but to all objects throughout the universe with mass. You ponder whether you need to use rocket engines to push a spacecraft forward when it's weightless (but not massless) in space. You begin to see gravity in a broader framework and connect it to other inverse-square laws in physics such as the law of electricity. It's possible to understand something but not be able to apply it.

- **Application.** Application is the extension of learning to new situations. For students, the application step occurs when you do homework problems and end-of-chapter exercises. Say I give you a problem to determine the effects of gravity on an object falling through the air. This is different from the effects of gravity on an object falling in vacuum. The object falling in vacuum gains a constant amount of speed (10 m/s) as it falls while the object falling in air eventually stops gaining speed and settles on a constant speed called the terminal velocity. Going through the jungle of sorting this out is an example of applying the principles of gravity. As you apply your knowledge to a variety of situations, you gain confidence that you really have learned it. It's possible to apply a principle but not apply it wisely.

- **Wisdom.** Wisdom is the prudent use of learning. You advise paratroopers to wear parachutes when they jump out of a plane. You tell NASA they need powerful engines to launch the Space Shuttle into orbit. You determine that you need smaller engines to launch off the moon where gravity is one-sixth that of Earth. You tell civil engineers they need a certain thickness of structural steel to withstand a million cars per week going over a bridge.

The reason I spend a lot of time in my college courses teaching by prototypes (analogies) is that it tells me how many onion layers my students have peeled away in their education. If students can peel down to the deeper application and wisdom parts of the onion, they are truly learning physics.

Now apply this to your own educational experience. How many times has this happened to you? You hear a lecture, think you now know something, nod your head, but when it comes to applying what you've learned, you're at a loss. Did you really learn it? Probably not. You haven't dug deep enough into the learning onion. It could be that you heard but didn't really listen. Or you heard and listened, but failed to understand. Or you heard, listened, and understood, but couldn't apply the knowledge to new situations offered on tests, projects, and homework assignments. Or you heard, listened, understood, and applied, but used the knowledge unwisely. There are five relevant steps—hearing what is taught, listening to what is taught, understanding what is taught, applying what is taught, and using what is taught wisely. Students don't advance very far in their education until most of the learning onion is peeled.

The Bible underscores the existence of learning steps. The author of Romans remarks that "Faith comes from hearing the message, and the message is heard through the word of Christ" (Rom. 10:17). Isaiah remarks

"[God] said, 'Go, and tell this people: Be ever hearing, but never understanding; be ever seeing, but never perceiving'"(Isa. 6:9). James says "Do not merely listen to the word, and so deceive yourselves. Do what it says. Anyone who listens to the word but does not do what it says is like a man who looks at his face in a mirror and, after looking at himself, goes away and immediately forgets what he looks like" (James 1:22–24). It's easy to identify the onion layers in these verses—hearing, listening, understanding, applying, and wisdom. Clearly, the apostles and prophets knew their vegetables.

STRATEGY #1: *Developing Effective Study Skills*

Entering college freshman generally have poor study skills. They've either never been shown how to study, or their high school courses didn't demand much studying. Effective studying is governed by principles similar to the laws that govern gravity. Cooperate with the laws and you get good results; ignore the laws and you will plummet to earth. Students are miles ahead if they learn and consistently follow the principles for academic success, starting with study skills. There are six principles involved with developing study skills.

ACTIVE LISTENING SKILLS

Listening is a significant part of the learning process. Venues for listening occur throughout your college education. The best way to listen is called active listening. By active listening I mean getting the most out of now. There is a saying that goes "Wherever you are, be there." The context is usually when someone isn't listening, as when a wife is trying to explain something to her husband while he's watching Monday Night Football. Forget it. Guys are notorious for tuning everyone out during football games. How many times have you talked and talked to someone only to find out that they haven't heard anything? Pastors can look out from their pulpits on Sunday morning and count the people in the sanctuary who are somewhere else during the sermon. They haven't really heard anything. It's that glazed, bored, distracted, and detached stare into space. The problems of the week have possessed them and Satan is stealing the nuggets of biblical truth we all desperately need every week. College students in particular seem riddled with attention deficit disorder (ADD), which is, in many cases, a fancy designation for a simple inability to stay on task.

The problem is lack of concentration. It gets so bad that most professors know that, for a typical M, W, F class, we only have Wednesdays to get our material across without losing a large fraction of the class to daydreaming, fatigue, and inattention. On Monday, students are recovering from the weekend. On Friday, students are looking forward to the weekend. Only on Wednesday can we accomplish anything productive. What a waste of time. Do you honestly believe you can learn a college-level subject with only one productive hour per week of professor-assisted education? It can't be done.

Professors learn that we have to repeat material several times before most of the class gets it. Only a small fraction of the class catch it the first time, a larger fraction the second time, and a majority of the class finally gets it when repeated for the third time. This is one of the major reasons we are covering significantly less material during a semester compared to a decade ago. Most students today would herald that as good, because less material means that there is less to learn and less to study come test time. Problem is, the rest of the world is staying awake during their lectures. Foreign students are eating our lunch and beginning to take over the world when it comes to the lucrative technical and professional jobs demanding high levels of competence.

The short attention span of college students is counterproductive in the long haul of college. A building will collapse if the infrastructure is weak and a college student will collapse if the critical concepts central to a discipline have not been learned in the first place. What to do? The short answer is that active listening takes deliberate and concerted effort. It develops by practice. At first, you may not be able to actively listen for fifteen minutes, but with consistent practice, it gets easier and easier. You also need to control the other parts of your life such as getting to bed at a reasonable hour and staying away from partying. Work first and party later is the best policy. You have time in college for all the things you want to do if you concentrate and time manage.

Note Taking Skills

Colleges are currently undergoing a transition from lecture-based to interactive and online courses. Driving the transition are software companies and colleges who seek to profit from millennials, who appear to learn best from media. That being said, most college courses still require students to take accurate and organized notes during lectures. There are several good reasons for taking notes.

Professors Highlight What's Important to Learn

The most utilitarian reason for taking notes is that you highlight what your professor might ask on a test. Professors organize their lectures around important points. We do this because we don't have the time in three fifty-minute lectures per week to treat all the possible nuances discussed in textbooks. Professors handle the time constraint issue in one of two ways—they either cover a lot of chapters superficially or choose the most important things and treat them in detail. I'm of the latter persuasion. In either case, professors emphasize what is important for students to know, and this is what you should take notes on.

Note taking skills have degenerated so much that every year I find myself saying "You need to write this down" more frequently. When I do this, I'm trying to teach my freshman students how to take effective notes. Part of the problem in my courses, if you want to call it a problem, is that I make all my lecture notes available so my students can actively listen and think with me during the lecture and not just take dictation. Sad to say, I'm not sure it would be too different if I didn't supply the notes. Even when I spoon-feed my students with prompts, hints, and allusions to "This would be a good test question," it's frequently the case that students either don't take me seriously, don't care enough, or don't indicate in their notes that what I was talking about was important, and this presumes students come to class in the first place. If you don't come to class, you can't take good notes. Trust me. Getting notes from a classmate is not the same as taking them yourself.

Note taking is more art than science. Avoid two extremes—taking notes on everything and taking notes on nothing. Beyond that, your note taking strategy should change appropriately with the course. Courses with lots of mathematics require meticulous and comprehensive notes. Courses in the liberal arts require general notes, such as what was talked about in class or discussion groups. Note taking is best learned by experience and by evaluating how your notes stack up with what helps you do better on tests. Experience with professors and the course material will show you what is important. Comparing your notes to your tests will show you what you should have been writing down. It's an iterative process that gets better with practice.

The best professors will help you learn what is important to learn. I simply tell my students which parts of the material are important and to emphasize it in their notes. If you have a professor who is poor at leading students, most textbooks offer useful, almost tediously redundant, end-of-chapter outlines and summaries of key points and important terminology. Start with that if you are clueless. The problem is not that help is unavailable but that most students don't take advantage of it, opting to let education come to them rather than going to education and seeking help when they need it. To be successful in college, you have to be active and not passive. You have to pursue what you need and not think it will magically come to you.

NOTE TAKING KEEPS YOU ACTIVELY ENGAGED DURING CLASS

Note taking is a form of active listening. You stay engaged with your education by taking notes. Writing down important points keeps you busy and fights boredom. Professors can almost predict when students are going to do poorly on tests by the level of note taking we observe. When I see that glazed and detached look on my students' faces, I know they are missing vital information. Taking notes can prevent your mind from wandering away to the party last night or the argument you had with your girlfriend.

What I am talking about here is staying on task. There are several ways to maintain focus. The method that has worked best for me is to be interested in my courses. Rather than considering core courses as unnecessary irrelevance to your degree, think of them as teaching you important information that every college-educated person should know. Give your subjects a chance to interest you. Here's what can happen.

Characteristically, students say to me after my physics course that, while they hated having to take the course at first, they later found it refreshingly interesting, stimulating, and filled with insightful examples of how physics is used in everyday life. Granted, it takes a good professor to bring out the joy and relevance of a subject, but you can learn something useful from every course. When I was in college, I wasn't exactly thrilled about taking Russian, Western Civilization, and History, but I was glad later that the curriculum designers forced me to take a broad range of courses. They were useful to raise my view of the world and courses you would never take unless you were in college. There is precious time later in life to appreciate the range of knowledge that has made our world great, and you never know what skills you might need for your future. Heed the advice of returning students when they say that learning the second time around gives you a totally different view about a broad liberal arts education.

Note Taking Helps You Retain Important Information

A huge body of empirical data supports the notion that retention depends on how many times you are exposed to concepts and ideas. Retention refers to how much of what you learn you remember. Exposure refers to how much you interact and think with the concepts and ideas. When you take notes in class, you receive information by the ear, eye, and hand gates. As you review your notes, they become part of you as you expose yourself to them over and over.

The word is repetition. Note taking reinforces repetition. Think for a moment about how you know the words to songs such as "God Bless America." The answer is that you hear them over and over and over again. Repetition, repetition, and more repetition. Eventually, they become part of you and are pleasurable to sing because they are like old friends. The same is true of the information you learn in college. At first, it's a struggle and there is resistance from the newness of what you are learning, but as you spend time with it, it becomes second nature and you retain what you need for your life.

Good teachers will help you with retention by constructing their lectures with periodic reviews. A take-off point for most of my lectures is to review what we learned last time and how it relates to the material of the day. Tests are also reviews. The problem with most college students is that they don't spend enough time with new material to make it familiar. You don't repeat it enough. You don't live with it enough. You don't think about it enough. Taking notes forces you to interact with course material time and time again. It's like when you first meet someone you have a crush on. The interaction can be horribly uncomfortable and intimidating at first, but as you talk and get to know each other, it becomes enjoyable by the end of the evening.

Note Taking Organizes Your Thoughts into a Personalized, Logical Framework

Don't laugh, but when I was in college, I used to recopy my notes in important physics courses when I got back to my dorm room. While this is terribly inefficient, and I'm not recommending it, the procedure helped me reiterate the lecture, reorganize it into a form I could better understand, and personalize it to my particular way of learning. Later, when I found myself having to teach the same material in college, my recopied undergraduate course notes provided a valuable resource for composing my own lectures. I could look back and see what I didn't understand and tailor my teaching to address the difficulties when I was a student first learning the material. Former students remark often that they go back to their course notes when attempting to solve a problem in their post-college job. Course notes provide a useful historical record that you will reference again and again in your field when you need to review how something works.

Course notes make for easy learning and help you study for tests. Rather than having to go back over the textbook, it's easier to go to a set of well-composed notes which give you the high points without all the verbiage. You get to the point quicker. Outlines and notes are especially useful for memory-intensive courses or courses with a logical progression of ideas. Oftentimes, it's only the skeleton of an argument that's important, and notes provide the schematic. I would hate, for example, to try to learn what is involved with a complex electronic circuit by reading about what each of the resistors, capacitors, and inductors are doing in the circuit by words in a textbook. But give me an electronic schematic of the circuit and everything gets easier due to the terse way a schematic organizes information. In short, it's usually a diagram, figure, or interactive situation which facilitates learning, and notes provide the necessary framework for this visualization.

READING AND STUDYING TEXTBOOKS

Due to the number of mediocre physics instructors I had in college, much of my early physics education was achieved by reading textbooks. Fortunately, there were excellent physics textbooks at that time which were well written. When you have a below-average professor who has trouble communicating in the classroom, teaching yourself from a textbook is often your only option. Before giving you advice on best ways to read a textbook, it's useful to give you a brief general perspective on them. There are pros and cons to the story.

Today's textbooks are generally superior to textbooks of the past in terms of helping students learn. There's more study aids, more solution manuals, more Websites with examples and visual simulations, more study questions, more everything. Publishers for the leading college textbooks can easily break the backpacks of students with ancillary study aids. The materials make more money for the publishers and attempt to make learning easier for students. They are not only pedagogically better but the full integration of computer technology into textbook publishing enables spectacular graphics, photography, and visual aids which motivates learning and provides oomph to college-level material.

Regrettably, a minority of students take advantage of the better textbooks. It's rare to find students who study their books unless professors use a big stick. Instead, students employ all other sorts of methods when studying, such as using notes only, studying old tests, talking to other students, using tutoring services, and studying in groups. Nothing wrong with this, but a learner eventually has to go to the primary source of information for full understanding, and that's usually a textbook. Another con is the high cost of textbooks. You can easily go broke buying new textbooks, which are almost rammed down students' throats due to the frequent editions and bundled ancillaries forced on students by publishers. In fact, the "new and improved" editions are merely money making schemes offering few substantive changes from edition-to-edition. The textbook I use in my Dave Letterman course, for example, is in its fifteenth edition and is getting worse as the editions pile up. What is the best way to use a textbook? Here are a few suggestions.

To Fill in the Blanks of Lectures

Professors lack the time in lecture to give all the details. Textbooks fill in the details and add extra illustrative material. The graphics, photographs, figures, and drawings in textbooks today are better than life. Good pictures are worth a thousand words. In the case of physics, students who want to know how a particular mathematical equation is derived can find accurate derivations in textbooks. There are scores of worked-out examples, instances of where physics is applied in the real world, and hundreds of study questions that professors can't cover in lecture. I frequently have my students read the insets in physics textbooks on the life of famous scientists to show them that not all scientists are nerds. The insets have some of the most interesting material in the course but almost nobody takes the time to read them. Do yourself a favor and read enough of your textbooks to get the sense that you know your author as a professional who loves his field and seeks to show you how it can benefit your life. Few authors make much money on writing textbooks and it's largely a labor of love to their fields and students.

For Additional, Worked Out Examples

A good professor will pepper his lectures with worked-out examples and illustrations. But after we show you how to work out a couple of problems, you need to try your own hand in order to develop confidence and build comprehension. Under such circumstances, a textbook takes the place of direct tactile involvement such as my graduate students get when working hand in hand with me in the laboratory. There is no substitute for interacting with the material yourself instead of watching your teachers do it for you. Textbooks provide an optimum source of questions and exercises to stretch your learning experience and help you understand the material. Good students avail themselves of the opportunities. It's common knowledge among my AU students that, to do well on my tests, you have to go beyond the required homework assignments and try some additional problems and questions. Textbooks make that possible.

To Aid in Organization of the Course Material

Professors usually can't remember how difficult material is to learn the first time and fail to provide the logical, step-by-step progression needed by most students. They have forgotten what needs to be learned first, what second, and what third, because they use the material every week and have long forgotten the important, intermediate steps to learning. Textbooks usually make up for this shortcoming because authors have the time and space to organize their thoughts and get editorial feedback along the publishing process about how to explain things effectively. They have the time to reflect on the correct ordering of material and provide study aids in the form of chapter goals and objectives.

To Get the Correct Language and Terminology

Professors know that students have studied the course material when they use proper vocabulary and terminology. This is important when answering discussion questions on tests and, in general, is prerequisite to becoming a literate, educated member of society. Imagine how it would look to a recruiter if you lacked the proper vocabulary to express yourself during a job interview. Professors see the lack of expression when students attempt to answer test questions without knowing the appropriate terminology. It sticks out like a sore thumb and gives us a good reason to knock down your test score. A common complaint I hear from my students, after seeing low scores on discussion questions, is that they knew the answer, but didn't know how to express it properly. This is due to a lack of vocabulary and can be corrected by studying your textbooks.

THE AMAZING DISAPPEARING ACT

WHAT ABOUT MEMORIZING?

As a physics teacher, I usually have a fraction of students who, when polled, say they have had a year of calculus. But then when I start to talk about the simplest calculus concept, such as the technique of integration, there are blank faces throughout the class. What happened to that year of calculus? It's as though Houdini waved his hands over my student's heads and pronounced "Now you see it, now you don't." Where did it go?

It was never there. Instead of learning calculus, what really happened was that you memorized a series of steps to solve a problem to pass a test to get a good grade. You never peeled back the learning onion successfully. That kind of learning never stays. It's completely unsatisfying. It's like sitting down for a meal of prime rib, mashed potatoes, creamed corn, and home-made biscuits but you can't taste it because your nose is stuffed up. It's not learning at all but rather playing the game of school. I ask my students "Why would you spend a year in calculus and not learn anything satisfying, anything lasting, anything with meat, anything that applies to everyday life? What a wasted year of effort. That's why you hated calculus. It stops here. We're not doing that in my physics class."

Students memorizing everything in sight and calling it learning begins early. An ACT study (2007) found that high school teachers consistently rate knowing facts above process and inquiry skills such as understanding a theory of science.[69] That's just what I'm talking about. Students used to succeeding in high school by memorization are blown out of the water by college professors who prefer thinking skills. Let me make this concrete to show you the difference between comprehension and memorization. Don't hemorrhage because it's a calculus example. Be daring, and keep reading. You don't have to know calculus to follow my logic. Let's consider what is called integral calculus. At its core, integral calculus is really nothing more than advanced addition. When you do an integral, as it's called in calculus, you are simply adding up the areas of rectangles. The rectangles have broader meaning, which in physics means connecting the rectangles to real, measurable quantities such as energy, but it's nothing more than addition. How simple can it get?

Say you want to know how much energy it takes to do something, such as lift a bag of groceries from the floor in Wal-Mart. In physics, you find the answer by determining how much force your muscles exert during the lifting process multiplied by the distance over which you lift the groceries. This is the definition of energy in physics. If, in the most complex case where the force varies along the distance you lift (by say, lifting hard at first and soft at the end of your lift), you can come up with an exact answer to the energy required by doing the calculus integral operation. Translated into mathematical language, you would determine the integral of the force F times the distance d, a calculus operation called "integrating F over d." It's written as $E = \int F \, dx$, where E is the energy, F is the force, and dx is the incremental distance moved by the sack when using force F. If I give you the functional form of how F varies over the distance you move the grocery sack, which is called F as a function of x, and written as $F(x)$, you can use the calculus rules of integration to solve for E, the energy.

Most calculus students will memorize the rules of integration and be able to come up with an answer but have no idea what the answer means or that integral calculus is connected to addition. There is little connection of mathematics to reality, no idea of what doing an integral means, and no clue to why this might be important in life. There is nothing of lasting value to take with you to other courses which depend on calculus. Learning is merely memorizing a set of instructions to pass a test. Not! You can never hope to enjoy your college studies and accumulate a broad education for life if you so stumble through your studies. Choosing the path of least resistance is not an appropriate or satisfying way to get through college. Yes, I know, part of the problem is poor teaching. It's not all your fault. Nevertheless, millennial students have been trained from kindergarten to rely on memorization instead of comprehension, which takes a lot more effort.

Memory and Learning Contrasted

Students have had it drilled into them that memorizing is tantamount to learning. Nothing could be further from the truth. Memorization deals with only the outer hearing and listening parts of the learning onion. Some memorization is necessary to give you the raw materials to think with, but students who equate memorization with education are profoundly mistaken. The memory gymnastics you do in college to pass tests are largely temporary, dealing only with short-term memory. When short-term memory is not converted to long-term memory, it vanishes and you are left with nothing. You're smitten with collegiate Alzheimer's disease. It becomes hard to function in college courses when you try to memorize the prerequisite knowledge from previous courses. You're dead in the water and hopelessly behind from day one. It's a horrible feeling.

There is another side to the memorization coin, consisting of the essential information that must be memorized in every discipline. Think of how handicapped and frustrated you would be, for instance, if you were an X-ray technologist and had to look up where the liver was located on an anatomical chart every time you had to take a patient X-ray. If you wish to keep your sanity and optimize your learning in college, you have to memorize some critical information. This was brought home to me as an undergraduate when I found myself constantly looking up the physical constants used in physics. It got to the point that I finally made a list of the most-used physical constants and memorized them. While it goes against the grain of most physicists who are against any kind of memorization, it served little purpose to keep looking up everything needed to do physics problems that you tackle on a daily basis. Memory is therefore a critical part of college courses. The sticky point is what and how to memorize. I let expediency and context guide me.

Expediency. Expediency refers to the necessary actions required to achieve a desired result regardless of whether you believe they are correct actions. Expediency means that, in some college courses, professors simply require memorization to do well on tests and exams. You're forced into it if you want a good grade. While memory-driven courses minimally contribute to deep and insightful education, when you have to do it, you have to do it. A more difficult question is what to memorize when you have courses that are less memory-directed. This relates to the issue of context.

Context. Context means to decide what to memorize depending on the situation. In my case, the context decision was based on efficiency and whether the course was important to my major. Most students who take my physics courses are not going to be physics majors, so I advise them not to memorize too much unless it leads to major inconvenience. It would do my students little good to memorize, say, the conversion between pounds and newtons, or the value of the charge on the electron, or the mass of a proton, or how many protons are in the nucleus of a sodium atom. You're only going to use the information sparingly. It might be prudent, on the other hand, for students to take to heart the major laws of science, such as Newton's laws. Newton's laws are used so much in a physics course that students might as well learn them without having to look them up every time. Knowledge of the laws of science provides the mental raw material to examine a whole class of events in the physical world. Without a discipline's raw materials, it's difficult to think and reason about the great ideas of educated society. Imagine trying to be an effective writer without knowledge of vocabulary and grammar. Or a mathematician without knowledge of algebra and trigonometry. Or a forestry major who doesn't know the different varieties of wood. Or a pastor without knowledge of the books of the Bible. You get the idea.

Is there a best way to convert short-term into long-term memory? There are a variety of theories that seek to explain what happens in the brain when you learn. Rather than discuss the theories, which would require a whole book, my goal here is to give you some practical tips. The important concepts involve repetition and emotional involvement.

Memory obviously depends on repetition. Say you are a basketball player and want to learn to swish more free throws. How best to learn this skill? First, you would have a knowledgeable basketball coach teach you the proper techniques of shooting. Second, you would practice the techniques by shooting free throws. Hundreds of them. Thousands of them. That's repetition. Whatever you can do to repeat college material during a semester is useful. One suggestion is to carry a stack of note cards. There are always slots of time in a busy schedule where you can pull out your cards and review. For courses such as organic chemistry and anatomy where rote memory skills are required, it simply takes practice, practice, and more practice. Use whatever methods work to make memorization easier. Mnemonics often help. I've always remembered the music scale with the mnemonic **E**very **G**ood **B**oy **D**oes **F**ine and the astronomical star types by **O**h **B**e **A** **F**ine **G**irl, **K**iss **M**e. One mnemonic in the South is GRITS (**g**irls **r**aised **i**n **t**he **s**outh). Mnemonics are usually corny but that's what makes them easy to remember. The key, involving memory and the necessary practice, repetition, and review cycle is, to be disciplined.

A second method to enhance your long-term memory is by getting emotionally involved with the material, meaning that you learn something by living with it over a period of time. When you live with something, you get emotionally involved with it. You move in with the course material. Scientists have found that memory and emotion are biochemically linked with hormones such as adrenaline involved in forming the neurological patterns we call memories. James McGaugh, a leading neurobiologist at UC–Irvine says "Any kind of emotional experience will create a stronger memory than otherwise would be created."[70] This explains why nearly everyone remembers where they were when the planes hit the World Trade Center on 9-11 or when President Kennedy was assassinated in Dallas in the sixties. One of my pet theories for why students find college work so onerous is that they never get emotionally involved with their courses. It never gets to the level of passion. Students can't wait to get out of many of their courses. When you hold something with contempt, push it away, and refuse to become engaged with it, you're not going to develop an emotional connection with it. When a subject isn't important to you, it's like pulling teeth trying to learn it. In contrast, when you enjoy a subject, the repeated exposure cements it into your mind by familiarity. Whatever you live with becomes part of you, not by memorization but by repeated exposure. An illustration. Think back to how you "learned" about your best friend. Did you fill out note cards on that person describing their personality, tastes, likes, and dislikes? Of course not.

You spent time with them. You ate with them, went to movies with them, roomed with them, shared your disastrous blind dates with them, prayed with them, worked with them, and shared life secrets with them. You learned by experience. Likewise, when I teach a concept in physics, say the law of conservation of momentum, I never suggest that my students memorize a verbal statement of the law, such as "When only internal forces act on a system of moving objects, the total momentum is conserved." That means almost nothing. Verbal definitions are filled with jargon and result in virtually no education when students try to memorize them.

STUDY GROUPS AND TUTORS

There is a growing body of research which indicates that learning in groups is better than learning in solitary environments. Group work allows for discussion and comparison of ideas which reinforces education and enables students to correct wrong notions of how something works. Many disciplines require working in groups on projects that are time critical and depend on the input of a variety of people who are experts. Think *The Apprentice.*

There's nothing wrong with learning in groups. I strongly encourage it for students who learn better in group environments. But there are downsides. Take science labs as an example. It seems that just about every article written on science education nowadays addresses the advantages of students working in teams of three to four students doing hands-on, tactile, touchy-feely lab activities. The idea is sound in principle. After all, one of the best ways to learn about how a car engine works, for example, is to take it apart and see how the component parts fit together, such as the battery, spark plugs, water pump, and crankshaft. You get a totally different education when you put your hands on something than when you read about it in a book. But here's the rub. Everyone in a lab or study group has to participate to make the lofty team learning experience a reality, and that's not what happens in most study groups. Most students stand off to one side and hope someone in their lab or study group knows what's going on. This means that only a few students in a college lab get anything useful out of it, and the others just copy from them. Even in that situation, there is some value, as the students on top of their game end up teaching those that are not. But group study is not what it's cracked up to be and can actually be detrimental to students because they remain on the sidelines and then deceive themselves into thinking that copying something is the same as learning it. So beware of group study.

Concerning tutors. Here are some guidelines on whether you should seek them. First, it's better to do something than nothing when you need help in college. Many students err by wringing their hands instead of seeking out the plentiful help offered by colleges. We all need help sometimes, so it's better to swallow your pride and admit you're lost, but whom you admit it to is important. It nearly makes me crazy each semester when students who are lost in physics come up and ask me who I would suggest as a tutor. My answer is me. And I'm free. Somewhere it seems to be written that you can't ask your own teachers anymore. Professors should be your first line of defense. That's part of our job, what we are here for, and some of us enjoy helping you. Unless I have an exceedingly busy week, I want my students to come by for help and hate it when a semester goes by and I only get to know a small fraction of my students. I'm always telling them, "I can't imagine spending fifteen weeks with you and not getting to know you, so please come by for help or just to say hello. And if you can't come by, then email me some of your best jokes."

That being said, I'm aware that some professors are less than helpful, or students are just more comfortable working with a tutor. Where do you find a good tutor?

- **Recommendations of Fellow Students.** This is where living in a dorm, fraternity, or sorority is helpful, because fellow students usually know who the good tutors are and where they are located. Walk down the hall and ask a suite mate.
- **Bulletin Boards.** Graduate students who are available for tutoring often advertise by flyers on bulletin boards around the campus.
- **Individual Departments.** In most cases, each department has a list of graduate students who wish to be tutors. In my department,

we have a list of suggested tutors for various physics courses posted in the physics department office.

- **Your GTA.** In large universities, it's graduate students who teach recitation and laboratories. They know other graduate students who would be good tutors.
- **The University Itself.** It's amazing how many student support services exist today compared to when I was in college. At AU, for example, we have scores of services for students who are struggling academically, and they are nearly all free, because you paid for them with your tuition. At AU there is Study Partners, Tutoring Services, and about ten other programs to help students academically. The bottom line is that there is no excuse for students not getting help if they need it. The resources are there, but you have to reach out. In college, you are an adult, and we won't force ourselves on you, but we will happily respond if you ask.

STRATEGY #2: *Time Management*

Time management is crucial to success in college. If I had to pick one area where college freshmen fall short, it's in organizing time. You've never had to do it before because you lived with your parents and they tended to organize your time. In college, when students learn that parents are no longer supervisory, the new freedom goes to your head. There's too much to choose and not enough maturity to choose wisely. Fun comes before studying. Football Saturday comes each week in the fall. Sororities and fraternities have weekly activities. You have to spend time with your boyfriend or girlfriend. Cell phones are ubiquitous. There is your part-time student job. Successful students learn that you have enough time in college to do all the things you need to do, but you must manage yourself. Decide on what four to five things are important and stick with them. There's not time for much else.

BUILDING A SCHEDULE

When writing this section, I started by trying to think of any successful person I knew who didn't work from a schedule. I could think of none. Not one. If you want to be successful in college, scheduling is paramount. Without scheduling, your life turns into chaos, frustration, and inefficiency. Either you control your time or it will control you. If you choose to live without a schedule, which many people think is confining, you're the one who is enslaved. You are in bondage to the whims and forces in your life that deal your cards for you. There is no way a college student can survive for long without a schedule because there are too many time-critical things that can't be ignored without paying a stiff penalty.

Take assignments and tests. Every semester a raft of students tries to hand in papers that are late, messy, chaotic, incomplete, and done in haste. Students are disorganized and forget to do what is important. They don't carry a calendar or keep a schedule. Some college students are so used to having mommy get them up, remind them to eat their vegetables, wash their clothes, and a host of other maintenance things, that they don't know how to manage their own lives.

Everybody who works from a schedule does it differently. Management is a personal activity. Some use pocket calendars, some use Blackberries, some use their computer, some use roommates, some use a secretary, some use phone calls from mommy. A simple method I've used for years is to purchase a DayMinder from an office supply store that I keep in my briefcase. This is a small, black, spiral-bound notebook that allows you to see an entire month at a glance and gives you space in each day block to write what is important to do that day. I can't live without it. Many students use calendars they carry in their purse or backpack. The important point is not your particular scheduling method but that you have a scheduling method. Keep it simple and portable. Fancy schemes offered by computer software are usually more trouble than what they're worth and, unless you carry around a laptop all the time, not very portable.

Take each course syllabus after your first day of classes and block out all the important assignments, project deadlines, tests, final exams, field trips, laboratories, football games, concerts, trips home, haircuts, tanning bed appointments, and so on. Use a pencil so you can amend when things change, such as when professors change the date of their tests at the end of the semester. Each night, before your head hits the pillow, check your calendar to make sure you're not overlooking something tomorrow or the day after tomorrow. Look ahead to see when tests are scheduled and projects are due in order to stay abreast of the power curve. You will find security and solace in keeping a calendar, and it will free you up to do the things in college you enjoy because you are efficiently using your time.

Taking Responsibility

Taking responsibility means to take charge of your life and quit depending on excuses, girlfriends, mommy, or roommates when it comes to the daily tasks of living. Responsibility is not a dirty word. It's a badge of courage showing you are breaking free of the bonds of your parents and beginning to live as an adult. It has special meaning for Christian students who are seeking God's will for your life. God is handicapped in growing you up if you continue to cling to the safe haven of home. There is a transition from being a teenager to being an adult, from being dependent to being independent. The transition doesn't have to be brutal, obtuse, difficult, or dreadful, but something to look forward to as you see God work in your life. He is getting you ready for greater service.

Responsibility is learned with time and trouble. Each person has to get that sickening feeling of not hearing the alarm go off, or the gut-wrenching punch in the belly when you haven't prepared for a test and discover that nothing looks familiar, or the shock and awe when you take your first physics exam and find out you got a 55%. We learn best in the caldron of adversity. College offers God the perfect pressure cooker to grow you up as a Christian. Allow Him to teach you.

One of my pastors taught me an early lesson on how to handle difficult situations with students. He told me not to play God and rescue everyone. I wanted to rush in and solve the problem my students were facing, which usually amounted to granting leniency on missed tests and assignments. While there is wiggle room for special circumstances, I learned that bailing out my students hurt them more than it helped because it usurped what God wanted to do in their lives. I was playing God. One of the problems in college is that a steady diet of overlooked lax behaviors and low standards result in students who can't fend for themselves or take responsibility for their actions. It's always someone else's fault, and I was contributing to the problem. Own up to the situations you've created, and allow God to teach you to be a better Christian steward. He loves you and will carry you through the difficult learning curve everyone faces in college.

BEING FLEXIBLE

Being flexible for a college student means to go with the flow. Some mountains are not worth dying on. For freshmen who are the low man on the totem pole, there are times when you have to defer to your junior and senior classmates. They have seniority and should get priority for football tickets, parking spots, and enrollment in critical courses required for graduation on time. This means you have to be flexible and not get bent whenever you think you're being treated unfairly. When it comes to a bureaucracy, everyone gets treated unfairly. Allow God to build your patience and character. You should take the dark days with a positive attitude and a grateful heart that God is in control.

Flexibility is especially needed during course enrollment. Enrollment is getting better every year due to computer software that manages course schedules, and college students now enroll and manage course schedules largely by themselves. The software checks for required prerequisites and blocks students from signing into classes without first seeing a counselor or when the necessary background courses are absent. While this is a pain for many students, it prevents frustration for students who fool themselves into thinking they can handle a course. Students often think they know more about curriculum design than the professionals who look at the big picture and determine what courses are prerequisite in various majors.

Let me tell you how lucky you are compared to how it used to be. When I was an undergrad at Michigan State, the entire population of the university (forty-five thousand) was expected to show up at a single building on campus (affectionately called the class card arena; better described as the Roman Coliseum) and get in line for class cards that guaranteed admission into courses. The class cards were like American Idol tickets.

Students would camp out overnight to grab the precious slips of cardboard. For popular courses like business and marketing, the lines ran around the outside of the building for something like fifty yards. Enrollment for those courses could take the better part of a day. Physics majors, by contrast, could walk right up to the physics table where nobody was in line. If your high stress visit to the class card arena wasn't enough, most universities then were on the quarter system, which meant that you had to enroll three times per year instead of twice. Further, this was Michigan where it gets cold in the winter. Talk about wanting a course. Students today are spoiled. You should be kissing IBM, Apple, and Intel for making your life a comparative breeze during enrollment.

THE PROCRASTINATION CYCLE

Procrastination means to defer action. You put off something until a later time. It's lethal to a college student. There are few things in college that will hurt you more than procrastination. It's a self-fulfilling prophesy that dooms you to failure. You do yourself an enormous favor if you forever conquer procrastination.

Procrastination puts you in bondage and keeps you on defense in pursuit of your education. You lose control of your life; instead, the list of postponed tasks controls you. Your list of "to-dos" becomes a list of "haven't dones." Procrastination haunts you, dogs you, saps your strength, and then moves in for the kill. As more put-off tasks accrue, it becomes increasingly difficult to catch up. You drown in academic quicksand. Wild, uncontrolled flailing only sucks you down deeper. Once the downward spiral begins, it takes such an enormous effort to reverse the giant sucking sound that few students can hack it. This is the procrastination cycle.

Procrastination is increasing as people find more gadgets to kill time. University of Calgary professor Piers Steel remarks "That stupid game Minesweeper—that probably has cost billions of dollars for the whole society."[71] He adds that the U.S. gross national product would probably rise by $50 billion if the icon and sound that notifies people of new email suddenly disappeared. Some of his findings show that people who procrastinate tend to be less healthy, less wealthy, and less happy. Psychologist

William Knaus, a recognized expert on procrastination, remarks that he found it harder to wean chronic procrastinators from the habit of delaying than to get alcoholics off booze.[72] That's like the pull of a black hole. There are several root causes of procrastination:

Laziness. People who are lazy are easy marks for procrastination. If you have poor work habits or are used to having someone else do your work then procrastination lurks at your doorstep. The millennial generation is particularly at risk because helicopter parents have fostered and tolerated dependent behavior from their children. They now face the difficult mountain of effort required for success as a college student.

Poor Management Skills. Disorganization leads to procrastination. If you lack management skills, you overlook important tasks. Say you have a time-critical project due for a design class and forget to write down the due date in your calendar. Then, at the last minute, you remember it's due tomorrow. Your lack of organization has forced you into a procrastination scenario. While you didn't back into procrastination by being lazy, the end result is the same. You have fallen behind and created enormous stress in your life. Your project ends up being hastily thrown together. You end up hating the project. You get a poor grade. And the more tasks you overlook the more you have to play catch-up and the more you fall behind.

Poor Personal Discipline. Discipline refers to an orderly, controlled, and efficient way of doing things. It is the ability to put first things first and to tackle tasks that are hard to do before things that are easy to do. Discipline is the ability to stay on task. One of the best definitions of discipline is given by best-selling author and pastor Chuck Swindoll, who observes: "Discipline is control gained by enforced obedience. It is the deliberate cultivation of inner order. It is training that corrects and perfects our mental faculties or molds our moral character."[73]

Control gained by enforced obedience. Yup, that's it. Discipline means getting control of your college life by forcing yourself to study. It means to put aside your natural desires to pursue a course of action that requires sustained effort. To turn off the TV when you need to study. To say no to a party if you have an important test on Monday. To cut short a visit with your girlfriend if you have a project due. To refuse to let the masses lead you with their herd mentality. Discipline is an important life skill. Identify a successful person, and you will find a disciplined person.

Fear of Failure. Fear is a major reason for procrastination. For students, the major fear is the fear of failure, which creates inaction and freezes progress. When you are afraid of something, you put off confronting it. You procrastinate. Think of a time when you wanted to break up with a guy you were dating but were afraid to broach the subject with him for fear of the pain. Or someone who thinks they have an illness but is afraid to go to the doctor. There are numerous sources of fear for college students. Some are afraid of hard work and whether they can cut it in college. Some are afraid of leaving home and being on their own. Some are afraid of growing up. Some are afraid of being pushed out of their comfort zone. Some are fearful of disappointing themselves, their friends, and their parents. And some are afraid of the level of competition in college. With each passing month, the competition gets stiffer as the system eats up the weaker students, and the stronger ones survive. It's academic Darwinism. There is a natural selection process that occurs in the first couple of years of college as students jockey for easier majors or drop out of college. We call it the weed-out stage. Students are freaked out when they find that the big bad world demands work to achieve their dreams.

Being Clueless. Procrastination results when students don't know what to do when faced with unfamiliar situations in college. The novel circumstances paralyze you momentarily while you ponder your next actions. The deferred action results in procrastination. For example, students often spend the better part of their first year employing study habits that worked in high school but now are failing them in college. They don't know how to study for tests or what to do when professors move so fast they're lost. When students are clueless on how to be successful in college, they often fumble around in their purse for solutions or twiddle their thumbs and do nothing.

College Stresses. Students who deal with stressful relationships with parents, boyfriends, roommates, and teachers are ripe for procrastination. If you're depressed, it's difficult to get up in the morning, let alone go to classes and study for tests at night. It takes emotional control to roll with the punches that come with relationships. Relationship turmoil can drive students to stay with one partner throughout college or not to get seriously involved with a boy or girlfriend until after college. For students who are messed up on drugs or alcohol, procrastination is part of their daily life. Do you really think you can stay aloft in college when you're drunk or high most of the week? Sometimes when I see that lost, unkempt, and vacant look in my students who are addicted, I want to put my arms around them and lead them over to Student Services to get some professional help. Professors can almost tell who is going to make it in college by looking around the class during a test.

Gadget Proliferation. The increase in chronic procrastination correlates directly with the rise of electronic gadgetry in society. Toys that make for easy procrastination are everywhere. Who, for example, would rather sit in a library and study when you can play computer games, chat on the Internet, gab on a cell phone, or watch TV just about anywhere? While the new technology is powerful and life changing, it also comes with downsides depending on how it's used. Technology is like drugs. Use it wisely and it makes you productive. Abuse it and it takes over your life and turns your brain into mush. Choose to make it your slave and not your master.

Given the root causes of procrastination, we can now deal with it. Rid your life of the root causes. This means changing your reward system. If you make defeating procrastination more appealing than continuing with procrastination, you will reorient your life. You'll find that the rewards for staying on task outweigh the anguish you feel when procrastinating. As the rewards for good behavior and punishment for bad behaviors pile up, procrastination becomes something you choose to avoid rather than coddle.

Say laziness is the chief cause of your procrastination. When you're lazy, every late assignment, every hastily-completed project, and every poorly written essay results in emotional anguish. Anyone Christian who has pride in doing a good job can't feel good about doing sloppy work on a regular basis. Since college consists of completing scores of time-critical tasks, you either feel bad all semester or you find ways to combat procrastination. Laziness in college gets so uncomfortable that you either drop out or rise to the occasion and determine that you're sick and tired of deferring action.

Take a millennial student who is procrastinating because he loves to play computer games which are sucking away ten to twenty hours of his life per week. It's impossible to do well in college when half your work week is glued to leisure activities. Crunch time will inevitably come when you have to decide what is more important—to play games for four years or work toward a degree. Do this. Choose a couple of your least favorite computer games and determine not to go there that week. Instead, spend some time completing your math assignment. You'll have to force yourself to do this at first, but imagine the peace of mind when you hand in your paper and get an A on the assignment. Then dump another computer game the next week and work on your English essay. Force that one too. The reward you get when your essay comes back saying "well-composed and reasoned arguments" will start into motion a cycle of positive reinforcement. The more work you get done, the more positive feedback will pry you away from procrastination and toward accomplishment. I often rewarded myself in college for a job well-done by doing the very things I enjoyed that were once detrimental to my success. By putting work first and play later, my enjoyment of the things that were once tormenting me was exponentially greater. First things first, works.

Try this for one month to banish procrastination. It's simple but effective. It's worked for thousands of highly effective people, and I guarantee it will produce results for you:

- Write down all the things you need to do on a given day.
- Prioritize the items on the list. Determine what things are the most important to do. What things have to be done today?
- Make an ironclad decision with yourself or an accountability partner that you're going to complete the chosen tasks if it kills you. Go to number one. Finish it before you go to number two. Go to number two. Finish it. Go to number three. Finish it. If you need further information to finish an item, put it in a separate pile for pending action. As the relevant information comes in, finish the

task. Complete each task as fully as you can before going on to the next task item.

- Observe how you feel. The positive emotions when you get your work done will be wonderful. Liberating. There's nothing like it. It's so good that you seek it by completing more and more of your assignments on time. It works like a drug. Eventually, your entire student life transforms from laziness to efficiency because you've changed your reward system.

The best one-line advice on procrastination has been offered by Zig Ziglar, a best-selling author on leadership issues: "If you do what you ought to do when you ought to do it, then you can do what you want to do when you want to do it." It's difficult to improve on Ziglar's advice. His homespun wisdom offers the secret to winning at college and setting a godly tone for your life.

The Bible on Time Management

Managing your time is important to God. Time is equated to life in the Scriptures—your time equals your life. Anything that intimately associated with life is valuable. Time is a precious commodity, perhaps the most precious commodity. When you look at your watch tick away, you are watching your life tick away. You can run out of just about anything in life except time. You can make more money; you can make more friends; you can make more children; you can replace broken and worn-out goods; but you can't make more time. For the common man unfamiliar with Einstein, time is a universal constant of nature. You can't save it; you can't store it; you can't stretch it; you can only spend it. It goes in only one direction.

Facing up to the facts on time changes your life perspective. It's difficult for college students, with the bulk of your lives ahead of you, to understand this natural law, but if you embrace just a few of the implications, it will radically change the way you live. Managing your time is a life skill worth the effort to master. To see how valuable time can be, consider the following:

- Ask a pro athlete with a severed ACL the value of a career.
- Ask a middle school student who flunked eighth grade the value of one year.
- Ask a mother who lost a premature baby the value of one month.
- Ask the editor of a Hollywood tabloid the value of a few hours.
- Ask an unemployed person who was late for a job interview the value of one hour.
- Ask a person who just missed a bus or plane the value of one minute.
- Ask a person who just avoided a serious traffic accident the value of one second.
- Ask a runner who just lost the gold metal in the hundred meters the value of 0.01 of a second.

It's critical that Christian college students establish proper time priorities. Here are two significant Bible passages on time to help you. "Live purposefully and worthily and accurately, not as the unwise and witless, but as wise (sensible, intelligent people), making the very most of the time (buying up each opportunity), because the days are evil" (Eph. 5:15–16, AMP). "Man's days are determined; you have decreed the number of his months and have set limits he cannot exceed." (Job 14:5). Job says that God has deposited a certain number of hours in our life's time account. The bad news is that our life on earth is finite. We won't live here forever. Everyone will face the grave at an appointed time determined by God. The good news is that we can quit worrying about our life and live each day with fearless abandon. We won't die before our time. Our appointed time is in God's hands and nothing can snatch anything from God. Yes, I can hear your questions regarding free will and the sovereignty of God. "Are you saying that it doesn't matter how we live?" "If a person smokes thousands of cigarettes, doesn't take care of himself, drinks like a fish, uses dangerous drugs, and likes to drive 100 mph, are you saying that it won't affect his life span?"

This is a difficult question. Intellectuals throughout history have wrestled with the riddle of sovereignty and free will. It's best to admit that both ideas are accepted by the Scriptures; in that sense, sovereignty and free will are similar to the trinity and the hypostatic union. Nobody understands them. The human mind is insufficient to fully comprehend how God determines our span of life and yet allows our free will to live irresponsible lives. Christians who take the Bible as God's Word, however, will admit that both ideas are consistent in the larger mind of God. It's the clay trying to understand the potter. We are no match for His intellect. In Psalm 118:24, David gives us an important lesson on how to approach time. "This is the day that the Lord has made; let us rejoice and be glad in it." God gives you 86,400 seconds = 1,440 minutes = twenty-four hours each day. While He determines the broad extent of our lives, we are given the choice on how to spend the individual days. But you only get one chance to choose how you spend your days. You can choose to use time wisely or choose to fritter it away, and most college students fall on the side of wasting time. This has to change if you expect success in college.

David hints at a key principle on how to time manage. He says that appreciation is an important starting point. Start each morning by thanking God for another day. It's a rare day that I don't kneel in grateful appreciation for God's provision of life. If you have trouble finding reasons to praise God for the gift of time, spend some time listening when people share prayer requests. You'll hear petitions involving every conceivable tragedy, hurt, and pain. You'll see how lucky you are to have your health, your family, your opportunities, your college, and the bulk of your life ahead of you. You'll develop a godly perspective and come to see that how you spend your time absolutely matters. You'll see that time is finite. You'll see that pleasing God requires a sobering reconsideration of time. For most of human history, the lot of man on earth was difficult and painful. You have it good as a college student in the twenty-first century. Thank God for your fortunate situation. David's advice will result in doing better in college. When I share his prescription with my students, I usually get a "that's it? It seems too simple" Nope. It's simple in principle but hard in practice unless you practice. Be grateful for every minute of your life, and you will manage it properly.

STRATEGY #3: *Test Taking*

Tests are an integral part of college. The faster you learn to master tests the better you will perform in college. There are only two choices; either you master tests or they master you, and there's little worse for a student than to be repeatedly victimized by tests and exams. Few students come to college with effective test-taking skills. With some changes in the mechanics of how you take tests, you can radically improve your performance. Understanding the origins of poor test-taking skills goes a long way toward improving your college performance. We discuss the most common test-taking problems and offer tips to improve your examination skills.

WHY STUDENTS DO POORLY ON TESTS

NOT STUDYING ENOUGH

The first reason students do poorly on tests is because they don't spend enough time with the course material. It's that simple. There are few substitutes to getting down and dirty with the material you're expected to learn. Problem is, I rarely see this with college students. Instead, they determine how little effort they can make to get the grade they are shooting for in the course. The presumption is that spending the minimum amount of time will suffice when set against all the fun things students can do in college. But this strategy breaks down in most substantive college courses. You simply can't spend a minimum amount of time in, say, electrical engineering and expect to do well in your courses. Rule number one for success on college tests is to quit living off shortcuts and honestly put in the hours of time necessary to learn the material. If you fail to prepare, you prepare to fail.

USING THE WRONG STUDY STRATEGIES

Students often bomb my tests despite the fact that they studied forever. This is due to ineffective study strategies. All students should go back after the first test in a course and compare what you were asked to what you studied. You'll be surprised at the findings. My students usually find that they tried to memorize, rather than apply, the laws of physics during their study time. They see that I don't ask rote memory questions, but I do ask a lot of conceptual questions that deal with how physics works in practical situations. They find that I have a discussion section on my tests which deals with applications. My students' study strategy was flawed.

The effects of faulty study strategies are readily evident when I teach our Physics for Engineers course. This course is known as freshman physics in most universities and is required by engineering majors who have had calculus as a pre or corequisite. Most students presume that I will throw hundreds of problems in their face during the semester to help them learn physics. Surprise. I don't use plug and chug methods; instead, we learn physics with a minimum of mathematics. You should hear the complaining after my first test. Students used to learning science by rummaging through formulas and plugging in numbers to find the odd solutions in the back of the book now have to think. Thinking is novel. Thinking takes work. It's different from mindless plug and chug exercises. It takes about half a semester to convince students that what I'm trying to give them is valuable, and then students are still not really comfortable with my system. Finally, near the end of the semester, it dawns on my students why they are in the predicament they find themselves. Eventually, you have to know what you're doing or spend the rest of your college days as an actor in a Shakespearean tragedy.

LACK OF PREREQUISITE SKILLS

Students lack the necessary background skills for some courses. If you lack key prerequisites you will get off to a bad start, and the problems multiply during a semester. When I say you lack the prerequisite skills, I don't mean that the prerequisites are absent from your record but that you never learned them. It's an unfortunate given in most of my courses that I have to go over unit conversions, unit consistency, scientific notation, the metric system, and many basic skills that should have been learned in prerequisite courses. Some of my math professor friends in the adjoining building tell me that students are rarely ready for calculus even though they had algebra, trigonometry, analysis, AP, and pre-calculus in high school. The result of not learning the prerequisites is that you're handicapped, fall behind, and never get caught up with the power curve in a course.

Low Concern for Your Education

Students do poorly on tests because they simply don't care about learning anything in college. They want As but aren't willing to work for them. Or they are in school to have fun. Or they don't know what else to do with their lives. Or they want to find a husband or wife. Or they want to postpone the future. Or sponge off their parents for a while longer. Or prolong the comfort zone of college as long as possible. Such students are the most difficult to work with because they simply don't show up at class, don't turn in assignments, skip labs, and refuse to crack a book after 5:00 p.m. In so doing, they ask you to flunk them. I have little choice but to oblige. It's easy to identify why these students flunk if you examine my grade book. My failing students are the ones with zeros across the board for many of the course requirements. They are precisely the ones who should flunk and why professors should give Ds and Fs.

Regular Diet of Taking Shortcuts

Shortcuts are defined as doing the minimum needed to survive in college. When students find themselves drowning, they resort to whatever desperate strategies they think will work to improve their grade. The trouble with desperation strategies is that they offer only short-term solutions to long-term problems, and that's if you call them solutions in the first place. Shortcuts to your college education treat symptoms and not causes. Take, for example, a health condition, such as insomnia. You can treat it by taking sleeping pills or drinking until you fall asleep, but these solutions never address the root problem and, in fact, probably makes it worse. A better strategy is to get to the underlying cause of the sleeplessness, such as reducing the worry or stress in your life.

Shortcuts take several forms. A common college shortcut is studying for a class by relying on old tests instead of learning the material itself. No matter how much I preach to my students about studying old tests, it's still the preferred way for college students who are too lazy or don't have the time to study. Commonly, every sorority and fraternity has stockpiles of old tests given by professors on campus. When faced by time constraints, desperation, or laziness, students pull out the old tests and memorize the questions and answers with the hope that professors will ask the same questions each semester. Problem is, when you take the shortcut of studying old tests, you are gambling with your education in several ways.

First, the professor may not ask the same questions. Then you end up flunking because when you try to live by memorizing, you also die by memorizing. Better to learn the material. Stockpiled tests are a large thorn in my professor's side every semester because it forces me to make up different tests in order to level the playing field for those students who don't have access to them. But I do it because I'm not going to give an advantage to someone who belongs to the right fraternity.

Second, you never learn the material. Shortcuts might work to take pressure off the short-term emergency, but a steady diet leads to problems later because learning builds on prior learning. You can't survive forever by shooting yourself in the foot. This is especially true in quantitative courses which rely on a stream of concepts which have to be learned sequentially.

Third, if you think you can succeed by playing the game of school rather than by working for it, that attitude will color other areas of your life. You will develop a habit of shortcuts and learn to fake it rather than simply buckling down and doing the work. For Christian students, relying on old tests is also an ethnical dilemma, bordering on cheating. Yes, you argue, if a professor is stupid enough to give similar tests each semester, it's not your fault for taking advantage of them. But that's like saying that because you can get away with it, stealing is not against the law. Would you want to face the Lord with that argument?

MASTERING TEST QUESTIONS

Most college tests are based on multiple-choice questions, essay questions, and problem-solving questions. Mastering each type of question will save you frustration and ensure success. Since class projects are becoming more common as grading criterion, we also offer some comments on how to generate successful projects.

MULTIPLE-CHOICE QUESTIONS

Students make life difficult when doing multiple-choice (MC) questions due to a variety of misdirected strategies and superstitions. Following are several of the common mistakes and how to avoid them.

NOT READING THE QUESTION CORRECTLY

Students are so anxiety ridden during exams that they read the test questions incorrectly. This can be suicide when taking MC tests. For most MC questions, there are key words or qualifiers that change the meaning. If you don't catch the key words or understand their significance, you will underperform. Science and engineering MC questions pose a particularly difficult problem because of the exact terminology in those disciplines. A key overlooked word can make the difference between getting the question right and getting the question wrong. The solution is to slow down on the test, breathe, and read all the words in a question. Here's an example from one of my tests.

A truck is moving at constant velocity. Inside the storage compartment, a rock is dropped from the midpoint of the ceiling and strikes the floor below. The rock hits the floor
  a) exactly below the midpoint of the ceiling
  b) ahead of the midpoint of the ceiling
  c) behind the midpoint of the ceiling
  d) more information is needed to solve this problem

The correct answer is a). When I return the test to my class, the students who answered incorrectly tell me that they missed the question because they didn't notice the qualifier "at constant velocity" which changes the entire meaning of the question. Constant velocity means the truck always moves in the same direction at the same speed, say 50 mph. If the truck turned suddenly, the rock would continue to go straight while the truck turned and wouldn't hit the floor below the midpoint.

ANSWERING A DIFFERENT QUESTION

Students miss MC questions because they try to answer a different question than the one asked on the test. Students who try to fly through the test as fast as they can in order to leave the room and get on with college life are prone to this error. It's similar to contestants on *Jeopardy* or *Family Feud*. Before the entire question gets out, they push the buzzer to be first and frequently get burned because the second part of the question changes its meaning. When students only partially read the question before answering, they also get burned because of the rush to judgment. The solution is to force yourself to read the entire question, even if you think you know what's being asked. Examine this question.

> A pair of tennis balls (one regular and one lead-filled) fall from a
> tall building. Air resistance just before they hit is actually greater
> for the
>   a) regular ball
>   b) lead-filled ball
>   c) is the same for both

The correct answer is b) because the lead-filled ball falls faster through the air and air resistance increases with speed. A common mistake is that students try to answer the wrong question. They try to answer the question without the words "air resistance." They don't see this crucial phrase if they speed through the test because many physics test questions say to neglect air resistance. But the question specifically asks to account for air resistance. Students in a hurry read right over this phrase and miss the question, thinking I am asking about dropped objects in the absence of friction.

NOT KNOWING KEY CONCEPTS IN THE QUESTION

My students typically remark that my tests are difficult at first and that my first test borders on the impossible. But this is absolutely not the case, as students find out on later tests when they get A's and B's instead of D's. What is actually the case is that they progressively figure out that they have to learn concepts in my course. The flowering of understanding is especially evident when, for the final exam review, I go over all the old tests in the course. Most of my students are embarrassed. They wonder in amazement why they ever circled their originally wrong answers. The point is, when students learn concepts instead of trying to memorize everything, what they thought were difficult questions later turn out to be embarrassingly simple. Here is an example.

> An apple weighs 1 N. When held at rest above your head, the net force on the apple is
> a) 0 N
> b) 0.1 N
> c) 1 N
> d) 9.8 N
> e) none of these

The correct answer is a). For the liberal arts majors out there, the N in the question refers to "newtons" which is a measure of force in the metric system, comparable to "weight" in the United States. The question is trivial if you know the concept of net force. Here is a test-taking hint. When doing MC questions, don't even look at the list of possible answers at first. Rather, focus on what the question addresses, in this case the net force, and then form a tentative answer before looking over the multiple answer choices. In this instance, the first question out of my mind is "Do I know what net force means?" Then I define it to myself, "The net force is the sum of all forces acting on an object, directions accounted for." Next I determine how many forces are acting on an apple when you hold it over your head. There are two forces, the force of gravity (its weight) and the force of your hand holding up the apple. Since the apple is at rest, the two forces must balance out, which means the net force is zero. If the net force were not zero, the apple would be moving, but the question states that it's at rest. Students who learn to do MC questions by focusing on key concepts will find that the correct answers fall out of the sky like manna from heaven. You blush at why you missed them in the first place.

Employing Superstitions in Lieu of Learning

Students try the craziest things on tests. Some actually believe they can increase their chances of success by strategies best described as superstitions. This is particularly the case when students haven't cracked a book and are clueless about the course material. Here are a few of the common superstitions. Some students circle a given answer on a MC test because of the pattern of a)'s –e)'s on the answer sheet, thinking that professors will never have three a)'s in a row, for example. Others believe professors never use the e) choice, which is usually the "not enough information to answer" selection. Don't count on it; I use the e) choice often because it shows whether you have confidence in your answer. A big superstition is when students believe their first hunch on a MC question is probably the correct one. They are reticent about changing their first answer even when they reconsider the question and think another selection is the best choice. The list of superstitions goes on. Let me say this. Superstitions vanish when you know the material. Did you read that? Students employ superstitions when they don't know what is going on. Only in rare cases are answer pattern superstitions due to deliberate question construction on the part of your professor. Ask yourself this. If you really knew your stuff on a MC test, would you resort to superstitions? No way.

Belief in Trick Questions on Tests

Students believe that professors are out to scam them on tests by using trick questions. This results in misguided time trying to predict how a professor works rather than how the material works. When you believe that college tests are filled with ploys, tricks, and traps, you play defense when you should be playing offense. You try to anticipate rather than study and get angry in the meantime, which adds to the problem. It's similar to an army general who can either choose to sit back and predict how the enemy plans to attack his forces or get his troops off their fannies and attack them first. By playing offense, you take control of your education instead of letting a professor's presumed tricky questions direct your steps and your sanity. While I'm not so naïve to think that professors never ask tricky questions, it's rare that professors deliberately try to deceive students in order to weed them out, for example. This is a common college misconception. The actual case is that, what students think is a trick question is actually a question that tests whether you know the material thoroughly. Here is an example of what some of my students have called a "trick" question.

> You're driving down the highway in a Hummer and a bug splatters as it hits your windshield. Which delivers the greatest force during the collision?
> a) the Hummer
> b) the bug
> c) both the same

The correct answer is c). Students call this a trick question because it goes against every intuitive cell in their bodies. Try asking your friends this question. Virtually everyone on the street will say it's a no-brainer. Of course the Hummer delivers a bigger force during a collision with a bug. The truck is huge, it's going fast, and it weighs a ton. The bug gets flattened while the truck barely knows it got hit. Ah, but that's the genius of Newton. He saw through this situation and postulated Newton's third law, which states that whenever one thing hits another, equal forces are involved during the collision. This means that you can't hit anything harder than it hits you. Never. When I explain this to my students they're usually still not convinced the question is fair. They retort that surely something is different during the collision, because the bug gets smooched while the Hummer is unharmed. True, but the thing that's different is not the forces involved, which are the same, but that the bug's speed changes to zero rapidly while the truck's speed is hardly affected. This is called acceleration in physics. The difference is in the huge deceleration of the bug. My students eventually see that my test question was actually straightforward once you buy the third law. It was not a trick question. What I am trying to show you is that, when you truly understand something, the less you believe the question is a "trick" question. But that's what tests are for; to determine if you know the concepts.

DISCUSSION QUESTIONS

Essay (discussion) questions allow for written or oral expression on tests. They are employed to determine if you can articulate your thoughts and use logical reasoning skills when arguing for or against a position. Literature students are well familiar with essay questions such as "Evaluate the theme of hypocrisy in Hawthorne's *The Scarlet Letter.*" It will surprise you that even though I teach physics, my tests typically contain discussion questions, where I ask students to explain a commonly observed physical event. Here is a sampling of the kinds of discussion questions on my tests. Note that each question requires you to know, reason, and apply, and then to state your answer succinctly using correct terminology.

- Explain why a flimsy shower curtain nearly attacks you during your morning shower after you turn on the water?
- In the old days, on a cold winter night it was common to bring a hot object to bed with you. Which would be better to keep you warm through the cold night—a 10 kg iron brick or a 10 kg jug of hot water at the same temperature? Explain.
- Consider a very large wooden barrel, such as the kind used in wineries. Should the "flat" ends be concave (bending inward) or convex (bending outward) to make the strongest barrel? Explain.
- Explain why you shouldn't spin your tires when trying to get your car moving on an ice-covered road.
- Why is it that the canvas roof of a convertible bulges upward when the car is traveling at high speeds? Use physics principles in your answer.
- If liquid pressure were the same at all depths, would there be a buoyant force on an object submerged in the liquid? Explain.
- Using physics principles, explain how a suction cup sticks to a wall.
- Would it be slightly more difficult to draw root beer through a straw at sea level or on top of a very high mountain? Explain.

- On a sensitive balance, weigh an empty flat thin plastic bag. Then weigh the bag when air is in it. Will the readings differ? Why?
- Water will boil spontaneously in a vacuum—on the moon, for example. Could you cook an egg in this boiling water? Explain.

Are there specific test strategies students can employ to improve their performance on essay questions? The answer is yes.

BEGIN BY REFERENCING THE APPLICABLE PRINCIPLE

Discussion questions usually require the application of a general principle. They proceed from the general to the specific. If you begin your answer by stating the relevant principle, that will get you going in the right direction and at least get you some partial credit. Partial credit is the name of the game when answering discussion questions since graders generally give you credit for saying something correct. While students dislike essay questions, they like the idea of partial credit, so take advantage of the situation and say something. Let me illustrate by using one of my discussion questions.

Why will a watermelon stay cool for a longer time than sandwiches when both are removed from a cooler on a hot day? Explain.

Answer. A watermelon will stay cool for a longer time because it's composed mostly of water, which has a high specific heat. The specific heat measures how difficult it is to change an object's temperature. Objects with high specific heat change their temperature with difficulty, while objects with low specific heat change their temperature readily. This means that the water in the watermelon doesn't want to change its temperature when removed from a cooler, and the watermelon which, starts out cool, stays cooler longer. The sandwiches start out equally cool but, in contrast, have a low specific heat and change their temperature rapidly when removed from the cooler. They readily heat up to the ambient temperature outside.

Note the important features in my answer.

- First, I answered the question. Many students dance around the question, and I never do see an answer. That tells a professor that you either don't know the answer or lack confidence in your answer. It's better to answer a discussion question wrong with some kind of reasoning, however incorrect, than to dance around in your answer.
- Second, I identified and defined the relevant principle, in this case the specific heat.
- Third, I applied the specific heat to the situation to answer the question.
- Fourth, I articulated the answer with an economy of words and accurate terminology.

It's to your benefit to follow a similar systematic framework when attacking discussion questions.

WHEN STUCK ON A QUESTION, AT LEAST SAY WHAT YOU KNOW

If you are clueless on how to answer a discussion question, at least write something that you know. Never leave a discussion question blank. If you do, you leave us no choice but to give you a zero on the question. Professors are prone to grant you credit for some attempt. When assigned to analyze irony in Dickens's *A Tale of Two Cities,* if you aren't familiar with the book, at least try to define irony. You will get some partial credit. On the other hand, professors hate snow, loosely defined by Shakespeare as "much matter, with little substance." Snow doesn't go. Many students think that the more they jabber on in discussion questions, the better score they will receive. Not. If you insist on wasting our time with a gabby, wandering answer we will respond appropriately. The best strategy is to use just enough correct terminology and reasoning to answer the question. Then stop. We're looking for quality, not quantity.

USE PROPER ENGLISH AND TERMINOLOGY

Every subject has distinctive terminology. Vocabulary is fundamental to higher education. Without learning new vocabulary in college, you will be handicapped when embracing the lofty ideas of mankind and unable to answer college test questions. A rich and diverse vocabulary is an essential part of professional discourse.

I observe that college students "know" the answer to test questions but can't articulate the answer. The basic problem is that students don't know what words to use and/or are weak at forming coherent arguments. This is due to the ineffectiveness of American schools when teaching vocabulary, grammar, logic, and writing. The writing skills of many college students are deplorable. Shocking is another description. Professors wonder what happened during the years when students were in elementary and secondary school. Few college students can compose a sharply written sentence let alone answer a discussion question requiring logic and analysis.

If you are weak in writing and reasoning, there's no easy solution. You either go through college trying to avoid classes where writing is required or you play catch-up. I recommend catch-up. The difficult solution is to now learn in college what you should have learned in secondary school. That's a tough road to hoe, but you have few good choices. If you are a weak writer, do your level best to learn to write in your freshman composition courses. Refuse to gloss over new vocabulary. Slowly build up and reinforce your ability to speak and write clearly by practice. If you need to, swallow your pride and take the remedial courses that universities offer in English. When I was an undergraduate, I was like many of my students, wondering why I had to take classes like composition, history, and foreign languages when I was going to become a scientist. What did science have to do with writing? The answer is everything. I do more writing as a scientist than you can believe. There are reports, papers, updates, presentations, and research proposals to generate monthly. I wasn't at the time, but in retrospect, I'm eternally grateful to the Michigan State curriculum designers for exposing me to a broad education involving the arts and letters. To do well on college discussion questions, it's imperative to learn and use the proper terminology peculiar to each discipline.

LEARNING FROM MISTAKES

A universal finding of educational research is that learning is most effective when there is feedback. The return side of the educational process is as important as the delivery side. The delivery side refers to the transmission of material by hearing lectures, reading textbooks, studying Websites, and doing problems and exercises. The return side refers to the evaluation of learning by means of tests, feedback, and discussion. Most students believe that the brain learns only during delivery. Nope. The brain learns on both ends of the process. The synaptic pathways are stimulated in both directions. Effective professors will exploit this by providing stimulating learning experiences both before and after covering a body of material.

I try to help my students with test questions by posing similar questions during my lectures. The latest trend in science education is to provide each student in large classes with a "clicker" for instant feedback during lectures. The professor poses a question and students select their answer in real time by clicking on the answer. The distribution of answers is compiled by a computer and a histogram is displayed on a board in the classroom. This strategy provides instant feedback and enhances learning by evaluating what was right and wrong about you or your peer student's responses.

What happens in college courses is that everyone gets lazy when it comes to learning from mistakes on tests. The pace of college is so rapid that almost nobody takes the time to go back over tests to see what and why they missed it. You're doing well enough just to keep up with new material let alone figure out the old material. But this speaks to time management. Look at it this way. What coach or college athlete doesn't go back to see what went wrong after getting their clocks cleaned in a game? Most football coaches spend Monday in the film room looking to see who missed blocks, why they missed blocks, why there were turnovers, and who missed their coverage. They grade each player's performance. Learning occurs when you see where you went wrong. Students should factor in some film room analysis with your returned tests. You will improve your test taking skills.

REDUCING TEST ANXIETY

College students have major anxiety when taking tests. They can freeze before the test is passed out or during the test when they come up against difficult questions. Your anxiety overcomes you and paralyzes your thought process. It grips and owns you. Test anxiety is debilitating and frustrating. For a Christian student, it's not in keeping with God in you, as 2 Tim. 1:7 states that "God has not given us a spirit of timidity, but a spirit of power, of love, and of self-discipline."

Anxiety is the fear you feel when being forced into a circumstance you don't feel prepared to handle. The definition hints at the solution. It's preparation. If anxiety and lack of preparation go together, then preparation will negate anxiety. Let me illustrate. A couple of summers ago my pastor asked me to substitute preach for him. While I was honored to be asked, it initially caused me anxiety because, despite the fact that I've taught Sunday school for years, I'd never been asked to preach. The pastors in my life have been world-famous preachers with huge television and radio ministries. They don't share their pulpits with a rookie. I was anxious because I didn't know how I would measure up as a pulpit speaker and because of the high respect I held for my pastor. I didn't want to disappoint him. Further, my church has three services, each with hundreds of listeners sitting in the pews and thousands if not millions around the world through television. The thought that millions of people might be listening to me was overwhelming.

How did I deal with the anxiety? I got busy. If I was going to go down in flames and look stupid during my message, it wasn't going to be because I wasn't ready. I selected a message I was passionate about and had wanted to share with a group of believers anyway; I anticipated that Dr. Purvis would eventually need someone to pinch hit and I had composed a couple of sermons in my head. I had been ready, by God's help, for the circumstance. The points I wanted to make during my sermon had been brewing in my mind for months. When I realized that I had a subject I was passionate about, knew a lot about, and one I was comfortable talking about, then I knew I could do it. Preparation made the difference; viewing preaching as similar to teaching made the difference. When I walked onto the platform of our church, I had my message down and nearly couldn't wait to start talking. What started out as anxiety turned to confidence as my preparation and confidence in God's help increased. God used the experience to grow me.

It's similar for all areas of life where anxiety rears its ugly head. Preparation dispels anxiety. Not a month goes by that I don't get a report from a former education student who was once scared to death to stand in a classroom. But get a few trials under your belt and it becomes second nature. It becomes enjoyable. There is easy power and fulfillment. Some mornings, you can't wait to get to the classroom. Think of three P's to deal with anxiety—**p**reparation, **p**ractice, and **p**assion. Whenever I watch bestselling author and pastor Joel Osteen preaching to the vast throng at Lakewood Church in Houston, it tells me I also can face the public speaking tasks God gives me to do. Joel is so good now that he makes it look easy, but I know it took time and preparation. He worked in the background of his dad's ministry for years, never aspiring to be a public speaker. When the Lord took his dad to Glory, he balked at assuming the mantle of leadership at Lakewood. It was an emotional and mental battle with confidence. But thank God Joel rose to the occasion and, by His help, he is now the most natural speaker you will ever see. You'd never know he once was uncomfortable in front of people. If you asked him for his secret, he would tell you that it was preparation, practice, passion, and the compulsion of God in his life. Here are some practical tips to reduce anxiety in your student life.

RUN THE RACE OF COLLEGE SLOWLY

Some of the best advice to reduce anxiety was offered by my high school track coach. It's a formula that will work for any anxiety. My coach had moved me up to the quarter mile from the 100 and 220 yard dashes. What he didn't tell me was that the quarter mile is one of the most difficult races in track. It's a sprint with guts. To be successful, a runner has to run as far as he can as fast as he can, which is usually for about 330 yards. The last 110 yards are pure guts, running form, fighting off the lactic acid buildup, and iron determination.

After one of our first meets, Coach pulled me aside and said if I wanted to get to the next level, I would have to change my philosophy of the race. He told me I was running the race too fast. I can still hear his voice "Bozy, run the race as slow as you can, not as fast as you can." What? Surely he was kidding or not working with the drugs. Run the race slow? Was he nuts?

It was pure genius. He explained "Look, try this. During the race, while your body is working as hard as possible, your legs pumping as fast as possible, and your feet pushing off the track as forcefully as possible, your mind should be like you are laying on a calm sea…peaceful…graceful…quiet." Let me translate. Coach was telling me to stay loose. Life can get incredibly hectic, with people, events, and decisions pulling at you from all directions, but if you run the race of life slowly, refusing to make a frenzied dash from one task to another, refusing to run from one harried event to the next, refusing to let your schedule control you, then you will not wear yourself out and instead have unusual energy and efficiency. Running the race slowly means to avoid getting caught up in the chaos and choosing to live deliberately and under control. If you don't believe Coach, take the case of Jesus. He did more in three short years to change the world than any person in history. His calendar and list of accomplishments stretch forever, but you never see Him in a hurry, never harried, never late for an appointment, even when raising Lazarus. Christ knew how to stay loose by relying on the Father's strength and power in His life.

A THIRD DEGREE BLACK BELT IN PLANNING

Anyone will feel anxiety if they're not prepared for the task. Anyone. Even professors can feel anxious. I'm an expert at experimental surface physics but, if I don't spend some time before class reviewing my lecture notes before facing a class of graduate students, I can feel tentative and anxious. The same is true for a pastor in front of his congregation, a doctor when examining his patients, a lawyer when presenting a case, a salesperson trying to cut a deal, or anyone in any walk of life. Four-time Super Bowl winning coach Chuck Noll of the Pittsburgh Steelers put it best when he said "Pressure is something you feel when you don't know what you're doing."[74]

Paste that on your dorm room mirror. Preparation is a biblical concept. When God prepares a task for His children He prepares His children. Joseph spent seventeen years in the halls of Pharaoh before saving His people and the citizens of Egypt during seven years of drought. Moses required eighty years to get ready for forty years of ministry. David underwent innumerable trials for years before he took the throne of Israel. Joshua was born into Egyptian slavery and was overshadowed by Moses for years before being anointed to be Moses' successor. Jesus Himself was barely visible for thirty years while God prepared Him to save the world. The Bible says that when Christians prove faithful as stewards over a few things then God will make them rulers over many things. Our patience during our preparation leads to our promotion.

Preparation implies planning. The conquest of Canaan was carefully planned and skillfully executed by Joshua. Joshua first led his army straight across the Holy Land to conquer and divide the territory by isolating the north from the south. Then he conquered the cities of the south and turned to invade the north. He used guile, surprise, cunning, and sound military strategy. It takes planning to accomplish the will of God in your life. A sage observation is "When the pilot doesn't know what port he's headed to, no wind is the right wind." Students should know their destination port. Academics require preparation for success. It's imperative to put in adequate practice (study) time to reduce your test anxiety.

STUDYING BETWEEN SEMESTERS AND DURING BREAKS

Students look at me with stunned disbelief when I recommend, if you anticipate an absolutely crazy semester, to get going on courses before the semester. It's not possible to use this strategy for all courses, but if, say, you know you're going to use a certain textbook, as in the second semester of a two-semester course, it's advantageous to work ahead and read a couple of chapters before the course starts. During my junior and senior years in physics, my goal was to get two chapters ahead in each of my upper-level courses before the first day of classes. By getting a head-start, I could spend more time on difficult parts of the course without feeling pressure to keep up with the frenetic semester pace. I found that a two-chapter lead on the material would put me roughly even with the course pace at the end of the quarter. This did wonders for my sanity and reduced my anxiety during the school year. It allowed me to control my studies instead of my studies controlling me. For fellow party-animal friends who accused me of needing to get a life in college, I replied that studying ahead gave me a life. Who wants to always be playing catch-up? Catch-up is horrible. It's like being in debt. Having money in the bank gives you peace of mind and generates options. Debt puts you in bondage.

HAVE A SET OF STUDY GUIDES HANDY

Some professors are less than helpful when it comes to explaining a subject. It could be a foreign professor who struggles with the language. It could be a graduate student who is a rookie at teaching. It could be a professor nearing retirement who just doesn't care anymore. It could be a professor with a bad attitude toward teaching and thinks students just get in the way of research. It could be a poor textbook choice for the course. Or it could just be hard material.

The mistake students make in these circumstances is to do nothing. For freshmen, it's usually a case of not knowing what to do. What do you do when your teacher or textbook is so bad that you're not learning anything? The answer is to get proactive. Say you're in a math class with a professor from India who is just learning the language. Since the professor has a Ph.D. in mathematics, he is competent in the subject but lacks understanding of our educational system and how to be an effective American college instructor. You don't understand the lectures, can't do the homework, and are, in general, lost and frustrated in the course. The whole thing seems like a waste of time. But since you need the class and there are no options to transfer to another instructor, you are stuck.

Don't just stew and fret. Do something. We've all been there with poor instructors. By something I mean to get some resources that help you to learn on your own. Head to the campus bookstore or library and peruse some other math books, preferably ones with a lot of worked-out examples. Find some easy-to-read textbooks, reference books, tutors, or roommates. Do whatever is required to avoid letting a poor teacher ruin your education or your GPA. There are several good resources. It depends on the subject area, so I can't make general recommendations but, in my day, many of us in science and engineering were saved from disaster by a set of reference books called the *Schaum Outline Series,* which are still available in college bookstores. The *Schaum* Series[75] has useful study helps for all kinds of college subjects, from tensor analysis to nodal theory to quantum chemistry to classical mechanics. They are the equivalent of Cliff's Notes for science and engineering and are chocked full of worked-out problems and examples. I amassed about twenty of them during my college career and still use them as sources of homework problems for my physics courses. So get off your fanny, take charge, and try to learn as much as you can in a bad situation. It's good practice, as you will eventually find yourself in the job world with a boss who gives you very little direction but still requires you to make things happen. College is a microcosm of the real world you have to eventually face.

HAVE CONFIDENCE IN GOD'S PLAN FOR YOUR LIFE

For Christians, reducing anxiety is a balancing act between how much you do and how much God does. On the one hand, God expects you to do your part. If you don't study, you won't be successful in college. It's the same with nature. If you jump off a tall building, you won't survive. God rarely suspends the laws of science to save you. While God still works miracles, He asks you not to test Him and prefers to work through His established physical laws.

Look at the life of Joshua. Why did he have so much confidence when conquering the Promised Land? The enormity of the task would reduce the strongest person to a puddle of anxiety. There were dangerous, brutal, and capable enemies to fight and Joshua only had a ragtag band of uncertain warriors who were formerly slaves in Egypt. They weren't professional soldiers. But because he knew it was his mission in life and was anointed by

God to lead the charge, Joshua was confident. Believing in your mission and allowing God to empower you dispels anxiety.

How about David? A casual reading of the Psalms shows that David had every reason to feel anxious. He was forever running from Saul and was a fugitive who lived on the move to stay alive. Imagine the anxiety level if the American military was hunting you down to kill you. Most of us would be paralyzed by fear, but the Psalms, while recording the full range of David's emotions during this time, are full of David's assurances of God's care.

It works the same way with college anxieties. When anxiety rears its ugly head, consider why God led you to college and remember that those He leads, He empowers. During my darkest days in college, it was useful to spend some time alone with the Savior and remember that He put within me the desire to become a physicist. Surely He would help me to succeed. With vision comes the provision.

PLAY YOUR OWN GAME

College students make it hard by displaying pack behavior and by playing the comparison game. If everyone seems to be studying in groups, you think you should be studying in groups. If some students fly through a test in fifteen minutes, you think you should fly through the test. If a neighbor is on question number twenty during an exam and you're only on number eleven, you think you need to hurry and catch up. This creates anxiety.

Refuse to play the comparison game. Don't look around at everyone else during a test. Most students who finish a test in fifteen minutes are the ones who are clueless and simply throwing in the towel early. Students who fly through test questions make silly errors and shoot themselves in the foot. Working in groups reduces to one, maybe two, students who do all the work and the others who copy them. Little education occurs in groups unless all parties make an honest contribution.

Playing your own game yields dividends. Let me give you an example of how not to do it. While studying for his physics Ph.D. comprehensive exams, one of my grad students noted that his peer students were studying in groups by working physics problems together. He believed they knew something he didn't, so he joined them, but it turned out that collective studying was not a good strategy for him, largely because he sat by and watched others do physics. He became a spectator and not a participant. When you work in groups, you aren't able to spend time with your own weaknesses but instead go where the strongest students in the group take you, which is usually to their weaknesses. The result was that he flunked his comps and had to switch to engineering. He lost out on his dream because he chose the wrong study strategy for an important test. The next time you watch ESPN, notice how many athletes remark in post-game interviews that they lost because they weren't playing their own game. Everyone learns differently and only you know best what works for you. Refuse to blindly follow the pack, who probably don't know where they're going anyway.

Resist All-Nighters

No two students are the same in what works for them. Some students need pressure to study. Lots of pressure. Whence the all-nighter, that caffeine-filled, pressure-packed endurance session to see how much information you can stuff into your head before a test. All-nighters are a time-honored part of college, but there is little I can think of that would cause more anxiety than to stay up all night before a test cramming. The motives are all wrong.

Students who think cramming works for any long-term good are fooling themselves. They are short-circuiting the very reason for being in college. Test cramming is symptomatic of poor organization. Tactically, it may get you through the immediate crisis, but do you really think that cramming addresses the larger, more important question of whether or not you learned anything? Would you want a surgeon who crammed for anatomy and physiology to operate on you? Would you want an aircraft designer who fudged his way through strength of materials to be the engineer of the plane you are flying? You see the point.

All-nighters are designed to chase the almighty GPA. With so much information stuffed in your brain at the last minute, all-nighters are prime anxiety generators because it's now a sink-or-swim, now-or-never proposition. You've lost the option of choice. You now have to study or else, and the "else" is the sickening feeling that you should have known better. Imagine when you come up against problems in learning the material, such as how to solve a particular class of homework problems. Your options are limited. Too late to visit the professor; too late to think through your difficulty or consult other books, tutors, or study helps; too late to take a breath. Prayer offers little solace.

A study at St. Lawrence University (2007) showed what is obvious to any college professor—all-nighters are not effective for success in college.[76] The author of the study Pamela Thacher concludes "If you use all-nighters, your GPA is slightly lower on average…pulling all-nighters compromises your (overall) sleep" and makes it difficult to reach your full academic potential. Retention after a crammed test is near zero. There comes a time when you have to learn something to be successful in college. Cramming is like wolves that track you, wear you down, ruin your life, and eventually move in for the kill. While it's a fact of college life that sometimes your schedule gets away from you and you're forced to play catch-up, a steady diet of all-nighters should be avoided unless you want to spend your entire college career going from one stressful set of circumstances to another. Avoid them.

STRATEGY #4: *Using Campus Resources*

WHAT IS AVAILABLE TO STUDENTS?

There is a wealth of campus resources available to students who need assistance during their college education. The problem is not a lack of resources but rather that students are unaware of them or are afraid to admit they need them. There is a diverse range of services that can help in all phases of college life—resources that address academics, remedial education, alcohol and drug problems, marriage and relationship problems, career counseling, placement services, religious services, leisure services, clubs, intramural sports, and the list goes on and on. Since you paid for most campus services with your tuition, you should avail yourself of them when the need arises. Broaden your view of campus resources. We discuss a few that are particularly helpful for students, just to give you a flavor of what is out there.

COUNSELING SERVICES

Students should rely on course and career planning regularly during college. The good news is that colleges have course counseling. The bad news is that effective course counseling is rare. Hardly a week goes by that I don't talk to a student who has received poor advice when signing up for courses and, as a result, loses valuable time, money, and credits by taking unnecessary courses. There's also loss when students transfer from a junior college or change majors and attempt to determine which credits transfer. Poor counseling can lead to disaster for students whose only sin is trying to find out what courses count toward their degree program. Academic counseling is the Achilles heel of most large universities.

My first exposure to college course planning was during my freshman year. I had to sign up for courses leading toward a degree in astrophysics. I'll never forget it; it was the stuff of a stand-up comic. The secretary of the physics department directed me to the office of my academic counselor to help me sign up for classes. What a joke. The first task was to find the counselor. I knocked on his office door, heard a voice that said to come in, but, when I entered, nobody was in sight. After thinking he had invented a cloaking device, I heard a voice coming from the direction of the floor. I looked down and there was my counselor, lying on a mat, using some undergraduate physics books as pillows. He had a recurring back problem and needed to lay flat for thirty minutes daily, and I happened to come by during the therapy session. He kindly offered me some quantum physics books to use as my pillow and asked me to join him on the floor while we talked, which I appreciated, but decided a chair would work better. When I told him I was a freshman who needed to find out what classes to take, I knew it was going to be a long day. Turned out, my assigned counselor was a freshly minted astronomy professor who just transferred from Harvard to Michigan State. Since he was new, he barely knew where the men's room was located, let alone the credits, requirements, and courses particular to Michigan State. I quickly found out that academic counseling meant reading the University Bulletin together to wade through the various and sundry credit requirements for a bachelor's degree in astrophysics. Before I left, I joined him on the floor with several quantum physics pillows.

Things haven't changed much in the world of counseling since I was in college. Universities still utilize faculty to do much of the counseling with much of the same deplorable results. Counseling is viewed by many college administrators as a necessary evil that sucks up money and is unnecessary when there are well-paid professors who can do it. Counselors are the last to be hired and the first to be fired. What's a student to do when it comes to academic counseling?

First, lower your expectations and get proactive. By this I mean to take charge of your situation and not allow nonexistent or poor counseling to hinder your progress. As much as it will bore you to tears, it's to your advantage to read the college bulletin, add up the credits required in your academic area, and keep track of your progress. It's tedious spade work but well worth your time. Think of it this way. If you take courses that don't count toward graduation, you waste incredible amounts of time and money. Every semester I hear horror stories about students who took courses that counted for nothing because they didn't double-check to see if the courses counted toward their major. It's worth your time to get it right.

Second, college departments usually have flowcharts of suggested courses of study. The flowcharts list the prerequisites, how many electives are available, and how everything fits together in four years. The first thing a student should do is visit the department office in your major and pick up whatever information they offer on course requirements. Getting to know your department secretary is an excellent strategy. Secretaries know more than bureaucrats when it comes to what classes students need since they are the first line of inquiry in a department and have been asked nearly every question.

Third, there are always questions that can't be answered from the college bulletin or by talking to faculty counselors. A common inquiry is whether you can take a course outside of your major and still get credit toward graduation. Find the Dean's Office in your major and ask to speak to a professional counselor in that office. Those are the advisor superstars who really know their stuff. They talk to students all day. The Dean's Office counselors are like gold for a confused and frustrated student. Use them.

Fourth, attend the freshman orientation programs run by nearly all universities. In our case, it's called Camp War Eagle. It's offered the summer before freshman enrollment and gives you a general introduction to the university. You are signed up for classes, get practical knowledge about college life such as where to find things to help you, and you get a one up on the power curve of freshman life.

STUDY HELPS

Universities offer useful programs to help students up their academic performance. Study Partners (SP) and Supplemental Instruction (SI) have been particularly successful at AU. SP is a free tutoring service where students teach students. An SP is an outstanding junior or senior student who has successfully passed the more difficult courses in the core curriculum. If you need help in freshman chemistry, say, the chemistry SP will offer a free, walk-in, chemistry help session a couple of times a week for several hours in the evening. The object is to allow for student questions, to get help with homework, and to interact with other students taking the course. Students know what difficulties arise when learning new material, so it's often true that a student SP can explain things better than a professor. The downside is that the nightly sessions get so large that you can miss the personal attention they were originally designed to give you. SP can also degenerate into doing students' homework for them. This is one reason I don't put a lot of grading weight on homework. I never know who is doing the work, whether a roommate, SP, tutor, boyfriend, girlfriend, or engineering major. One thing I do know, however, is that many students benefit greatly from SP.

SI is a program designed to supplement the lecture in large courses lacking recitations or study sessions. My SI sessions are taught by handpicked students who recently had my course and got an A. I won't choose an SI teacher that doesn't have passion and an aptitude for teaching. SI consists of a study session taught by student teachers and offered twice per week. To encourage attendance, I offer partial credit to students who attend some fraction of SI sessions in my Dave Letterman course. What is amazing is how many students fail to take advantage of it. It's true that students have packed out schedules and often can't make it to SI, but many students are either too lazy or too afraid that SI will cut into their after-school social life. That's the major problem with all the academic resources available at a university. The assistance is there in droves but students have to step up and ask for help when they need it. You are adults, and we can't force help upon you, but from where I sit, there's no excuse for a student who receives poor grades in college given the huge amount of assistance provided to students. The message is to educate yourself on the resources offered by your university, and then use the resources to help you successfully navigate through college.

YOUR PROFESSOR AS RESOURCE

TAKING ADVANTAGE OF OFFICE HOURS

Professor office hours should be viewed as a university service. Office hours refer to specific times set aside by professors to help students. They are like dollars in your pocket. You get to visit with the very person who is trying to teach you and ask whatever is on your mind about the course. You can't get a better or more knowledgeable person to help you. Yet, every semester I ask myself why more students don't take advantage of my office hours. Almost nobody shows up, and it's not due to an inconvenient time, since students can come by to see me anytime. In fact, I almost beg my students to come in for help if they are not doing well in my courses. But most semesters, only a few percent of my students bother to show up at my office door. Why?

When I first began teaching, my office hours were well attended. One reason was that I brought my office hours to the student by meeting them on their turf. I would schedule my office hours at 9–11 P.M. at a centrally-located dormitory, with an open invitation to attend for help with problems, studying, or just to chat. These were wonderful sessions. Talk about bonding with your teacher. Since students keep late hours it was right at their prime time. We usually ordered pizza and talked for hours about physics, math, science, and just about everything else. It was the best way to do education. But not anymore. I haven't offered dorm office hours in years. The reason I stopped is not because I lost interest but because I couldn't get but two to three students in a class of over a hundred to show up. Students today are busy with things having little relationship to school-work in the evenings, such as watching sitcoms, working, visiting their girlfriends, gabbing on the computer, watching sports, going hunting, or they simply don't care. Here are some other reasons why students are missing in action during office hours.

- First, some students have to work to put themselves through school and are saddled with impossible hours. Although my office hours are virtually anytime, some students still don't have adequate time to take an hour. My advice is to stop working so many hours.
- Second, students have been burned by professors who humiliate them during an office hour. Deriding students is inexcusable behavior; no professor should ever debase a student. On the other hand, if you as a student allow a bad-apple professor to negatively impact your education by never giving other professors a chance, then it's your fault. You want people who love you to affect your behavior, not a pompous, full-of-himself professor. Give some of your other professors a chance. Our profession has both good and bad apples.
- Third, some students don't really think professors can help them. This occurs when a professor is a foreigner, has trouble communicating, has no patience explaining material, or has absolutely no bedside manner. It was obvious to me when I was in college that some professors were not going to be very helpful during an office call, but I went anyway, if only to let the professor know I was trying. Sometimes, a professor cancelled a homework assignment because some of us went to him and told him how impossible it was to work the problems. Professors forget how difficult it is to learn material the first time around.

When students fail to take advantage of office hours, they shoot themselves in the academic foot. Students can usually tell if a professor honestly wants to help them and, for those professors, there are few excuses for not coming in for help. In my case, I want you to visit my office hours, but I'm not going to beg you. You have to man up and knock on my door. It's part of growing up. Some students tell me that they are too embarrassed to come to office hours because they are so far behind in the course that they don't know where to start. Or that I will see how far they are behind and chastise them for poor planning. Or that I will think less of them. Or that I will see how dumb they are. Or that I will humiliate them. These fears are largely unfounded.

The truth be told, if you are a student who is courageous enough to visit my office hours and honestly tell me that you are lost in my course, my respect for you grows. Students who don't ask for help are the dumb ones. For courses that are numerically graded, there is absolutely no penalty for taking advantage of office hours. You can't hurt yourself. Professors don't "take points away" when you visit them and say that you're lost. There are no point values I can attach to "behind" or "being clueless" or "not cracking a book." I am forever telling my students that it doesn't matter what I think of them personally. When my syllabus is written, it shows that my grading system is based on raw numbers and not my subjective impressions of students. That releases students to get all the help they can from me.

A final point. Over the years, I have kept track of students who visited me for help. Without exception, they do well in my courses. A typical case is a girl who got an F on the first test last semester. She mustered the courage to come by, told me she flunked her test, and asked what she could do better. She found that I didn't bite and became a regular to my office hours. Long story short, she ended up with an A in the course. It's like clockwork for students who attend office hours. Nearly all of them get A's and B's and it's not because they become teacher's pets, but because they learn from my years of teaching experience and the one-on-one attention they get during office hours. Further advantages to office hours:

You Save Time. Instead of ringing your hands over a homework assignment or problem set you don't understand, why not come and ask? Time is short in college, and I don't want you to struggle for hours over something I could answer in a few short minutes. Too many students ask their professors last instead of first.

You Save Money. It amazes me when students ask me if I can recommend a good tutor for my class. Why would you pay for a tutor when you have the best possible tutor for the course in me? And you've already paid for me. Use your head and get your money's worth from your tuition dollars.

You Save Frustration. It's common for students to say that they don't know what or how to study. Why wonder? Ask me. If you spend time at my office hours, you will see what material is important, you will learn what I tend to ask on tests, and you will see how I think. It never fails that I give my students any number of simpler ways to learn something because I had to come up with simple ways to learn something when I was a student. Take advantage of my years of experience in learning physics to save you hours of frustration.

You Develop Motivation. The more you know your professors, the more respect you will develop for them and their subject area. It's easier to study for someone when you respect them. Think of the old coaches you've had in your life. If you respected them, you wanted to win for them. A good example is Tony Dungy, coach of the Super Bowl winning Indianapolis Colts. During a recent interview,[77] someone asked Peyton Manning how the team was able to hold together over the course of a difficult season. His answer was simple. He said that the team worked hard because the players respected Coach Dungy so much that nobody wanted to disappoint him. The same is true for courses and professors. I hope I can motivate my students to do well because they respect me and know that I have their best interests at heart.

You Get Personal Help. When I have a struggling student across the table from me, I can assess where he's having trouble and how many layers of the learning onion he's peeled. It's usually something easy to correct, such as not reading a test question accurately, trying to break the land speed record when taking my tests, not reading key words, or being rusty with calculations and unit conversions. The personal interaction is what education should be about, when the highest ideals of college education are realized. When you don't come to my office hours, you don't get my professional help with your learning.

STRATEGY #5: *Navigating the Career Process*

Navigating the career process refers to figuring out what you want to do with your life. Few students approach the career process systematically despite the fact that most people are in college to pursue a career. They typically fall into career choices by hit and miss, trial and error, and one step forward, two steps backwards approaches. The lack of career foresight wastes time and breeds frustration with college life. If you don't identify a specific career goal early in your college life it makes everything more difficult. You'll either waste a lot of time trying a variety of majors or you'll be so far behind your peer students who know what they want to do that you'll always feel behind the power curve. Students should narrow their career choices early. In this section, we offer a systematic procedure to help you find your place in the career universe.

WHAT'S INSIDE YOU?

Self-inquiry is the first step toward a career choice. Self-inquiry refers to the process of determining your wiring. Unless you know where you want to go in life, it's very difficult to navigate successfully through it. If you're trying to figure out how to get to New York, for example, you first have to know that New York is your destination. The first crucial question in the career process is often the most difficult for people to answer. The greatest thinkers in history recognized that self-knowledge is paramount to a successful and fulfilling life:

- Socrates believed that fulfillment in life is obtained when we "Know Thyself."
- Confucius taught that the key to a satisfying life is to "Control Thyself."

- Christ said that the secret to life is to "Deny Thyself" (Matt. 16:24–25).

Truth be told, successfully navigating college for a Christian student requires all three elements—knowing thyself, controlling thyself, and denying thyself. Translated, this means knowing what you want to do, disciplining yourself to work toward it, and accepting the necessary deferred rewards along the way. We focus in this section on knowing thyself.

It's common to find people in their twenties, thirties, and forties who still don't know what to do with their lives. I meet them every week. Not knowing what you want to do for your life's work is tragic.

- It's tragic because it leads to a life of frustration as you wander through life and wonder what's wrong with you.
- It's tragic because you look with envy at people with satisfying careers who have found their niche.
- It's tragic because you mourn the years you've wasted while you were waiting for something to grab your interest.
- It's tragic because you count the money you could have been earning if you only knew early what you wanted to do.
- It's tragic because you hate the dead-end job you currently have that has drained your will and sucked you dry for years.
- It's tragic because you feel like the wedding has occurred and you're still standing at the altar.
- It's tragic because you've missed the will of God for your vocational life.

Few questions in life are more important than determining your talents, interests, and aptitudes and how they translate into a rewarding career. Career dissatisfaction is epidemic today.

- A recent Conference Board survey[78] showed that < 39% of employees below age twenty-five considered their job "satisfying," the lowest level in the survey's twenty year history.

- A survey from CareerBuilder.com (2007)[79] found that 84% of workers aren't in their dream jobs.
- A poll by the research firm Maritz (2005)[80] showed that only ~ 10% of Americans "strongly agreed" that they looked forward to going to work.

Are you serious? You mean that ~ 90% of American workers have trouble getting up in the morning and receive very little satisfaction from half of their waking hours? Since one-third of your life is sleeping, one-third is working, and one-third is personal time, wasting that much of your life in an unfulfilling job is a personal disaster.

If you don't know who you are, you wander through college, trying this and trying that, while wasting time, energy, and money. The lack of direction tracks you into adulthood. A major reason employees jump job ships is because people haven't found their passion. Even if you've decided what career is best for you, the going is still hard. You have to have the opportunity, courage, and savvy and not succumb to your fears, your millennial ego, your comfort zone, or the almighty dollar. There are three important steps in the career decision:

- Finding your passion
- Having the courage to pursue your passion
- Matching your passion to a paying vocation

Nearly everyone who finds themselves in a boring, unsatisfying job falls short in one or more of these areas. We'll talk below about finding your passion and matching your passion to a paying vocation. These are the easier steps in the process because you can work at them. They require time but are conquerable by effort. The courage step, however, is a different animal. Courage is a gut check, an inside job that exposes what you're made of and how you approach risk and adversity. Courage refers to a fearless pursuit of your career choice. It means to move toward your career goal regardless of adversity; to be brave and refuse to wilt under the pressure when the resistance comes. The resistance can take several forms:

- Your close friends tell you your passion is strange.
- Your parents are convinced you'll never make enough money.
- People tell you your passion requires too much time and effort.
- Society convinces you that your passion is not prestigious enough.
- Your ego argues against your passion being sexy enough.
- Your comfort zone is too comfortable to take a risk.
- You believe everyone else who thinks they know what you should do.
- Your biological clock says it's too late.

I heard at least half these arguments when I told people I wanted to pursue physics. Everyone wants to put in their two cents and talk you out of your passion when it doesn't fit their mold of what they think you should be doing. Everyone thinks they know better than you about what you should do with your life. It's good that I never listened to the arguments. Truth is, nobody knows better how to live your life than you. Nobody else walks in your shoes, they're not the ones putting in the effort, they're not the ones with your talent, and they're usually the last ones who should be advising anybody about career choices. The people who try the most to discourage you from a vocation are usually the ones who don't have their own career act together. Nothing wrong with getting advice from people who know and love you, but the final choice is yours and yours only after consultation with the Lord and your family and loved ones. Below are some reasons students find career choices difficult.

NOT KNOWING YOURSELF

The first reason students find career choices difficult is because they don't know themselves. This means they are struggling with questions of identity. Identity questions are always thorny because they go to the core of who you are as a person. They are gut checks. You have to look in the mirror and see what is there, good and bad, real and imagined, warts and clear skin. It's about being honest with yourself. It's how you see yourself when you are all alone in the quiet of the night looking at the ceiling. Some of the identity questions students ask:

- Who am I?
- What am I here for?
- What is my purpose in life?
- What are my passions?
- What does God want me to do in life?
- Where do I fit?
- What gives me the most satisfaction?
- Should I choose money over satisfaction?
- What will my parents think if I go against their career choice?
- Will my parents cut me off financially if I choose a career they disapprove of?
- What is really inside of me? What am I made of?
- Will I take risks in my career choice, or will I play it safe?
- Will my fears and confidence level determine my career choice?
- Will the level of work required limit my career choice?
- Do I have the drive to pursue my passion?
- Do I want to get married more than choose the best career for me?
- Am I smart enough to become a _____?
- Will I work hard enough to become a _____?
- What is the most important job criterion to me?
- Do I want fame and celebrity?
- Do I want to make a lot of money but not have to work hard to get it?
- I'm interested in _____ but afraid I can't make a living at it.

Finding your identity optimally occurs during the childhood to adulthood transition. When you're in college, you're breaking free of your parents and learning to stand on your own. The pressure builds as you're expected to know what you want to do. A lot is at stake; it's like dragging around a weight. It's difficult to hear the anguish of my students over what to choose as a career. They have spent precious little time thinking about what lights their fire. The solution is to start your pondering early. Deliberately take time to consider what drives you as you work through the core curriculum in college and are exposed to a variety of majors, careers, students, professors, and experiences. Find out what you love to do and what challenges your imagination. Consider taking one of the interests and aptitudes tests provided by collegiate academic services at your school. The pertinent question is "What would you love doing so much that you would do it even if you weren't paid?" Is it helping people? Is it teaching? Is it writing? Is it acting? Is it singing in a band? Is it heading up a start-up company? Is it software development? Is it film editing? Is it becoming an astronaut? Is it being a news anchor? Is it serving the Lord as a pastor? Is it being a stay-at-home mom?

One more clue. CareerBuilder.com[81] asked people to describe what their dream jobs would look like. They found that dream jobs were "surprisingly reminiscent of childhood wishes for many workers." No surprise there. For Christians, God has a mission for us in life. He gives us abilities, skills, aptitudes, and interests that match His goals for our life. Those skills and abilities show up during childhood before the realities of the world set in and discourage us from our childhood first loves. That was my case; I knew what I wanted to do since about eighth grade. I had an early aptitude for science and decided to be a scientist or a science teacher. There was no debate and no wringing of hands; turns out most of us scientists make our ultimate career decision during the middle school years. But my experience is rare. Extremely rare. For most people, the transition from confusion to clarity is long and agonizing. Partly what college is for is to help you see the larger world of opportunities that yearn for consideration as your life's work. Make a concerted attempt to take advantage of your college experiences to study yourself and make a viable career choice that fits your talents and God's will for your life.

FINDING YOUR PASSION: PREOCCUPATION LEADING TO OCCUPATION

Finding your passion is so important it's useful to continue with this line of thought. A college student without passion is like a ship without a rudder. There is power without objectives and loads of wasted, fruitless effort. Few students today know what they want to do even after four years of college, despite the fact that God clearly states that He has tasked every Christian student with an important role to play in life. Some of Paul's observations on finding your passion: "We are God's workmanship, created in Christ Jesus to do good works, which God prepared in advance for us to do" (Eph. 2:10). "But in fact God has arranged the parts in the body, every one of them, just as he wanted them to be" (1 Cor. 12:18). "For it is God who is at work in you, both to will and to work for His good pleasure" (Phil. 2:13). These passages show that God created each of His children for important and productive work. He has given us abilities and talents and wants us to use them for His glory. It's contrary to Scripture that God would put us on earth without a passion for something that we should pursue as a profession. The most satisfied people are those who find their passion and turn it into a paying vocation. They have the best of both worlds.

The mistake Christians make in finding their passion is to sit back and wait for divine revelation to tell them. Waiting on God is one of the hallmarks of a Christian, but it doesn't mean doing nothing. There is passive waiting and there is active waiting. It's rare that God tells His people to do nothing while waiting for His direction. Waiting on God really means to pause for further instructions. While you're pausing you do things. You get yourself ready to receive the blessing and work with a plan of attack. You get off your fanny and try some things. In the case of students, it means thinking deliberately about what ignites your interests and it means to expose yourself to careers and occupations to see what suits you. In the section ahead we discuss practical ways for students to match interests to careers. My thrust here is to give you direction on how to find the will of God in your life. Your passion in life will match the will of God for you because He has made us to serve Him with our gifts and abilities.

It doesn't take a personality test or spiritual gifts inventory to find your passion. Use those if you must, but you have only to observe yourself and take note of where you spend the majority of your time. Where do you gravitate? What do you enjoy doing? What consumes you? Where are your intense interests? When you have spare time, what do you like to do? What can't you stay away from? What was your childhood first love? That will lead you to the right answer. Everyone is wired for a specific purpose in life from the Creator. If you follow the wiring diagram

God placed in you before you were born, you will find your passion. Nobody says it better than Solomon, "A gift opens the way for the giver and ushers him into the presence of the great" (Prov. 18:16). Solomon is saying that, if you pursue your gift, it opens the world to you. There is nothing more fulfilling than doing the things for which you were created. You are ushered into great and mighty endeavors for the Lord that would be lost had you not pursued your passion. Accomplished people from all walks of life pinch themselves daily for the opportunities afforded them. Never in their wildest dreams did they think they would meet the people they have, do the work they do, and accomplish the great things they seem to attain so effortlessly.

For me it was astronomy. I loved the stars, made my own telescope, memorized all the nearest and brightest stars, read college books on astronomy as an eighth grader, and spent many nights observing the heavens. One of my friends spent most of his time helping people in his college church. He helped the college minister with planning, organized social events, helped as a backup teacher, and served to counsel other college students with personal and academic problems. He nearly spent more time at church than attending his college courses. Let me ask you as the reader. What is my college friend's passion in life? It's obvious. He's happiest when serving the Lord in a church. You would advise him to consider a career in ministry. Or take another friend who, from an early age, kept data on all things college sports, such as how many Heisman candidates went to USC, who was the MVP of the college world series in 1985, or how many years Lou Holtz coached at Notre Dame. When he got to college, he volunteered to keep statistics in the Michigan State press box during football games. What is his passion? Sports information. If you were to advise him, you would suggest he look for a job in some facet of the sports world, such as a journalist or team statistician. He ended up being the assistant sports information director at Michigan State.

Point is, God gave some to be pastors, teachers, encouragers, authors, athletes, businessmen, CEOs, generals, stay-at-home moms, guidance counselors, and presidents (Eph. 4:11). You only have to look within yourself to find your passion, to travel back to your youth and remember your childhood dreams. When your preoccupation becomes your occupation it's like you died and went to heaven. Life stands up because you are doing what God designed you to do.

PERSISTENCE: WILL STRONGER THAN SKILL

There is an adage which states that success is 10% talent, 10% luck, and 80% persistence. Is that true? Let's ask an expert—the most successful coach in Auburn University sports history. And before you think it's one of our storied football coaches, try again. It's not John Heisman, not Shug Jordan, not Pat Dye, not Terry Bowden, and not Tommy Tuberville. Our most successful coach is Dave Marsh, recent coach of the AU swim team. We have lost count on how many national swimming and diving championships Coach Marsh has to his credit in the seventeen years he was at AU. It's something like ten. In recent years, both men's and women's swim teams have won the national championship in the same year, several times. By anyone's definition, Coach Marsh has produced a dynasty in aquatics at AU.

Was the going always easy for Marsh? No way. Recently, Marsh announced his departure from AU to tackle a new challenge, opting to take a position with the Mecklenburg Aquatic Club in Charlotte, North Carolina where he will serve as the head elite coach and CEO of the program, which established the U.S. Olympic Committee Center of Excellence. In this role, Marsh will direct the development of future U.S. Olympic swimmers. It's a dream job. He has nothing left to accomplish at AU. We all wish him well. During comments made in a press conference announcing his departure from AU, he said "The hardest part of all this is the thought of departing from Auburn. Auburn's where I gained my self-esteem in the sport of swimming. Auburn's where I have found my profession in coaching…Auburn's where I came to faith in the Lord. Auburn's where I courted my wife and where my three children were born. And Auburn's the one who believed in me. I had 15 letters of schools turning me down before Auburn hired me."[82] I've often wondered about the fifteen schools that turned Marsh down. What were they thinking? Consider the ramifications had Marsh quit after opening the fifteenth rejection letter.

AU would have lost one of the top coaches in college swimming history; Marsh would have lost the opportunity to be at a university and live in a community he came to love; hundreds of young collegiate swimmers would have missed having him as a coach; and AU would have lost their ten national championships.

If you don't have persistence you'll never accomplish anything of value in life. It's that simple. Persistence keeps you going when the going gets tough. Persistence renews your energy when you are weak and beat up. Persistence tells you not to give up when everything looks bleak. Persistence means throwing your heart over the high-jump bar and refusing to take no for an answer. Persistence is more important than talent and brainpower. It's better than wealth and status. Find a successful, accomplished person and you will find someone who ranks persistence near the top of the list of qualities that separate the doers from the pretenders. Consider the words of the boxing great Muhammed Ali, who advises: "Will must be stronger than skill." My own career in physics would have died on the vine without persistence. Clearly, I was nowhere near the brilliant students in my physics graduating class. A physics problem that took them thirty minutes to solve took me hours. There was hardly a book in my house growing up. My dad was a factory worker who made ~ $15K per year when he retired with five children to feed, clothe, and house. The stucco house where we lived had ice on the inside bedroom wall during cold Michigan nights. I slept with my brother and our dog to keep warm. There was nothing of the silver-spoon upbringing that many genius-caliber physics students possess. I was blue-collar and probably closer to black collar or no collar at all.

But I tried. I stayed with it. I didn't quit, even though I lived most weekends in the library with a crushing burden of homework problems that I had little competence to solve. One time I estimated the number of hours required to read a single page of one of my senior-level physics textbooks. It was well over an hour and sometimes several hours as I struggled to fill in the math steps. Consider that the average physics major takes four senior-level courses, each covering roughly two hundred pages per semester, and you see the problem. Just to keep up I would have to study for hundreds of hours per semester, and then there was homework, studying for tests, and working for professors in their labs. It was tedious, mind-numbing work. Without an iron will and an accompanying fear of failure, no way was I going to make it.

EVALUATING CAREER OPTIONS

PLACEMENT SERVICES

A few students have a general idea of what they want to do in life but can't translate it into career choices. This is because they lack information about careers. I usually see this when students come to me with a gleam in their eye about a job-related experience. The conversation goes something like this: "Dr. Bozack, you should have seen the kids I met at the hospital today. They were in serious car accidents and had head injuries. Many of them were relearning how to talk, learn, and process information. It was amazing to see the progress after a few short weeks of therapy. I loved working with them." When I subsequently ask if they ever considered going into speech or occupational therapy, I get the quizzical, "I've never heard of those occupations." Students are frequently ignorant of what occupations exist to match their interests.

When I hear that kind of passion in my student's voices, I know it's only a matter of time before we find the right matching profession. The first line of attack is to spend some time at the college placement center, which we alluded to earlier. Placement centers are libraries of information about employment options, careers, occupations, and all things vocational. In my generation a placement center had scores of filing cabinets with brochures describing all of the major professional occupations. There was information on salaries, required degrees, places of employment, prerequisites, regions in the country with the most openings, detailed job descriptions, typical paths to promotion, and on and on. Placement services arrange and host prospective employers as they interview students nearing graduation. They are a one-stop shopping brokerage for careers. Placement centers also have employment and vocational specialists to advise students on potential careers, and tests to help students identify their aptitudes and talents. It's well worth your time to spend a few afternoons at

Placement Services if you are having trouble identifying what you want to do vocationally. Much of the needed information today is online and not in filing cabinets.

CO-OP PROGRAMS

Cooperative education (co-op) programs are a second way to find out about occupations by offering on-the-job exposure to career choices. Say you:

- Are considering a career in textile engineering but need more information about what textile engineers do in the real world
- Are interested in a career in television production and want to see what it's like to work at a television station
- Are interested in space and wonder what working at NASA is all about
- Enjoy news stories and wonder what working at a newspaper is like

The co-op office at your university will work to place you with a company which agrees to hire you as a co-op student. Most co-op programs work on a semester-on, semester-off basis, meaning you attend college as a normal college student for a semester then work as a co-op student for a semester. It's a win-win for both parties. Students make some money, get a break from studying for a semester, and receive firsthand exposure to a potential career. In turn, the co-op employer gets to evaluate you as a future potential employee and receives cheap labor from an eager beaver student.

Employer assignments span the spectrum. An engineering company might assign a co-op student to a project that has been languishing for months because they can't afford to pull other engineers off time-critical projects. A marketing company might give you a list of clients to contact. A stock brokerage may assign a co-op student to work with account managers as they work with clients. A hotel management company might place you with one of their hotels for a semester. It's hard to beat the direct occupational exposure that a co-op experience provides. The downside is that co-op programs increase the time to graduation because you're working and going to school in series. Most students who choose to co-op can expect to spend one to two more years in college. For many students, however, it's better to try on a career before graduation than to find out afterward that your career choice, which looked good on paper, wasn't really what it was cracked up to be in the real world. If a student finds out during their co-op semester that their tentative career choice is unsuitable, they choose a different employer the next co-op cycle.

SHADOWING

A third way to evaluate career options is to shadow in a prospective vocational choice. Shadowing means to look over a professional's shoulder as they go about their business; it's passive while co-oping is active. You observe but don't participate. Some professionals love to answer questions and take time to explain their profession; others are too busy to answer anything. Shadowing is mostly associated with health-related professions (doctors, dentists, dental assistants, sonographers, X-ray therapists, etc.), but some students shadow with attorneys, pastors, farmers, builders, factory workers, and a variety of other professions. Shadowing arrangements are usually made on an individual basis between a student and the professional rather than through a formal university program. You target a given profession, choose a person in that field, knock on their door, and ask if they are willing to let you shadow with them. Many of our AU students have shadowed with professionals in their hometowns. It's easy for students from small towns who grow up knowing the local professionals to ask to hang around and watch how they work.

SUMMER INTERNSHIPS

Summer internships are co-op programs lasting a summer. Universities have established relationships with organizations who agree to hire summer interns. You apply to the intern program and select an employment preference from a list of compatible companies. If selected, you move to the company for the summer and work as a low-cost student employee. Common internships we are all familiar with are with summer camps, the

White House (Monica Lewinsky), Disney World, Six-Flags, cruise ships, and resorts such as Hilton Head. When I was a student, I had a summer internship at Tektronix, Inc., a high-tech company in Portland, Oregon who manufactures some of the best electronic test equipment in the world. I was assigned to work with a group of cathode ray tube (CRT) engineers whose goal was to develop the next generation of computer displays and oscilloscope monitors. My summer project was to determine the types of monitor defects expected when manufacturing CRTs in less-than-clean environments. I had to learn every step in the manufacturing process of a CRT, from the time a computer monitor came into the plant as pieces of plastic, glass, and metal to when it left as a working monitor. I spent the summer messing with the innards of CRTs and doing physics experiments on how contaminants affected the electron beam. The product was a report that characterized the beam distortions with ideas on how to get rid of them. You couldn't ask for a better experience on how industrial physicists and engineers work in a corporate setting. My internship confirmed for me that I was in the right area of science and propelled me toward my current subfield of physics.

NOT BEING ABLE TO HEAR GOD

A perennial problem for Christians is hearing from God during important life decisions. We wish God would talk to us like He talked to Moses. We want a burning bush experience. When He doesn't, we wonder what is wrong. Some Christians talk as if they have a hot line to heaven while others struggle most of their life to hear clearly from God. What is the deal with hearing from God?

College students aren't the only ones who struggle with hearing from God. Most Christians struggle with hearing from God. The reasons vary, but when I can't hear from God, it's usually because I'm not close to Him. God usually doesn't yell. His belief in freedom is so significant that He doesn't force Himself on us. He prefers to patiently wait for us to admit we need Him. When I'm having trouble hearing from God it's usually because I'm too busy to listen, too distracted to pay attention to what He's trying to say, or not spending enough quiet time with Him in prayer and fellowship. When you care about someone, you spend time with them. Think of your significant other. If you don't spend time with her, finding out what she's like, how she thinks, and what's important to her, it's difficult to "hear" her. Hearing from God is similar. That's why it's crucial for Christian students to carve out time with God no matter what else is on your plate.

Christians don't hear from God when they're lazy. Instead of spending time with the Scriptures, which are filled with God's wisdom on nearly every subject, including how to choose a career, we'd rather just have Him call us on our cell phones. When He doesn't, we blame Him for forgetting our number. We're so conditioned to buttons, instant messaging, and Googling for answers that we expect God to be our errand boy. We clap our hands and He answers. But God is not a lackey. He loves us and wants to be our Father, but He is also the Creator of the universe. OT believers did not have the Bible. We do. God talked to Moses directly but talks to us through the Scriptures. This is actually better than what Moses had because the Bible is a comprehensive treatise whereas Moses was asking about specifics. Christ said it was to our advantage that He go away, because He could only be one place at one time, but the Holy Spirit comes to reside in all believers. When we're having trouble hearing from God it's often because we are weak Bible students who are not putting forth the effort to learn the Scriptures.

We fail to hear from God when we're living in known sin. While this is a tricky issue because God doesn't expect us to be perfect before He listens to us, it's undeniable that the Bible is filled with instances where God's divine favor is hindered due to open aggression. Sin looks God in the face and taunts "I know better." Sin admits we're smarter than God. Sin means we're arrogant and selfish. Sin is the clay talking back to the potter. But God hates sin; He's offended by it. Sin changed everything in the Garden of Eden. Adam and Eve precipitated a downward spiral of bad experiences for mankind that continues to this day. One of the reasons life in this world seems so difficult is that we were never designed to live with the consequences of original sin, such as death, separation, and independence. Sin separates us from God until we seek forgiveness and reconciliation. It kills life, devours people, and destroys communication. Consider what happens to communication between a husband and wife when one party is caught cheating. Cheating kills communication and breeds estrangement. When God is knocked off our priority list, we replace Him with an idol and are spiritually cheating on Him. We've allowed a foreign god in our beds and then wonder why God doesn't want to talk. When you as a college student are in the process of making a career decision and need God to guide you, evaluate your relationship with Him and see whether the silence you hear is your self-inflicted sin.

Choosing Against Perpetual Adolescence

Students often avoid the career planning process in order to postpone adulthood. The struggle against growing up is especially acute in millennial students. Overindulged children have a strong sense of entitlement. They think parents should support them through college and after, often until they get established in their careers and make a living comparable to their parents. The sense of dependence can extend far into the twenties. It's shocking when students leave school and find that it takes years to match the wealth of their parents, so they return home and mooch off mom and dad awhile longer to save for a house. Not to put all the blame on students. Parents reinforce the slow crawl toward adulthood when they keep buying their kids cars, clothes, and apartment furnishings well after college. Many parents help buy their children their first home after graduation. Students who financially depend on parents for what seems like forever is becoming a natural law in American society.

Please don't stone me, but I have yet to find where it's cast in stone that parents must pay for the college education of their children. Many of us never received a penny of parental help, and we seemed to do fine, and an argument could be made that we are better off for it. People who have to face adversity and earn their way are those who most appreciate the cost of the journey. Perhaps the best advice I've heard for parents who believe that supporting their kids throughout college is a nonnegotiable entitlement was given by Warren Buffett,[83] the legendary investment genius and one of the world's richest men. He had it right when he said the correct amount of money to invest in children is enough "so that they would feel they could do anything, but not so much that they could do nothing." Buffett advises a balance between earning and getting. Parents who pay for everything during college rob their kids of the value of earning their education. It turns a privilege into an entitlement. Too little monetary support during college, on the other hand, discourages achievement as your child focuses on survival instead of the books. Best to be somewhere in the middle. While Buffett was specifically talking about how much money to leave children in a will, the principle still applies when deciding how much money to put aside when considering your child's college education. Why am I talking to parents in a book for students, you ask? It's good for students to overhear the discussion and appreciate the investment and sacrifice their parents have made for them.

Perpetual adolescence is encouraged by students who opt to party for a few more years before facing the responsibilities of adulthood. College life is pretty good. If you have parents who support you and you don't have to work, you can get up when you feel like it, go to bed when you feel like it, party when you feel like it, drink beer at all hours of the day and night, and choose to study or not study. The only thing you have to avoid is flunking out and even that can take years with the lax academic probation rules currently on the books in many colleges. The sudden rush of freedom in college is seductive, and many students fail to handle it constructively. Problem is, too much of a good thing quickly turns to regret and failure. There is time for both fun and work in college if you put first things first, but if you get stoned on the party scene and fail to address why you are in college in the first place, which is to get a degree, you will regret your actions someday when others get a great job, and you are left with a bunch of drunken fuzzy memories.

STRATEGY #6: *Setting and Achieving Goals*

SETTING PROXIMAL GOALS

Navigating college requires students to set and achieve reasonable goals. Goals are defined as what you believe is worthy of pursuit. Goals prescribe your destination. We talked earlier about career goals. Career goals are the broad, lofty goals we need to keep us moving toward something in life. Proximal goals, by contrast, refer to the nuts and bolts goals that students need to successfully navigate semester after semester through college.

College students should regularly formulate and review proximal goals. It's best to have both general and specific proximal goals and to lay them out in a tree structure. Say one of your general proximal goals is to achieve an A in chemistry. How do you get there? Those are your specific proximal goals. Let's lay them out:

General Proximal Goal
Achieving an A in Chemistry
Specific Proximal Goals
Regularly attend class
Take effective notes during lecture
Read the course text every day
Spend two hours of study for every one hour of lecture
Prepare for chemistry lab before getting there
Jump on assignments when they are handed out
Study for tests prudently and refuse to wait until the last minute to prepare
Ask for help from the professor or GTA when you are lost
Stay disciplined and develop at least a utilitarian interest in learning
  chemistry

GOAL SETTING TAKES DISCIPLINE

We saw above that discipline refers to an orderly, controlled, and efficient way of doing things. It's the ability to put first things first and to tackle tasks that are hard to do before things that are easy to do. Many incoming college freshman lack the discipline to stay on top of the rapid pace of college courses. Discipline and good work habits are the secret to conquering a lack of discipline. Consider these ways to increase your discipline.

PRACTICE, PRACTICE, PRACTICE

Discipline comes naturally to few people. Think of a person you admire for their success. Say it's Donald Trump in real estate, Bill Gates in computer technology, Billy Graham in evangelism, Duane Wade in basketball, Bobby Bowden in college coaching. In every case, discipline is the key ingredient. It may be the most important ingredient.

Most students know that discipline is important to success. That's not the problem. The problem is how to develop discipline. After the lax standards in high school, students have a difficult time finding the library to study. It's common to see freshman students who lack concentration, can't sit still for more than ten minutes, or fall asleep if they try to study in a quiet library. They succumb to the enticing distractions we all face. So how do you develop discipline as a student?

By practice and training. You start slowly and build up. Discipline isn't natural because it means you put aside the things you'd rather be doing to do the things you would rather not be doing. It's a deferred reward exercise. What you would rather not be doing is studying. Studying is hard work. It's lonely. It takes effort. It doesn't come easy at first for anyone. Say you want to lose a few pounds after pigging out over Christmas break by starting an exercise program. You join a health club and hire a trainer to set up a weekly program of cardio and weight training. After day one, you'd rather be dead. Your muscles are sore, you can barely walk, and every part of your body is crying for relief. You can't move without something hurting. It's horrible. Nobody enjoys exercising when they first begin, just like nobody likes studying.

But it gets easier with practice. During the second week of exercising you feel a little better as your muscles get used to the work. The third week is even better. After a month or so, exercising becomes an integral part of your weekly routine and makes you feel so good that you don't want to go without it. What was once drudgery and pain now becomes enjoyable and productive. On top of it all, your body starts to look better and the pounds begin to evaporate. The positive reinforcement cycle engages as you see your body change, which in turn motivates you to higher levels of performance. That's discipline taking root. Eventually, your laziness is replaced with achievement as you see that it's better to get with the program than remain on the sidelines. You force yourself at first, and it gets easier with practice.

At the beginning of my freshman year, I could barely sit for fifteen minutes and study. My mind kept wandering, and it was difficult to focus. Much of the time I was overwhelmed by the amount of work. But I kept at it. I reasoned that if I could study for fifteen minutes on Tuesday, then on Wednesday I could extend it to twenty minutes. And if I could do it for twenty minutes on Wednesday, then I could do it for thirty minutes on Thursday. At the end of my freshman year, because I continued to hammer at the problem, I could study for hours at a time. In my prime, I could put myself away in a library and study for eight to ten hours with good concentration. But you have to be legalistic at first.

VISUALIZE THE END RESULT

Discipline is easier to develop if you have a clear picture of what you want to do after college. Visualize yourself doing the things that you are training for in college. If your goal is to work for NASA, visualize yourself heading up a team to build the next Hubble Telescope. If your goal is to be an industrial mathematician, visualize yourself working for AFLAC doing actuarial calculations. If you want to be a top fashion designer in NYC, visualize yourself working for Versace. If you want to be an actor, visualize yourself working for MGM and starring in a Hollywood movie. If you want to be a high roller, visualize yourself as Donald Trump. If you want to be a great soldier and statesman, visualize yourself as Colin Powell. Get a collection of people in your mind that you respect and want to emulate. The power of visualization is incredible. It's a general law of life that you tend to become the person you visualize yourself to be. Successful people keep going by visualizing where the work will get them. They focus on the end goal, the finish line, breaking the tape, and not the blood and sweat.

Focusing on the means, rather than the end result, is demoralizing due to the sheer magnitude of the task. You tend to quit. Take the Olympic skater Michelle Kwan. Nobody will ever know how many times Michelle had to get up at 5:30 A.M. for practice, how many thousands of times she fell while mastering a triple axle, how many sore muscles and leg bruises she endured, or how many heartaches and disappointments she experienced in her long skating career. Michelle herself doesn't know, because successful athletes don't focus on the pain but on the gold medal. Successful people visualize the goal and set aside thoughts of the work required to achieve the goal. The work to get to the goal is the means to the end, the price you pay to stand on the winner's platform. If you as a student focus on all the work, all the test preparation, all the late nights studying, and all the pains of deferred rewards, you will crush under the load. But if you have a firm visual image of what you want to accomplish, where you want to go, and who you want to emulate, the means become secondary and the goal becomes primary. The picture of who you want to be won't let you quit.

A personal example. Focusing on what I saw myself doing in life kept me going during the long years preparing to be a physics professor. The secret for me centered on "chair time." Chair time is my cherished period of renewal at the end of a long day. No matter what happens on a given day, I always make a point to have some personal time set aside at the end of the day. It's what kept me grounded and sane during my college years. Chair time usually amounts to donning a set of headphones and listening to music in a favorite rocking chair. I blame chair time mostly on my mom, who used to rock all her kids to sleep when we were babies. We're all rockers.

What happens during chair time is not about the rocking or the music. It's about renewing, recalibrating, and reaffirming where I am and where I want to go in life. Chair time is when I review my goals and regain the energy and strength to get there. It's when I let my mind soar to great heights and imagine myself doing the stuff of my dreams. Usually, I don't even hear the music. Chair time is when I visualize myself being successful in whatever endeavor God has for me. During those dark days as a student when I didn't think I would make it, I would spend a little time each night in the chair and imagine myself being a physicist, teaching large classes, solving equations that were impossible, and making significant discoveries for mankind. I saw Dr. Michael J. Bozack on my business cards. I saw myself giving presentations to large audiences of other scientists at conferences. Visualizing who I wanted to be kept me going during the thousands of hours in the library. Visualization is to discipline what fuel is to an engine. Be sure to keep your gas tank filled during your college years.

VIEW LEARNING AS IMPORTANT

Working toward a goal is easier when it's important to you. If what you are studying in college is not important to you, it will be difficult to find the discipline to learn it. This is a particularly a problem for freshman and sophomore students taking the required suite of core courses. Many students think the core courses are a waste of time and money. Stupid requirements to make the university more money. Irrelevant classes that have nothing to do with your prospective occupation. Courses outside a major are often simply not important to students. This viewpoint is cocky, short-sighted, vocationally oriented, and presumes that you know more than the professionals who developed your curriculum.

To show you the correlation of importance and discipline, consider when you met your current significant other. If you are a guy, you wanted to know all about her. You wanted to know what she liked to eat, what she liked to wear, what her favorite subjects were, what music she liked, what you could do to help her, and what she wanted from the man in her life. You would go the extra mile to learn about her and work to make her life easier and please her. Disciplining yourself to do the things she liked was easy because she was important to you. In fact, you wouldn't even apply the word discipline to her. It's the same with college. Unless you care about your studies or care about doing well in school or care about something related to your college life, it will be difficult to find the discipline to be successful.

PRIORITIZATION IN GOAL SETTING

The mechanics of managing your weekly schedule is important. When you are organized, huge amounts of time and frustration are saved by efficiently handling the tasks you face as a student. The word is efficiency. Efficiency means to produce the desired result with a minimum of effort, expense, or waste. Efficiency is defined in physics as the ratio of energy output to energy input:

$$\text{Efficiency} = e = \text{Energy Output/Energy Input}$$

When the energy input equals the energy output, the efficiency is one and all the energy directed toward a given task goes entirely to where you want it. No energy is wasted. You get the most bang for your buck. The goal of every college student should be to maximize efficiency. Efficient study saves you time because the energy you expend to learn something goes right to where you want it to go, toward good grades and success.

Prioritization is primary to efficiency. Prioritization means to order a group of tasks according to what is important. The tasks that are most important are given high priority and tasks that are least important are given low priority. Washing your clothes on Sunday afternoon, for example, is probably of lower priority than studying for a major exam scheduled on Monday morning. Seeing your boyfriend on a given night might be of higher priority than going home to see your sister. We all make decisions based on what we think are valuable and significant; we prioritize. There are two primary ways to prioritize your life, which can be classified by the terms rank order and equal significance.

RANK-ORDER PRIORITIZATION

Most pastors I know suggest Christians prioritize their lives by rank order. The rank-order scheme goes something like this:

God
Spouse
Family
Work
Play

Rank ordering these priorities means that God comes first in your life, followed by your spouse, then your sons, daughters, and in-laws, then work, and last play. Higher priority items trump lower priority items. The rank-order scheme offers a straightforward way to solve conflicts. Say a father is involved with a time-critical presentation at work which conflicts with a school play where his son is performing. With a rank-order system, the solution is to choose the higher priority task (family) over the lower priority task (work) which means that the father should cancel or postpone the presentation in lieu of attending the play. Or say that you haven't done your daily devotions but a particular film you've wanted to see for months is scheduled for TV that night. You are torn about what to do, either watch the movie or read your devotional book. The rank-order scheme answers by saying you should do your devotionals and catch the movie at another time.

EQUAL SIGNIFICANCE PRIORITIZATION

Prioritization by equal significance, by contrast, recognizes that there are several crucial priorities in life that cannot be easily ranked by order. Rather than viewing, say, studying as more important than work, it's better to view both tasks as mutual responsibilities that demand their fair share of time and effort. Equal significance means to order your priorities in parallel rather than in series, to say that they all are equally important to success in college. None can be neglected without loss of performance. This is conceptually different from the rank-order approach, which is largely a series approach. I am probably in the minority among Christians on this point, but I believe it's better for Christian college students to prioritize their lives by an equal significance scheme.

Here are my reasons. There is never enough time in college. There is too much to do and not enough time for everything. In a rank-order system, something important winds up taking a back seat to a priority that is ranked higher, with the result that the lower priority task is neglected. But a college student cannot neglect anything important; to do so would result in unfortunate consequences such as poor grades.

For example, take the case of a Christian student who has to decide whether to miss a Wednesday night prayer meeting or study for an important test on Thursday morning. In most rank-ordering schemes, worshipping is higher than studying. The downside, however, is that the rank order guarantees poor results on the test due to the loss of valuable study time. This is in part why Christian college students are not excelling at college level work. They rank worshipping God before studying. Nothing wrong with that lofty posture, but why not have the best of both worlds? It's possible and, in my judgment, far better to treat worship and studying as parallel tasks which both demand their share of time and effort. My advice is to both study for the test and worship God, maybe not during a Wednesday night prayer service, but rather by sitting and meditating with a devotional book at the university arboretum between classes. In other words, adjust your schedule to do both important tasks rather than putting one above another when up against a time constraint.

My rank-order friends would argue that to make up for the lost study time, God would somehow honor their devotion and priority to Him and get them through the test even with reduced study time. I'm not so sure. Yes, God can intervene miraculously, but God doesn't usually change the laws of nature to fix our dilemmas; in fact, the Bible cautions against relying on divine miracles. The Bible says not to test the Lord, the exception being the tithing law in the OT book of Malachi. Rather, He expects us to do as much as we can before petitioning Him for a miracle. The applicable verse is "having done all, then stand." While you can choose to pray on Wednesday night, it's not likely that God will bail you out with a good test grade.

ENGAGING IN YOUR EDUCATION

Engaging in your education refers to being a participant and not a spectator in college. Too many students sit passively during lectures, labs, and projects, trying to learn by watching. They never engage the material. Watching gives you only the lowest, most superficial, level of learning.

Students frequently say they have read the chapter, studied their notes, made note cards, did the homework, but yet do poorly on tests. This is often because they tried to memorize everything. Memorization is passive and thinking is active. Here's one way I try to explain the difference. Imagine you are watching an NBA basketball game. It's true that you can learn something about basketball by watching the game from the stands. There are lots of armchair quarterbacks who think they understand basketball by watching from the stands. But imagine the difference in education you get when you get on the court with a bunch of six feet five guys. That's where you get a real education in basketball, when you get pushed around, muscled to the floor, out rebounded, and get your shots blocked back in your face. The same is true in college. You learn best when you engage the material by getting on the court instead of staying in the stands watching the game. While I'm not trying to turn my students into professional basketball players, I am trying to get them up to SEC standards and onto the college court.

Christians should know instinctively that the best way to learn is by doing and not just watching. That's why God takes us through valleys; we don't learn the lesson otherwise. Take the case of Pharaoh. It was one thing for Moses to tell him that ten plagues would come if he didn't let the people of Israel go, and quite another to be personally attacked by insects, covered with boils, and have his firstborn killed by the death angel. Or take Jonah. When he tried to escape the command of God to preach in Nineveh, God took him into the belly of a whale until he learned that God wasn't kidding. The same thing is true of us in the NT world. We learn best in the caldron of adversity, when the bottom falls out and we are forced to depend on God. Our faith in God grows, and we please Him by becoming more like Christ. God's goal for Christians is to grow us up in faith, and He will use all the tools in His vast arsenal to get us there.

STRATEGY #7: *Changing Bad Student Habits*

Success in life depends on minimizing mistakes. Corso and Herbstreit are forever saying on ESPN that turnovers will play a large role in the outcome of the Saturday football games. Turn the ball over and you lose. Hang onto the ball and you win. The same is true for college students. Those who do best in college make the fewest mistakes.

Students know to avoid mistakes in college. That's not the problem. The problem is how students define mistakes. What a professor calls a mistake a student calls his rightful exercise of freedom. If students disagree with professional educators about what behaviors are self-defeating, there will be little justification to change. Exchanging bad habits for good habits occurs when students buy into the reasons for good habits. If students deny or redefine the reasons for constructive moral action, it will be difficult for them to take on more constructive behaviors. The whole issue is a question of values.

Changing bad habits for some students works like drug addiction. When someone is addicted to drugs, it modifies their view of reality. An addicted person has a full range of emotions, from feeling like Superman to being so paranoid that you refuse to leave your dorm room. When you plead with your addicted friend to get off the drugs, they reply that they know better. Arrogance and ignorance together is difficult to overcome. There is stubborn refusal to see reality. College students display the same refusal to take advice. I want to save you the difficult learning curve by talking in this section about the most common mistakes students make in college.

CUTTING CLASSES

It's no surprise to any professor that one of the key factors affecting student performance is class attendance. It would shock most parents to learn how often their sons and daughters cut classes. It's become so serious that faculty members have resorted to bribery by making attendance a part of the grade or by offering extra credit. I have resisted begging my students to come to class, but even I'm starting to weaken. Students are paying for my course; they are adults and can exercise their judgment to attend class or not. It's part of growing up and learning how to live responsibly; further, taking attendance is a logistics problem in large classes. Some departments on campus try to help with the problem by paying someone to do nothing more than sit in on large courses and count students. Other professors, me included, would never stand for that. To be brutally honest, some of us almost want some students to act irresponsibly because they're the ones who will get the low grades. We would rather give low grades to students who refuse to show up than students who try to learn. You simply can't cut class and do well in most college courses. The correlation is strong and unambiguous. Students who cut class get low grades while students who attend class get high grades.

To show you how bad it's getting, Krystal Brooks, a senior at Oldham Country High School in Buckner, Kentucky won a Ford Mustang for perfect attendance. Nine-year-old Fernando Vazquez had perfect attendance in his Hartford, Connecticut school and was given the choice of a new Saturn Ion or $10K.[84] More and more schools across the nation are using incentives, but I'm guessing that even a car isn't enough to entice some students to attend class. My question is, "Whatever happened to truant officers?" These were police officer kind of people who would go out, find students who regularly failed to attend high school, and rudely deliver them to the schoolhouse door.

According to the latest dropout statistics, truant officers have apparently vanished. In a couple of dozen states, it's currently legal for sixteen-year-olds to drop out of school.[85] In the year 2007, roughly 30% (1.2 million) of teenagers did drop out. The numbers take your breath away. In a handful of big-city school systems, students have less than a fifty-fifty chance of graduating with their peers.[86] The cities include New York, Detroit, Baltimore, Milwaukee, Cleveland, Miami, Dallas, Denver, Houston, and Los Angeles. Researchers at Johns Hopkins[87] found that about 10% of all schools in the country can be termed "dropout factories," defined as schools where no more than 60% of the students who start as freshman make it to their senior year. The number is not due to students who transfer. It's inconceivable to me that, in the United States, the reputed world leader in innovation and technology over the last century, three out of ten students drop out of school and settle for low paying jobs. Research by the National Center for Education Statistics[88] show that high school dropouts had an average yearly income of $20,100 (2005) compared to $29,700 for persons who completed their education with a high school diploma or GED. Based on money alone, there are strong incentives to stay in school and graduate.

Who are the dropouts? A study in *Education Week*[89] reports that dropout rates are lower in the suburbs than in the inner cities, lower among Asians and whites, and lower when compared to blacks and Hispanics. There's also a gender difference—nearly 75% of girls make it through high school but only 66% of boys. The dropout demographics threaten to create a blue-collar subclass of undereducated males. The reason? Most signs, as discussed earlier, suggest that boys are not equipped to succeed academically when they get to high school. Another reason for dropping out is poor reading skills. Most studies show a significant verbal gender gap between boys and girls in the area of reading. New York's reading scores (2007) show that just 51.6% of eighth grade boys are competent readers compared to 63% of the girls. In Massachusetts, a Rennie Center study[90] showed that 41% of fourth grade girls are proficient at reading compared to 29% of the boys. There are several reasons students are slack on course attendance:

- First, they can be slack. This is the first time students are in control of their own life, and frequently they are not ready for the responsibility.
- Second, some students think that going to class is a waste of time.
- Third, students keep late hours and it's all too easy to sleep through an 8:00 or 9:00 a.m. course.
- Fourth, after about the third week of the semester, most students are behind in at least one course and rob Peter to pay Paul by skipping one class to work on another.
- Fifth, some professors make it easy to cut classes with few consequences, or so the student thinks there are few consequences.

I may be partly guilty of making it too easy. For years, I've used a system of lecture notes to try to make learning easier and the lecture productive. This decision was a consequence of my own experience with poor professors, who stood at the board and copied their lecture notes from paper to blackboard. We dutifully copied the blackboard to our own notes. There was nothing going on in class but copying notes. No thinking, no reasoning, little discussion, mostly copying. What a waste of an hour.

When I became a professor, I vowed to make changes. Instead of turning the class into dictation, I worked to generate lecture notes and just gave them to the class. Students could now think with me during the lecture. This frees up my lecture time to offer analogies, stories, lecture demonstrations, and practical illustrations. The system takes art to avoid parroting the notes but if you master it, students show up to see the crazy professor doing his stage performance and learn all the short cuts and easy ways to learn physics. Students in my courses think they died and went to heaven because I give out my lecture notes.

Well, heaven must be flawed, because some students decide that, since they have all the notes, no need to come to class. Students are absent even when I argue that, come test time, they would have to go over the material anyway, so why not come to class and let the best possible tutor for the course (me) be their study session leader. I even promise that "I will make physics easier, and not harder, to learn…the lecture will be productive, not a waste of your time." Little effect. Students still cut class. Instead of benefiting from my generosity, many students take advantage of it, using my notes as an excuse to skip class. Such is the dark side of college student human nature.

FAILING TO HAND IN HOMEWORK

A second common student mistake is to fail to hand in assignments. There are several reasons students give for this self-defeating behavior.

UNDERESTIMATING HOMEWORK SIGNIFICANCE

Some students take a pass on turning in homework because they don't think it justifies the effort. Homework is typically assigned a modest fraction (say, 20%) of the course grade. Students reason if there are, say, five homework assignments during the semester, then each assignment counts only 4% of the grade. When faced with the choice of spending a couple of hours on homework or taking a hit on only 4% of their grade, students opt to skip out on homework. The risk is slightly decreased in curved grading systems where, if a large fraction of students fail to hand in homework, then the relative impact of skipping assignments is lowered. This means that students sink to the lowest common denominator and ride the curve.

Students who believe they can skip homework assignments and still do well in college are fooling themselves. Small chinks in academic armor lead to big cracks in your final grade. Most professors base test questions on homework assignments. When you skip homework, you opt out of your best chance to prepare for tests. If a professor gave you a copy of an old test over the material you are studying, would you throw it away? No. You would study the old test exhaustively because you reason the current test will be similar. Most professors take a lot of reflective time choosing homework assignments because they believe it will help you learn the material. If we spend that much time doing anything, we obviously think it's important and will ask you about it on exams. Some professors even tell their students that a certain homework problem will be on the test, but yet a large fraction of students miss it. Come on students. There is no excuse for missing a question that your professor point blank says will be asked. You'll never get a better deal.

Do the math if you don't believe that small hits on your homework can have big effects on your course grade over the course of a semester. Take the case of a curved grading system and consider the lab component of a science course. Students think they can skip a couple of labs during the semester with only minimal damage. Wrong. Say you end up skipping only one lab during the semester. On a curved system, if a student misses a lab and everyone else goes to the lab, they end up at the bottom of the curve for that lab's contribution to the course grade. This is because a curved system is based on relative performance. You are dead last on that scale and guarantee yourself on F on that lab's fraction of your course grade. This is why I tell my students that, with curved systems, assignments and laboratories act as work ethic components of the course. They measure whether you are willing to work rather than whether you are talented in a subject. Show up and do the work and pick up the nearly free points in a course. Choose to skip assignments and lose your free points. Going your own way is deadly to your academic success.

QUITTING ON HOMEWORK

The millennial generation often chooses to quit on difficult homework assignments. Instead of digging in when the going gets hard, students give up and say "It's not worth the effort to learn this." Little is more tragic. Imagine what a future boss would think if you told him it's not worth your time to put forth the effort on an assigned project. You wouldn't last long. Do you think your college professors should react differently? We don't. I am forever asking myself why students don't get in and talk to me when they're having trouble. Part of the reason is that some students don't care whether their work is done or not. When I get that "What, you didn't really expect me to do that assignment, did you?" look from students as I pick up a due homework, I know something is wrong with the millennial work ethic. No wonder our collective national butts are getting kicked by foreign students.

ABSENTEEISM

Students fail to turn in assignments because they are absent from class so much that they don't get the assignment. Students frequently blame professors for not getting the assignment to them and say we should post the course assignments on the Web. We respond by telling them that bosses usually don't call you at home to give you your next job assignment. They expect you to show up for work. I deliberately refuse to post assignments to the Web because I want my students to be in class. If students choose to cut class, that's their prerogative, but they also choose the negative consequences, one of which is to miss assignments. Some students think mercy is in order when the assignment is handed in late, all because they chose to miss class in the first place. Don't take your professors for fools. I know that students who miss class are going to miss the assignment and that helps separate the wheat from the chaff when I hand out course grades. Students who are AWOL make it easy for me to assign grades. I'm happy to give the A's and B's to students who have stayed with it and I'm equally happy to give the slackers the D's and F's they deserve. When you cut classes, you make our grade decisions easy.

PLAYING THE GAME INSTEAD OF LEARNING SOMETHING

Students in this category hand in homework but it's obvious they either copied the answers or had someone else do them, which is nearly the same thing as not doing the assignment in the first place. Professors hate it when students hand in plagiarized homework or assignments that are clearly someone else's work. Don't you think we know about the books you could copy from or the variety of sites on the Web where information can be cut and pasted? It's even sadder when students see nothing wrong with copying as long as they're not caught. Lest I didn't warn you, here is the true situation. Professors have seen nearly everything in their years of teaching and can spot cheating a mile away. It's not worth the risk and you cheat yourself in the process. Why take cheap shortcuts to your education when you can have more satisfaction by actually learning the material. This is what I call playing the game of school.

Once I was subbing for a GTA during an undergraduate physics lab. I was circulating around the room when I looked down and saw the lab report of a former student (call him Jack) who had taken physics from me a year earlier. The report had the completed answers to the lab exercise we were doing that day. The girl in question saw that I noticed the old lab and hurriedly hid it under some other papers. Rather than come down hard on her then, I asked her how "Jack" was doing. Talk about ten shades of red. She got the message, well sort of. While she seemed genuinely embarrassed when I caught her copying off Jack's old lab, I didn't get a warm fuzzy feeling she thought anything was wrong with the practice. She was embarrassed because she got caught, not because she thought it was wrong to cheat. I hate to estimate how many students try to learn by copying off other students' work, papers, and essays.

NOT ASKING FOR HELP WHEN YOU'RE LOST

Students who are lost or left behind by the high rate of information transfer in college frequently refuse to seek help from their professors. This is academic suicide. Part of a professor's job is to help you learn. The reasons students don't ask for help are numerous:

- Some students don't care enough about their education to ask for help.
- Some students prefer to play the game of school and get by with minimum effort.
- Some students are apathetic or too busy with work or other things.

- Some students have been burned by a professor who has humiliated them during class or an office hour.
- Some students are so far behind that they don't even know where to begin or what to ask.
- Some students are too cocky to ask for help, thinking they can learn it on their own.
- Some students are intimidated or shy around professors.
- Some students think professors are busy and don't want to be bothered.
- Some students think professors will be minimally helpful due to poor communication skills or by talking over their heads.

Fight the inclination to ignore your professor during the semester. Even in a class of over one hundred, which is frequently the size of my courses, I am always available to help my students.

CHAPTER AND VERSE OF EXCUSES

Students commonly react to the higher standards in college by offering excuses for poor performance. Excuses are explanations of behavior that try to free you of blame; to minimize or disregard an expectation or promise. Excuses seek to release a person from an obligation by offering a justification of performance that falls short of expectations. Excuses are rampant in college.

Not all excuses are bad. When a student has to be absent from class or hands in a late homework due to legitimate reasons, excuses are appropriate; they are an acknowledgement that education deals with real people who live in the real world where life is not smooth and seamless. Unforeseen calamities and emergencies arise that come out of nowhere. When a student is honest I am always happy to grant leeway and make arrangements for missed work. Those aren't the excuses we discuss here.

Students offer a whole host of excuses that are ridiculous. They offer ridiculous excuses because they got away with them in high school. It's only natural to try the same strategy on college professors. Trouble is, most professors won't buy them. A case in point. Students in my physics courses sometimes write on their test paper that they had no calculator during the test. The implication is that, since they had no calculator, they should be excused from doing the physics problems on the test. Are you serious? Anyone with any sense knows that physics deals with numbers. When students see me time after time doing example questions during the lecture involving calculations, you would think it would trigger a trip to the store to buy a calculator. Students seem to be able to find a calculator to do homework problems. How did they lose it before the test?

One student last semester turned in her first test in my class and informed me that our Office of Learning Disabilities excused her from answering discussion questions. She left them blank and said I wasn't allowed to give her a zero when I graded them. Oh, really? Imagine going through college and never having to answer discussion questions. How do you write an English essay, write a poem in poetry class, or compose an article in journalism class? How do you survive any professional vocation without the ability to write? How does a college with a straight face grant a bachelor's degree to students who cannot write? But yet, she actually thought she was immune to discussion questions; either that or she was trying to put one over on me because she didn't think I would check with the Learning Disability Office. Needless to say, after a call to Learning Disabilities, I found that there was no provision for students to tell their teachers what questions were acceptable per their disability.

College students are notorious for handing in sloppy, hastily-contrived homework. It's clear that a significant fraction of students do homework at the last minute by looking at the end-of-chapter odd answers and trying to work backwards. I've even observed students doing homework for their next class during my class. Students who do this are hoping that graders will simply look for the correct final answer and skip the intermediate steps. When I tell my graders to mark questions wrong that give the correct answer without any supporting work, you ought to hear the complaining. The argument is that we cannot mark a question wrong if it has the correct answer. What? You mean we should give you full credit on a question for merely copying the answer from the back of the book? You can't be serious. But yet, it's a common argument professors get when students get their papers back with low scores.

Choosing Trade-offs to Payoffs

Deferred rewards are one of the secrets to life, yet I find few students who appreciate the concept. Deferred rewards refer to the notion that it's far better to pay now and play later. It means to work hard in college (first) and then later (second) you can cruise. If you play now, by goofing off in college and treating it as a four-year party, you will pay, and pay dearly, later. Deferred rewards are a new concept to students because they had so much handed to them by helicopter parents. When they wanted something they usually got it. Immediately. In addition, American society has reinforced the "me first, and me now" attitude. The idea of waiting for something and enjoying the road to accomplishment is foreign.

Do this experiment. Ask any older, returning college student about deferred rewards. I usually have a few of them in my classes. They will invariably tell you that it's incredibly more difficult to go back to school after being in the job force. They would tell you to bear down and go for it now instead of returning to school later. They would tell you how difficult it is to go back when holding down a job and raising a family. They would tell you there's nothing like a college education if you want a high salary, good benefits, and a rewarding profession.

Not Treating School as a Job

Students would be miles ahead if they approached college with the same degree of responsibility that a regular job enjoys. Say your college job was working in the tool department at Sears or serving up nachos at Taco Bell. What do you think would happen if you were regularly late for work, reported sloppy work, or failed to be professional? You wouldn't have a job long. Why, then, do students think being a student is different?

A job imposes discipline from without but being a college student requires self-discipline. One is voluntary and one is obligatory. One is imposed responsibility and one is chosen responsibility. One involves legalism and one involves grace. One says must and the other says maybe. One involves choice and the other involves rules. Clearly, when it comes to deciding about what is best in the long term of life, students often make the wrong choices.

The solution? Give college the same level of respect as you would a job. You have to show up for work. Then show up for class. You have to do your job assignments. Then do your class assignments. You can't oversleep an 8:00 A.M. starting time in a job. Then don't sleep through your 8:00 A.M. class in biology. You have to pay attention when learning a new job. Then pay attention and take notes in your classes. You have to do outstanding work to get a favorable performance review in your job. Then do similar outstanding work in your college courses and get good grades.

Not answering the bell at college doesn't lead to immediate consequences, but the consequences will still come, and they are more far-reaching and serious than you can imagine. Students usually believe that slacking off in college is less serious than slacking off in a job because there's no immediate hand slap. It's the opposite that's true. The consequences of getting fired are merely immediate. You can get another job. You can make money anywhere. Slacking in college holds ramifications for your entire life. If you screw up your college studies you mess up for life. Successful students choose to sacrifice short-term pleasures to ensure long-term success. Don't trade your future for a steady diet of a few extra minutes of sleep or for gabbing all night with your friends. There will be time later for that.

PUTTING SOCIAL LIFE AND WORK AHEAD OF SCHOOL

Some college students put work before school, put social life before school, and put anything before school. When it comes to partying or studying, students choose partying. When faced with a choice of working or studying, you choose the money. It's again a matter of poor choices and misplaced priorities.

Take the case of work. Nationwide, 41% of full-time college students, and 81% of part-time students work.[91] Here is a common case. A student comes to me flustered and says she can't get to my office hours because she has to work all the time. She says she never has time to study for tests and can't complete her assignments. Simple solution. Quit working so many hours. Ask yourself why you are in college in the first place. Is it to work or to get a degree? Yes, some students have to work, but there are limits beyond which work turns into your worst nightmare, or at least an uncomfortable catch-22. You think you have to work to stay in school, but working too much works against you because there's little time to study.

Actually, it's fairly rare that I meet a student who is working to stay in school. More often, students work to buy things. Only in unusual cases is student employment a means to help financially-strapped families with college costs. Students more often work to maintain the standard of living their parents showered on them while they were living at home. They are working to drive a nice car, have nice clothes, buy good makeup, afford the latest cell phone, have money for tanning beds, to party at spring break, and to go out to eat several times a week. Students are big contributors to the local economy. They are big spenders. The millennial generation tends to view goods and services as entitlements that they're not going to live without.

Here is a question for my working students. Is it worth working so many hours to purchase things? Is it really that important to get the latest cell phone, to eat out at Olive Garden weekly, or to buy several pairs of shoes simply to keep up with the Joneses? Is it worth putting yourself under stress, hardship, and endangering yourself in college over a few extra bucks? Absolutely not. The things you want to buy will come later. What you are doing is trying to enjoy all the good things in life before you've legitimately earned them. Your parents took years to build up their wealth and you are trying to achieve their standard of living without putting in the work that they did. It's too early for you. You haven't earned it yet. Exercise patience and realize that, when your parents were your age, they were living on pork and beans and sleeping on borrowed mattresses. A date for them was eating at McDonald's or going to a dollar movie at a cheap theater. Yes, they love you and want to give you the best of their wealth, but realize it's now your turn to bear down and earn it. The moral is to accept less than the best and live within your means until you get into your vocation. Working in college to achieve a high standard of living is unrealistic and misguided. Better to work less hours and enjoy your college life more.

Putting social life before schoolwork could be the most common mistake students make in college. We all know students who party all the time, who drink every night, who cut most of their classes, and who are in school to have a good time. I'm not talking about them. They are nearly beyond help. They are the students who live at the bottom of my grade sheet every semester. It's only a matter of time before these students flunk out and end up working at Arby's or digging ditches in their hometown. Rather, I hope here to help students who have a hard time saying no when friends call and want them to come out and play when they should be studying.

Nothing wrong with having fun, but when social life becomes your major in college, it's a problem. A classic case is a student who loves sorority life. Sororities and fraternities can keep you busy seven days a week. The activities are well-intentioned and integral parts of campus life. They make college life memorable. You never forget the friends, the experiences, the fun times, and the roommate gags. But it comes with inherent dangers if you choose the wrong balance. Carve out the social events you wish to participate in and get them into your calendar. But don't overload. Studying has to come first, and socializing second, if you wish to succeed in college.

Last, entertainment is increasingly seducing students away from studying. Millennial students are raised in a culture of entertainment. Studying for college courses seems boring when compared to what is offered by the entertainment industry. When set against movies, surfing the Web, music, videos, MTV, MySpace.com, magazines, cell phones, and iPods, it's easy to see why students would rather goof off. But experts are seeing that too much entertainment gets in the way of schoolwork. A survey[92] conducted by Michigan State (2006) showed that 18.5% of students polled said that using the Internet and playing computer games resulted in poor academic performance. In comparison, 8.5% said drinking hurt their academics. Campuses are considering limiting the time students are online.

Praying Instead of Studying

As a Christian professor I would never discourage students from praying throughout college. Prayer should be a daily and integral part of your college life. Without prayer, you cast yourself into the fires of difficult coursework and secular college culture without tapping into the help and power of the Almighty. If there ever was a time when you need God and His wisdom, it's during college, where the tone of your entire life is set with so many crucial and influential decisions. When I was in college, I prayed about everything, from where to eat lunch to whom to go out with to whether I would ever figure out relativistic quantum mechanics. God should be an intimate friend to a Christian student.

There is a difference, however, in praying to God when you're in a bind and having a real relationship with Him. Flare prayers don't make for a healthy relationship with God. There's a difference between a sincere prayer and using God as an excuse for poor performance. There's a difference between working smart and asking God to bail you out on a test when you're too lazy to study. God isn't honored when you make a habit of asking Him to perform a face-saving miracle to save your butt. He expects you to do your part. For a student, doing your part means to put in an appropriate amount of effort on your schoolwork before asking Him to bless you with success.

It's a matter of order. God has a logical, ordered sequence for most things in life. The wrong order is to slack off and then ask for a miracle. The right order is to study first and then ask God to reward your work with good grades. Students insult the Creator when they don't do their part in college and then ask Him to fix things. True, we all get ourselves into tight spots on occasion. Some weeks are so charged with activities that we're thrown off our schedules. Emergencies arise. Personal and family issues come out of nowhere. God understands that we're not perfect planners and that modern life is full of distractions. What He doesn't understand is when we adopt a lifestyle of using Him. Praying instead of studying is like jumping off a cliff and asking God to save you before hitting the ground. It's like a baseball player who never goes to hitting practice and expects God to give Him a home run. It's like a lawyer who doesn't prepare for a case and expects God to write the final arguments. It doesn't work that way. The Bible rarely asks God's creatures to test Him with life's circumstances. That's because God has already passed the most important test—purchasing your eternal life by dying for you on the Cross.

Worshipping at the Altar of Summa Cum Laude

College students are a slave to the almighty GPA, allowing it to rule their life. The amount of grade grubbing is alarming. Students believe that it's more important to have a high GPA than to actually learn anything. The inordinate preoccupation with GPA is symptomatic of the false doctrine that a college education is like playing Vegas. Students worship the GPA golden calf by dropping hard classes, changing majors, shopping for easy instructors, and manipulating the system. It messes with your career goals and shows a dangerous lack of faith in God. Faith, in fact, has been described by best selling author Warren Wiersbe as "living without scheming." If you are scheming your way through college, you are not living by faith, and without faith it's impossible to please Him. Students worship the golden GPA calf for several reasons:

- GPA is a ubiquitous and quantitative metric of success in college. Everyone has a GPA and it's a convenient method to evaluate students on some level of equal footing. No getting around that.
- Students have had it drilled into their heads that getting low grades is not acceptable to parents and, since daddy usually controls the purse strings, there is enormous pressure to get good grades. No getting around that either.
- Most students believe that a high GPA is their ticket to money and success when entering the job market or getting into professional and/or graduate school. Further, the feel-good educational establishment has plied students with inflated grades for so long that they are addicted to them. When a low grade shows up during the freshman year, there is near-collapse psychologically as students face shock and awe for the first time.

- Colleges themselves send the messages that GPA is everything. A good example is Baker College in Flint, Michigan who offers students free or discounted rent at dorms for good grades.[93] Students who maintain a ≥ 3.5 GPA get free housing in residence halls. Discounted housing is offered to students with lower GPAs. The official reason given by Baker for awarding cash for grades is that it boosts graduation rates, but no matter how you cut it, it's like offering money to college athletes for good performance. Whatever happened to personal pride? Paying students for grades sends all the wrong messages and would be unheard of in earlier generations.

Let me debunk the GPA preoccupation. Better to rise from the summa cum laude altar and let your passions, not your GPA, rule the day. Here's what I mean. Every semester I have students who switch majors because they can't cut it. The conversation goes like "I really didn't know how much was involved in architecture" or "dental hygiene sounded good until I learned how much chemistry I had to take" or "my dad, not me, wanted me to be an engineer, and he is clueless at how much math is involved." It's usually not the case that students have truly lost interest in say, architecture, but rather that they don't want to put up the fight to work for it. The fear of a low GPA is a prime factor in the decision.

Students complain of being caught in a catch-22. Some are taking forever to get through college because they keep switching courses, majors, and instructors to protect their GPA. Dad is threatening to cut them off. Students afraid of getting kicked out of school cruise through puff courses to keep their GPA hovering above the minimum level to stay off probation. Students endangered by D's and F's in courses go ahead and ask us to flunk them. You read that correctly. They are asking for an F because colleges currently have a course forgiveness policy which allows courses with low grades to be "excused" from being counted in the GPA total. Better to GAP (Grade Adjustment Policy) the course so it will disappear from being a part of the GPA calculation. No joke. Apart from the wrong message, the problem in gapping courses is that it's not how the real world works. Tell most workers, when placed on a critical project, that they can walk away when the going gets tough, and they will be headed for the unemployment line.

Let's think biblically. You have a passion for something because God gave it to you. He has a mission for you to accomplish in life. Why, then, are you letting work stop you? Your God-given passion will not vanish by switching majors. You'll end up without God's best if your first reaction is to quit or switch to an easy major. You've made a life-changing career change and exchanged it for a face-saving ego boost that comes from saying you have a 3.5 or are graduating cum laude. It's not worth it. It's vanity and chasing the wind. You will look back on your life someday and regret your decision. The number on your transcript isn't worth opting out of God's will for your life. Why not buckle down, get the help you need, and let God lead you? You can do it if you work smart and refuse to give up.

Here's the real situation regarding GPAs. Paste this section on your mirror so you see it each morning before going to class. High GPAs are undeniably better than low GPAs. No argument there. Your GPA is a significant measure examined by committees who let you into law school, medical school, teachers college, and so on. No argument there either. But it's only one metric. There are other important qualities that employers and entrance committees consider when making hiring or admission decisions. That's the important point.

What's important to admissions committees? I was once the chairman of our admissions committee in physics and, while GPA is important, it's only one of several parameters. Some of the other things considered are as follows:

- The quality of your undergraduate institution
- Whether you took hard or easy courses
- Whether you write clearly
- Whether you speak with precision during an interview
- Your scores on the Graduate Record Exam (GRE)
- Whether you have favorable letters of recommendation

Admission committees weigh these parameters differently but, characteristically, a student with good letters who comes off positively during an interview will trump a less than stellar GPA. What pulls a student down is when we see a lot of puff courses on a transcript that shows us a student was trying to pad his GPA. A few fun courses to round out your college experience is fine, but when the number of "Basket-Weaving 101" courses is excessive, it's a red flag. We extract such courses from the GPA tote and recalculate a student's GPA in courses of substance.

Now take the case of a job. When I worked at Intel Corporation, one of my responsibilities was to hire and fire people as we were building the scientific infrastructure in the company. Who did I look for and what was the process? Applications to large corporations go first to Human Resources (HR) who, if you're lucky, route it to managers within the company who are looking for help. It's the managers who hire you. While managers are interested in your academic record in college, they are more interested in whether you can help them or not. A stellar GPA doesn't do much good if you can't work independently, be creative, carry the ball, communicate, work with others, solve problems, and have your act together. Employment also depends on technical expertise. In a study[94] of the top qualities employers look for in college graduates, the National Association of Colleges and Employers (NACE) reports that communication skills, both verbal and written, heads the list. Examine the NACE list below; GPA is nowhere to be found.

Top Ten Personal Qualities/Skills Sought by Employers

1. Communication skills (verbal and written)
2. Honesty and integrity
3. Teamwork skills
4. Strong work ethic
5. Analytical skills
6. Flexibility/Adaptability
7. Interpersonal skills
8. Motivation/Initiative
9. Computer skills
10. Detail oriented

I would rather hire a person who will work hard and is willing to learn than a Harvard hotshot who thinks he can set the world on fire. In a study[95] led by national higher education and business leaders, the Association of American Colleges and Universities identified four essential learning outcomes desired by employers—a broad base of knowledge across multiple disciplines; intellectual and practical skills such as teamwork and problem-solving; a sense of personal and social responsibility, including ethical reasoning; and experience applying what they learn to real-world problems. Increasingly employers are looking to hire veterans in their businesses.[96] Soldiers have leadership skills, and they are able to handle adversity and solve problems. Employers like the military work ethic. Sure, I like to see a high GPA on a transcript, but I would rather have someone who has passion, a thirst for knowledge, good work habits, dedication, common sense, and maybe even a little humility. Very low or very high GPAs raise a red flag. You read that correctly. Students with low GPAs in undergraduate physics courses may not pass our graduate courses and doctoral examinations which obviously doesn't help anyone. Students with super high GPAs makes me wonder if it wasn't gained by playing the system rather than by really learning something. A student who appears to breeze through courses is often not well suited for experimental physics due to the frustrations and seat-of-the-pants intuition required when building and operating one-of-a-kind research instrumentation. You fall off the horse daily in experimental science, and academic hotshots can't cut it in the blue-collar atmosphere of a research laboratory.

Finally, the higher the professional level you achieve in life, the less you'll get asked about your GPA. Do you think anybody ever asked Alexander Graham Bell, Donald Trump, Billy Graham, Thomas Jefferson, Isaac Newton, and so on for their GPA? I frequently tell my Ph.D. students that nobody will ever ask them for their GPA. What they will ask is where you did your graduate studies, with whom you worked during your dissertation research, the title of your dissertation, and the problem you solved. Consider the advice of Bill Gates, head of Microsoft and the richest man in the world. Gates gave a famous speech at a high school commencement. This is his list of life points.

Bill Gates Life Points for Youth

1. Life is not fair—get used to it.
2. The world won't care about your self-esteem. The world will expect you to accomplish something BEFORE you feel good about yourself.
3. You will NOT make $60,000 a year right out of high school. You won't be a vice-president with a car phone until you earn both.
4. If you think your teacher is rough, wait till you get a boss.
5. Flipping burgers is not beneath your dignity. Your grandparents had a different word for burger flipping—they called it opportunity.
6. If you mess up, it's not your parents fault, so don't whine about your mistakes, learn from them.
7. Before you were born, your parents weren't as boring as they are now. They got that way from paying your bills, cleaning your clothes, and listening to you talk about how cool you thought you were. So before you save the rain forest from the parasites of your parent's generation, try delousing the closet in your own room.
8. Your school may have done away with winners and losers, but life HAS NOT. In some schools, they have abolished failing grades and they'll give you as much time as you want to get the right answer. This doesn't bear the slightest resemblance to ANYTHING in real life.
9. Life is not divided into semesters. You don't get summers off and very few employers are interested in helping you FIND YOURSELF. Do that on your own time.
10. Television is NOT real life. In real life, people actually have to leave the coffee shop and go to jobs.
11. Be nice to nerds. Chances are you'll end up working for one.

Quitting on Courses

Frequently in this book I've mentioned that students quit on their studies. Let me explain what I mean and why it's a common student mistake.

INCREASED COMPETITION IN COURSES

Freshman students aren't prepared for the stiff competition in college. In high school, juniors are in classes with juniors, and seniors are in classes with seniors. Not so in college. It is common for freshman students to face competition from all four classes. Take my introductory astronomy course. There were one hundred students in the class last semester spanning all four years (freshman to senior) and two graduate students. Some students had completed calculus and some could barely divide two numbers. There were over twenty different majors represented in the course.

In college, there is a huge maturity gap between freshmen and seniors. It's a matter of experience. Seniors know how courses work, they are better at time management, and they know the unwritten rules of how to survive in college. It's almost always the case that my senior students do better than freshmen. They take the course as a fun elective and not something they expect to spend a lot of time on to assure a good grade. They have their post-college job.

When freshmen see the competition in college they are prone to throw in the towel. One reason is unrealistic grade expectations. Freshmen scan the classroom and see all the upperclassman and reason there's no way to get a good grade against that kind of competition. They believe classes with upperclassman are unfair; students with good math backgrounds have unfair advantages over students who are just now taking college algebra. Freshmen who find that college is not high school easily get discouraged. Here's my advice to freshman students who are prone to quit on their courses because they are intimidated by the competition:

- As a professor, I attempt to level the playing field in my lower-level courses by not using complicated math that will favor my seniors. The focus is on concepts rather than skills that rely heavily on prerequisite knowledge and experience.
- I remind my freshman students that they will eventually be seniors and have the advantage, and that the seniors in their courses were

once freshman who faced the same obstacle. The inequities will even out over a college career.

- I remind my students that college is a microcosm of the working world, where it doesn't matter to your employer if your coworkers have twenty or more years of experience compared to you. The job still has to be done. You can't use your age or lack of experience as an excuse.

- I encourage my freshman students to get in my face for help. Senior students rarely need or want help in lower level courses. If you work with your teacher one-on-one as a freshman, it helps to level the playing field and you learn how to deal with college-level coursework.

- It's often not how smart you are or how long you have been in college that makes the difference. Sound work ethics and good study habits can trump the experience edge of your upperclassmen.

INABILITY TO DEAL WITH THE HIGH EXPECTATIONS OF COLLEGE

A second reason students quit on their courses is because they are blown away by the high expectations and fast pace of college. Some students are like a deer in the headlights. No more feel-good education or gold stars on your papers. No more gummy bears for effort. No more rewards for slack work. No more waiting for slow students. It's a lot more serious. Sink or swim. Weed out courses. Buckling down. You're in the big leagues. Students crack under the pressure. College counselors who work with students have noted a marked increase in the number of students who seek psychological help. One of the chief problems is depression. A recent study[97] by Oregon State University found that 37% of their undergraduates experienced depression so severe it was difficult to function. Other national surveys of college students report similar numbers. Depression results when students are confronted by the sudden terms of accountability and high levels of performance expected in college. College seems like a long journey into night—the Jewish Day of Atonement.

What's a college freshman to do? There are few panaceas. You have to decide if going to college is important enough to get the help and resolve needed to survive. This takes concerted effort and willpower. Playing catch-up is never easy but your life's occupation depends on it. Take the advice I've offered in other sections of the book. Visit the student services center in your school and get the remedial work you need. It may require dropping back on courses and taking another year to finish. It may take eating a big slice of humble pie. But the reward is a higher level of satisfaction with college and confidence in your own competence. The extra year of college required to play catch-up is worth your sanity and future advancement. Better to work out your academic problems now rather than suffer through four years without the raw materials for success.

DECIDING AHEAD OF TIME HOW MUCH WORK YOU ARE WILLING TO DO IN COURSES

Students quit on courses because they underestimate the level of engagement required in some courses and then refuse to adjust to the situation. Take my astronomy course again. There are two primary teachers at AU who teach our introductory astronomy course. But say I'm a difficult teacher, and my colleague is an easy teacher; it's not really the case, but that's what some students believe. Then consider that I rarely teach the course. Counselors and fellow students recommend astronomy as an "easy A" course; it's packed to the gills every semester. Looks like a win-win situation, right? Students are getting A's, and bosses are telling the higher-ups that their courses are bursting at the seams because they're so exciting. The students are happy; the professor is happy; the boss is happy; the higher-ups are happy. Everyone's happy.

But there's a rub. I rotate into astronomy about once every three years. Students who thought they were enrolling in an easy A course find themselves facing a lot more work. Surprise. Students who expected, and consciously calculated, to do close to nothing in the course are now faced with a teacher who expects you to earn your A. They deal with it by failing to do homework and assignments, and then claim false advertising, bad advice, and disillusionment for doing poorly in the course. This is a mistake because you don't always know who your teacher will be and how the course will be taught.

IDEALISM VS REALISM

Finally, students quit on courses due to an inability to face reality. It's a rare semester that students don't tell me with an air of anger and disbelief that they are not a C student. The presumption is that it must be the teacher, the course content, or the counselor who told them to take the class that is morphing them into a C student. Not the student. Never the student. But the reality is that it's almost always the student.

You have a problem when a distorted view of your academic prowess results in quitting on your classes because grades are not viewed by professors as entitlements. In addition to a bad attitude, you now have to work to keep your daddy happy, but many freshman students lack the skills to work. The advice is clear. Expect to expend effort to achieve the high grades you got in high school or lower your inflated viewpoint of yourself. That sounds harsh, I know, but it's still the truth, spoken in love. Recognize that it's very difficult to get straight A's in college with the increased competition and course difficulty. Realize that your high school A's were largely feel-good grades based more on the feel-good system, sympathetic teachers, and a smaller competitive pool. That's what I mean by facing reality. The sooner you realize that the big leagues of college require quantum changes in effort and talent, the sooner you will adjust to the higher standards and rise to the occasion.

EXPECTING PROFESSORS TO SPOON-FEED YOU

A cardinal mistake made by freshman students is to wait for the professor to tell them what to do at each step of a college course. It won't happen. Most professors expect you to know how to study and exhibit adult behavior in your planning. At large universities, professors are experts in their fields and are too busy to spoon-feed students. They assume you are ready for college work and will balk at teaching what you should have learned in prerequisite courses and in high school. Further, many freshman courses have upperclassman that would be bored to tears if an instructor held the hands of freshman students throughout the semester.

Here's how a typical freshman student tackles my courses. In most of my freshman physics courses, I have four tests and maybe five homework assignments during the semester. The lectures parallel the textbook and, as noted earlier, I provide lecture notes so students can think with me during the class instead of mindlessly copying notes. The course schedule is laid-out in my syllabus and students know what is coming up, but there is little effort to, say, do the homework until the day before it's due. While I'm covering chapters of the textbook in the lecture, freshman students don't seem to know that they should be reading the chapters in the book. I usually have to tell them. Many students hardly ever crack the book. Upperclassman have learned to start studying a few days before a test, but freshmen don't start studying until the night before or when I explicitly say "Okay, it's time to start studying for test one."

While I try to be understanding, most of the time I scratch my head and wonder what happened in high school. The impression I get is that students have been told to do everything and rarely have taken a step beyond, or independently, of a teacher's directives. That's what I mean by spoon feeding. The inability of students to go beyond the minimum is particularly disappointing to professors. To make matters worse, we usually have to force students to complete even the minimum course requirements. You wouldn't believe how many times we hear the question "Will this be on the test?" It could be the most incredibly fascinating material, but the presumption is that, if it's not going to be tested, students aren't interested.

Let me illustrate. Once during my astronomy class I noticed that the text did little justice to the aurora borealis (northern lights), one of Earth's most beautiful wonders. The northern lights are giant curtains of undulating light in the far northern hemisphere sky that dynamically fold and unfold like the rolls in a theater curtain. They are caused by the interaction of the solar wind with the magnetic field of the Earth. Since most of my students are from Alabama or Georgia, few of my AU students have ever seen them. I took the time to find a beautifully photographed and narrated video, filled with interesting facts and real-time footage that few people are lucky to observe in a lifetime. The day came to show the video. I began class as usual and announced we would have a special video on the aurora borealis. The first question out of the box was whether it would be covered on the test. When I answered no, about ten of my one hundred students walked out of the class when I turned my head to lower the projection screen. Come on students. Man up enough to face me when you're walking out.

Parents are amazed when I tell this story during a seminar I run for prospective college students. They are embarrassed at the lack of respect. Yet I can't think of a time when some students didn't walk out during a video. That wasn't the case when your parents were in college. Most of your parents wouldn't think of packing up out of a class. Most professors have a thick skin after teaching for a few years and we've learned to expect such behavior. I don't take it personally anymore. But the worse part is the lame reasons given by the students who opt to walk away from course material not marked with a test price tag. Not only were they uninterested in anything that they didn't have to learn, but most were so far behind in other classes that they needed the time to cram for other courses, and I provided an extra hour by showing a video. Others had just pulled an all-nighter and wanted to go home and sleep. Some headed over to Starbucks for a coffee, which was more important than watching the northern lights. The rest were taking advantage of a break I was trying to give them from the usual material by having a movie instead of a lecture. No wonder professors lack compassion at the end of the semester when grades are due out.

PREFERRING SHORTCUTS TO HONEST EFFORT

College students are fond of taking shortcuts. It's like some students are on a race to the bottom. This makes me crazy as a professor. I hate it. Shortcuts rarely result in any long-term benefits for anything in life. Had I adopted shortcuts during my years in college, I'd have died an agonizing academic death. No person of excellence works by taking shortcuts. We talked earlier about the most common student shortcut, which is studying from old tests. Here are a couple of other reasons students take shortcuts.

No Interest in the Course

When students have no interest in a course they take shortcuts to get through it. It would be better to have a positive attitude. The professionals who designed your curriculum included the course in your list of requirements for good reasons. Trust their judgment.

Students have no interest in a course if their thinking is overly utilitarian. If a course seems to fit into your prospective occupation, everything is fine, but if not, then students will write it off as a burden. There are several things wrong with this viewpoint:

- First, you are too young to know what is useful for your future occupation.
- Second, a university education not designed to give you a junior college education. The goals of each institution are different. Universities are not vocational schools.
- Third, students prejudge a course or listen to hearsay opinions from other students that a course is boring. Any subject will seem boring if you don't know anything about it. How do you know a class isn't interesting until you take it?
- Fourth, we mentioned above that the average worker in America will change jobs several times in their lifetime. If universities don't give you a broad education, they do you a disservice and you're not getting what you paid for, which is preparation for a lifetime of employment.

I commonly hear my Dave Letterman students say they dreaded taking the class until they got into it; in fact, students frequently wait until their senior year to get my class out of the way because they believe they will get a low grade. But characteristically, many enjoy it more than they thought because they never knew physics rubbed against so many practical areas of life. The problem was they always heard that physics was hard and designed for nerds.

Doing the Minimum to Get a Given Grade

Students hope for tasks equal to their powers instead of powers equal to their tasks. This is a race for the bottom. What employer would hire someone who feigns excellence and is allergic to work? Shooting for the basement never helped anyone. It only promotes mediocrity.

Millennial students try to ride the curve in courses graded on a relative scale. You ought to see the class reaction when I hand back a test. It's bimodal. Students who are trying in the course are embarrassed by the low average; they shake their heads in amazement at such deplorable performance. The slackers in the course are singing hymns and spiritual songs. They are praying for a low test average because it means that their pathetic 40% may not be assigned the F that it deserves.

Whatever happened to shame? It's almost a badge of courage when students get low scores. When I was a student, I would be mortified by a test score under 80%. Not any more. For many students, lower scores are a hoped-for objective. It means that students can slack off and get a non-failing grade if the class is loaded with kindred slackers. If everyone in the class is bad, your performance doesn't look so bad. Problem is, students in other parts of the world have entirely different standards, and, in our emerging global economy, international students are going to get hired every time compared to the masses of American slackers.

After the initial shock of the freshman year when students find out that cookie-cutter A's are no longer the norm, C's become the new standard for millennial students. It's sad that a significant segment of students don't seem to mind when they get low grades; there's little humiliation or anger or anything. I'd rather deal with the angry and complaining ones. Professors get that apathetic and distant stare into space. Say it loud, I'm slack, and I'm proud. Students who do nothing in high school and adopt pop culture role models who get up at noon and write poetry have few motivators to work hard in life. When your role models are lazy, you're lazy.

CHEATING

Cheating is rampant on college campuses. People outside the university mainstream would be shocked at how much cheating is going on in college. A majority of today's students see nothing wrong with it. They have few qualms about downloading answer books, lifting term papers off the Web, or copying work from other students. It's a sad commentary that so many students, if allowed, will cheat their way through college.

Student attitudes toward cheating come partly out of millennial views concerning regulations. Millennial students are well aware of campus regulations but they pay only lip-service allegiance to them. There is little moral commitment to policies. The challenge for millennials is to find a way around the rules. The general student attitude is that cheating is okay if you don't get caught. Rutgers University professor Donald McCabe, who has studied cheating for nearly two decades, reports that 56% of business school graduates admit to cheating on tests.[98] You know that number is on the low end because it refers to graduates who actually admitted to cheating. McCabe finds similar percentages of cheaters in other graduate and professional programs, and the numbers are higher in college and high school. Southern Illinois University recently suspended the grades of all fifty-two first-year dental students pending a review of rampant suspected cheating.[99] The Josephson Institute for Ethics in Los Angeles recently reported[100] that 60% of the thirty-six thousand high school students surveyed in 2006 reported they had cheated within the previous year; 35% said they had done it two or more times. Nancy Cole, president and CEO of the Educational Testing Service, quoting a study by Stephen Davis, reports that between 75-98% of the eight thousand college students surveyed each year admit cheating in high school.[101] The research showed that students believe they're at a disadvantage if they don't cheat. Students consider themselves fools for not cheating in a cheat-tolerant system. The message is that cheating pays dividends and rarely gets called out. If you examine a large cross section of cheating studies, at least 60% of students cheat their way through school.

The problem starts early. Thousands of elementary and secondary students were recently found cheating on standardized tests in Texas. The *Dallas Morning News* found evidence of cheating by over fifty thousand students when it examined scores from the Texas Assessment of Knowledge and Skills given in the 2005-06 school years.[102] The *News* "found cases where 30, 50, or even 90% of students had suspicious answer patterns that researchers say indicate collusion." Cheating was most evident on the eleventh grade test required for graduation and on tests from Dallas and Houston. "The evidence of substantial cheating is beyond reasonable doubt," said George Wesolowski, a professor at McMaster University in Canada who worked with the *News* on the analysis. Amazingly, the Texas Education Agency won't do a thing about it without further proof. Their argument is that statistical analysis can't prove cheating. Apparently it's merely an amazing coincidence when neighboring students have the same sequence of codified answers. More evidence is needed such as getting teachers to document misbehavior. Get real. When authorities refuse to believe objective statistical mathematics, it's unlikely they will believe a subjective teacher's observations.

Students have become so blaze about cheating that they wear it like a badge. It's like if you're not cheating, you must be stupid or a religious fanatic. I've heard students openly brag about cheating on a test and getting an A without cracking a book. The pressure to get good grades at any cost breeds an environment that says cheating is acceptable. When students find out how much work is involved in getting high grades by legitimate means, cheating becomes the perfect short-term solution to the problem. The moral perspective adopted by students is that, if a professor is dumb enough not to prevent cheating, it's not their fault if they do cheat. Whatever is possible is permissible.

FIVE

How Professors Work and Why You Should Care

GETTING INTO YOUR PROFESSOR'S MIND

THE SYLLABUS

Professors use the first class day to go over the course syllabus. The syllabus provides a blueprint for the course and establishes policies. Experienced professors know that if they develop an organized syllabus, they save themselves a lot of time throughout the semester. This is because the syllabus serves as a legal and policy statement for the course. Rather then having to answer the same questions repeatedly, we let our syllabi do the talking. When students give me lame excuses for not handing in an assignment or not being able to find the first lab or not knowing when a test was scheduled, it's documented in the syllabus, and the excuses have no basis in fact.

A cardinal mistake of rookie students is to file it after the first day or to just use it to see how grades are determined. You err when you do this because simple mistakes such as missing the due date of an assignment can cost you during the semester. You also learn a lot about your professor and how to approach the course by reading the syllabus.

COURSE NAME AND CONTACT INFORMATION

The official name for my course at AU is Foundations of Physics but it's best known to students as Dave Letterman Physics. The popular name change tells you a lot about me and my approach to the course:

- That I view the course as dealing with the everyday science things seen on the *Letterman* show or *Mythbusters*
- To expect crazy demonstrations to illustrate the principles of physics
- That there will be few prerequisites for the course
- That there will be a minimum of tedious mathematics
- That I have a sense of humor and want you to have fun in the course

On some campuses, this course is called Physics for Poets. I ask to teach it every year because it offers a challenging teaching environment that stretches me. It's much harder to teach Dave Letterman Physics than the upper-level or graduate courses so cherished by professors. Try taking an incoming group of bored students who are scared to death of physics and convert them by the end of the semester to engaging students who actually enjoy science.

Course syllabi provide professor contact information. This means office number, telephone number, email address, and Website. By reading my syllabus, students find that I have several offices on the AU campus, but where I usually hang is my laboratory. This shows students that I'm a working research scientist who spends the bulk of my time doing experiments. When students show up for help, they get a much different impression of who I am outside the classroom because we're sitting in my lab surrounded by millions of dollars of fancy, nerdy physics instrumentation. It lends an air of credibility as students see me in my natural habitat.

By examining my Website (www.physics.auburn.edu/aussl), students gain an appreciation of my work as a professor. It's rare that students look at it. This is a mistake. Why would you spend fifteen weeks with a teacher and not learn something about him? I suggest to all students to visit the Websites of their professors. You will learn where they went to college, what they study, the area of their publications, and some personal information such as what they enjoy doing in their spare time. It helps you to see them as people. When I was an undergraduate, Websites didn't exist, but seeing my professors in their work environment helped motivate me as a student. When you respect a mentor and appreciate their professional accomplishments, you want to learn from them.

Course Outline

When a professor includes an organized course outline in the syllabus, it lets our students know that we've thought through the course and know our destination. It communicates foresight and gives students security. My syllabus lists the subjects covered each week and when the exams are scheduled. As we noted earlier, every student should keep a calendar and transfer the dates for tests, projects, assignments, final exams, and so on. The course outline shows you what a professor considers important to learn during the semester. Course textbooks usually have more chapters than what can be covered in a fifteen week session. We have to choose our topics carefully. The topics listed in the syllabus show you what to focus on.

When Professors Give Low Grades

You ought to spend some time in my office after the semester is over and the final grades have been posted. You can almost predict when the phone will start ringing and the calls are not from students who are complimenting me on being a wonderful professor. The inquiries are about the shock and awe when students receive a D or F in my course. Students are surprised to find that professors will actually flunk them.

It's usually not an in-your-face, belligerent phone message but you can hear the disbelief. It's often "Dr. Bozack, you must have made a mistake when you calculated my grade" or "Can you read me back the numerical grades on my assignments?" or "I had a C on all the tests and ended up with a D in the course. What gives?" or "Can you tell me what I got on my final exam?" Students don't really want to know what they got on their final exam, but rather why they failed the course. They are being polite until they find out how unmoving I am on changing grades. While I appreciate the polite inquiry of my AU students, it's obvious why they are calling.

The sad news is that my course is graded by numbers. Numbers are impartial, objective, and colder than ice. They slap you in the face. When I hear students talking and the question arises "What did Dr. Such-and-Such give you in chemistry?" my thought is that it's not professors who give you grades. It's yourself. Yes, I understand that some courses such as literature require that you "tell the professor what he wants to hear." But it's not my experience that most courses fall into such subjective categories. Even in literature courses, professors attempt to use objective metrics to grade you. The reason professors assign grades by a numerical scheme is precisely to take the subjectivism out of the equation. So I eventually return the calls and emails, and the conversation usually goes something like this: "Well, Mark, looking down at my grade book, I see that you missed one of the semester tests, got two D's and a C on the other three, missed three labs, and didn't hand in half the homework assignments. You also didn't qualify for my attendance bonus in the course. When you account for the missed work and note that you got a D on the final exam, it's easy to see why you got a D."

Next comes a moment of awkward silence followed by a litany of reasons why Mark can't tolerate a D. The reasons usually have nothing to do with Mark's actual performance in the course, but things like "They will kick me out of school if I get a D in your course" or "I will be on academic probation if you don't change it to a C" or "Is there any projects or extra credit I can do to improve my grade" or "You can't do this to me; my dad will kill me." I usually have to go through the excuses and tell the student why I can't do what they're asking. Let me save you time and your professors some grief by giving you my reactions to the main excuses.

First, it's almost never the case that a single grade in a single course will get you kicked out of college. If you are in danger of flunking out of college, it's because of collective and persistent poor performance. You have to work to get kicked out. The good news is that colleges have a number of services available to save you from getting to that point. The bad news is that students are oblivious of the resources or are too proud to admit they need help. The whole point of academic probation is to give you second and third chances before the axe finally falls.

Second, professors can't arbitrarily change grades after the semester is over just because you ask them. Think about what that question implies. Any student could come up to me after the semester is over and ask me for a grade change. If you were a student who worked hard to earn, say, a B in my course, is it fair that a student who goofed off all semester gets a higher grade just because he wants it? No, you'd be steamed. If I were to grant your request for a higher grade, on what moral grounds would I do so? What would happen to the integrity of the university grading system if I decided to give students higher grades just because they wanted higher grades? Changing grades undermines the whole reason for evaluation. And it's not at all how the real world works. Do you think a future employer will feel obligated to give you a raise just because you think you should get one? Society is based on standards and performance. We do you little good if we cave to a bleeding heart and feel sorry for you for not doing any work in our courses. When students accuse me of being unsympathetic for not honoring their grade change, I tell them that it's because I do care about their future that I have to deny their request. I care about all my students who worked hard for their grades, and I'll protect them from students who ask for freebee, bleeding heart grades.

Third, offering to do extra credit exercises after the course is over to improve your grade leads to ethical problems, ignores talent, and reduces college to busywork. It also doesn't correspond to the world you will find after college. Say I allow a student to do a research paper in order to improve their grade from a D to a C. Why should one student get that opportunity and not everyone? If I was really a fair person, I'd have to let all my students do research papers to improve their grade. No professor with large course loads is going to do that just because a few students didn't work in the course. Why didn't you work during the semester instead of begging for leniency now? No employer would accept extra credit when the job can be done correctly the first time. We're not going to do it either. How about working for your grade in college? This means that a grade can be guaranteed by a certain amount of work. The work can take several forms, such as assignments, problem exercises, homework, research papers, and so on. The important thing for most work-for-your-grade schemes is that you complete the extra exercises, not necessarily that you do the exercises correctly or can perform with excellence on a timed, closed book test. Students tell me that many high school courses were work-for-your-grade courses. If you wanted an A in algebra, you could do say, one hundred extra algebra exercises during the semester. If you wanted a B, then seventy-five would do.

Fourth, when you say your dad will kill you if you fail to get a C in my course, then perhaps your dad should kill you. Not literally, of course, but if he is paying the freight for your education, he deserves to know what he's getting for his hard-earned education dollar. Hardly a semester goes by that I don't talk to a shocked parent who wonders what went wrong with Little Johnny. The story is usually that it's my fault. Either my grading scheme was unclear, unfair, or that I made a mistake in calculating the grade. It's always interesting when the parent calls me personally to ask about the situation. It goes one of two ways. Either the parent tries to intimidate me to change the grade or the parent honestly wants to know what happened. When I explain how many assignments Little Johnny missed, how many times he was absent, how many labs he missed, the parent is usually shocked, but thankful that I was straight with him. There is a promise to talk to Johnny to get to the bottom of the story and a follow-up call to let me know that he is no longer taking for granted the gracious parental financial support without seeing documented effort.

Just to show you how bold parents can get when their kids' grades are involved, the worse case of parental interference occurred during my fifth year of college teaching. The semester was over and the final grades had been posted. There was a knock at my door and, when I opened it, there stood one of my students with a red-faced, obviously steamed father. The father demanded to come in and wanted an explanation for why his boy got a D in my course. Problem was, the door was not my AU office door, but the door of my home. The parent was so arrogant and used to pushing around high school teachers that he found my unlisted address and showed up on a Thursday night. I should have just slammed the door in his face, but I was so shocked that I let them come inside to talk. You can imagine the conversation. Hot is the kindest way to put it; fumes were going out the chimney of my fireplace. No way was I going to change his boy's grade, but his dad was loaded with two hours of reasons why I should and what would happen if I didn't. He left frustrated. The worst part was that his boy had to sit and watch his dad verbally battle for two hours. You have to feel bad for a college student whose dad fights his battles for him. Time for both of them to grow up.

PASSION AND TOUGH LOVE

One of the best times of the semester is when I read my instructor evaluations. It usually occurs about a week after the semester is over. In a small-town, land-grant college, this is the time of the year when only locals are left and you really find out who lives in Auburn. I usually go to a local hangout with close proximity to a stiff drink (figuratively), order some nuts and pretzels, and see what my students have on their minds. It ranges from hilarious to tragic. I've received everything from phone numbers of coeds to Mafia-like threats of what would happen if I didn't come through with a high grade. The most common sentiment goes something like this "Dr. Mike, you are a wonderful professor, but why are you so hard? You kicked my butt this semester." Let me explain, as it may help you understand why some professors do what they do.

First, my course isn't really hard. Hard is a relative term. Hard compared to what? Several considerations apply:

- When students say my course is hard, they mean that physics is hard compared to biology, literature, or history. True, physics involves logical and structured thinking, but so do many other college courses.
- My course is also not hard because, when I teach physics, I explain it using language that the common man off the street can understand; in fact, I tell my students to call home and explain to mom what you learned today using lay terminology. That doesn't sound too hard.
- My course is also not hard in terms of mathematics, because I use

only basic arithmetic and algebra, which every college student should have as prerequisite.

- Many students say my course isn't hard. When my students begin to study for the final exam by reviewing the regular course tests, they are shocked to see how easy the tests were and can hardly explain why they missed so many questions. What seemed hard at first is now easy. That means that education has occurred.

- My course is not hard compared to physics courses a decade ago. As noted above, there has been a progressive dumbing-down of science textbooks. I'm not criticizing the current texts, but it's clear that the freshman physics text I was using when I was in college was more difficult than the books nowadays.

- Finally, my course is not hard because I am unable to cover as much material as I did during my first years of college teaching.

Thus, I don't deliberately make my course hard. You just think it's hard. Forcing yourself to think is what makes physics, and my course, difficult. I insist that you learn something during the semester. It takes work, mental discipline, time, and patience. It goes against the grain of our attention-deficit, media- and entertainment-driven world. But thinking, not memorization, separates the achievers from the fakers, the participants from the spectators. You won't learn anything, and I don't help you, if I let you off easy by equating learning with memorization and not requiring you to think.

Second, professors don't help students by offering puff courses. Our job is to prepare you for the real world, and life is not a puff course. The real world is unforgiving, filled with traps, inequities, and unfair situations. My model for teaching is coaching. A coach sets the bar and helps his players to achieve it. He does little to help his players if he's more a friend than a coach, more interested in being popular than in being effective. Coaches have to be tough on their players to stretch their abilities, position them for success, and put them in situations that require competence and skill. Players need to build endurance, the ability to handle adversity, and how to work under pressure. There are few shortcuts. If there are no consequences to missing practice, failing to shoot free throws, and working on defense, there is no progress nor success in the SEC. It's human nature for people to take the path of least resistance and this is especially true for students. A coach is tough on his players to prepare them to handle the variety of things life will throw at you. It's really not that the coach is tough, it's just that he insists on accountability and a commitment to excellence.

Third, just as students will stoop to the lowest levels of achievement if they can get away with it, they will rise to the highest levels with the right incentives. Rewarding you with high grades for sloppy papers, careless assignments, late work, or no work, only enables you to remain in your comfort zone of just enough. But just enough is not enough. Why would you want that for your life? That's what you got in high school and why you're in trouble now. I care too much about you and your future to let that happen. The mediocrity has to stop and it stops with me.

Fourth, a professor can't teach important life lessons by rescuing you when you fail to perform academically. That would be like rewarding a child who continues to misbehave. The first time the issue arises is when I'm discussing my syllabus during the first class day. Students will often ask me whether I flunk anyone. What? This question used to floor me during my first years of teaching until I realized that feel-good grades were the norm in high school. Students weaned on the grade inflation cow had never received anything lower than a C. When I answer yes, you should see the looks of shock, disbelief, and the ringing of hands. In biblical terms, students would be tearing their sackcloth. By asking if I give D's and F's, students were really trying to find out if I'm an easy professor and whether I'm serious about grades.

But think about that view. Why should a student who rarely comes to class and refuses to crack a book get a good grade? An A means excellent, a B means good, a C means average, a D means poor, and an F means fail. If you were a student who did well on assignments and tests, how would you feel if someone who goofed off all semester received the same grade as you? You would feel cheated. But that is what students ask when they ask for a gift grade. It's not only unfair, it doesn't help anyone. Facing the consequences of actions is the caldron where we change our behavior and unfortunately, for many students, college is the first place where accountability is taken seriously.

Fifth, parents, teachers, friends, and pastors who care about you have to back away occasionally and refuse to rescue you. You need to feel the pain of treading water when you don't work, when you're lazy, when you don't study, and when you try to manipulate the system instead of making an honest effort. Better to learn the lesson in college than later in a job where the money and stakes are much higher. Take the case of a former student who came by one day to thank me for helping him with his drug addiction. His parents, who loved him, tried to help him. His girlfriend tried to help him. His church group tried to help him. The call home went something like "Mom, I'm out of money, can you send me more?" He was living out of his car, looked like a street person, and was trying to make ends meet with a burger-flipping job he could barely hold down. When his mom finally refused to send more money, he asked me to make up the difference. Begged me in fact. My heart went out to him but my better judgment told me he would just spend the money on more drugs. So I refused. He stormed out of my office and cussed up one side and down the other all the way out of the building. But now, months later, he was thanking me. By reaching rock bottom, he had to start looking at himself and allow God to help him. We play God as instructors when we let you slide by with a sob story. I'm not smart enough to play God.

Getting to Know Your Professor Personally

Students amaze me with their misconceptions of professors. One of them is that you can't really get to know your professor, especially at large universities. It's either too dangerous, too stupid, too impractical, too unprofessional, takes too much time, too this, and too that. Here are some of the reasons cited:

- Professors are too busy to bother with students.
- Professors only care about their research.
- Professors don't really care to have friends who are students.

- Professors just want to hang out with other faculty.
- Professors think students are too dumb to bother with.
- Professors are too smart to hang out with immature students.
- Professors are not really human.
- Professors are serious and have little sense of humor.
- Professors look down their noses at students.

Why wouldn't a professor want to get to know his students? Why would I want to spend three hours per week for fifteen weeks with my students and not get to know them? I wouldn't. Many people, and that includes professors, go into teaching because they enjoy students. They enjoy teaching, they enjoy seeing their students get to the next level, and they enjoy them personally. They want their students to do well and take pleasure in the educational trip with them.

I'm flattered when students take the time to know me. Teachers want to leave a legacy to our students. We have all kinds of experience and want to impart it to you. We've made all the rookie mistakes and have been through the same tough times you are going through in college. We want to steer you and save you time and trouble. We like being guardian angels. The sad part is that millennial students don't seem to want what professors have to offer. Either they don't think we have much to offer in the first place, don't really care, or are oblivious to the idea in the first place. We can't share the range of our collective wisdom unless you get to know us on more than a three-lectures-per-week-only basis.

Yesterday, one of our former physics grad students returned to AU to give our department a talk about his research. He is currently working at Mercer University in Macon, Georgia as a young professor of physics. The older members of our faculty all knew him and looked forward to seeing him. The room was heavy with respect for the faculty who mentored him and the pride his professors had in seeing where he ended up. Some of his former professors put him up in their homes and played a few rounds of golf the next day. Several professors' wives were there to hear his talk since they were also a part of his life as a student.

Would my colleagues do this if they didn't care deeply about students?

They wouldn't. Yes, not all professors are interested in knowing students. That's their loss. Yes, some professors give students the cold shoulder. They're missing out. Yes, some professors send the clear message not to bother them. They're unprofessional. Yes, some professors act like they're too important to stop for a minute and care about you. They're arrogant. But not all. That's the important message. Some of us love to know our students. We want to know you as a person just as much as we want you to learn our subjects. Many of us wait to learn about our students; we relish looking over our class rolls at the start of the semester and ponder how many new student friends we will make. I personally pray for each name on my class list before the first day of the course. There's nothing better for some professors than to make friends with our students and watch them develop throughout their college career. It's a kick. If you're a Christian professor, it's a mission—what you were made to do.

What are practical ways to get to know your professors? Is it okay to initiate a relationship with your professor? Ask him to lunch? Are there rules that prohibit faculty-student relationships? How is relationship defined in the first place? Is it important to know your professors? Here are my answers to questions involving relationships with professors.

RELATIONSHIPS ARE THE BASIS FOR LETTERS OF RECOMMENDATION

It's sad when an undergraduate student outside of physics asks me to write a letter of recommendation for a job or graduate school. It's not sad that they asked, but sad that they don't know a professor in their own department well enough to trust them to write a reference letter that reflects personal knowledge of them and their competence. One of the utilitarian reasons to know your professors is that we're the ones who write letters of recommendation, and letters of recommendation are often the most important factor in getting a job.

It's hard for us to write you a good letter if we don't know you. We mentioned this earlier, but such letters are generic, devoid of passion, and read like we're suffering through the writing. Some students prefer such a letter and nearly ask for it. They fear that, if a professor doesn't know much about them, they can't say too much negative about them. But what a deplorable attitude. If you were a potential employer, would you want a letter from a reference that claims a lot of nothing about a student? Not me. College students err when they spend all their time trying to get good grades without attempting to know their professors. When I hired people at Intel, I wanted to see an applicant's letters of recommendation before their grades. If I know a student personally and think he will do a good job, I often work the phones and try to find him a job. I can't tell you how many high school principals I have called with the message "You're crazy if you don't hire this person for your teaching opening."

Relationships with Professors Motivate Learning

College is more satisfying when you know your professors. We stated earlier that it's easier to learn when you respect your professors. Respect is built by knowing your teacher personally. Personal relationships provide a more accurate portrayal of the world of ideas and the people chartered to discover and disseminate new knowledge. You find that your professors are human, and their jobs are human endeavors. You see that they find learning new things as difficult as you do. You see the sweat and years they had to put in to be a professor.

Ignoring your professors as people reduces them to an impersonal slide presentation. You might as well be taught by a computer program. That's the problem with computer-guided instruction. A book or a computer program cannot impart importance and significance nearly as well as a teacher. When I'm talking about exploring the universe, for example, I always remark how courageous the Apollo astronauts were, who rode atop largely untested rockets in little more than a tin can. You can't get that perspective without a human teacher or a biographical video with good actors. Try learning how to throw a football by computer. It can't be done. Best to have a Joe Montana or a Dan Marino show you the art and science; to work with you on the technique and finesse required. It's hard to learn how to comfort a suffering grandmother who has just lost her husband of fifty years with a computer program that describes empathy. It takes a teacher, a person you respect and know personally.

GRADUATE EDUCATION IS THE BEST TEACHING MODEL

Sometimes I wish I could take my undergraduates into my lab to see how professors work with masters and doctoral students. It's close and personal. We work hand and foot daily with our grad students in a colleague and apprentice relationship. Undergraduate education has to be modeled differently than graduate education, but still, our undergraduates could learn a lot about how to approach college by employing a more graduate approach to professors.

In the graduate model, students work alongside professors to study a particular research problem or to accomplish a focused set of experimental or theoretical tasks. Say you are a media student who wants to learn how to make the amazing computer graphics and special effects conjured up in Hollywood studios, say for a movie like Star Wars. What's the best way to do this? By working for the experts and learning how they do it. If it were me, I would examine the recent list of Academy Award winners in media production, find out who they are and where they work, and then write them to see if they have a student internship program. If your passion is racing car engines, NASCAR has a school where you work alongside the master mechanics who work in the pits of such drivers as Gordon, Earnhart, and Burton.

This is how graduate education works. Students work beside experts who teach them the art and craft of their discipline. It's a human, personal, and intimate setting. And it's the best way to learn. A question for my undergraduates who doubt that getting to know your professor is valuable is this—do you think that the style of education in either a graduate or vocational setting is independent of close relationships with teachers and mentors? No. It depends mostly on close and personal relationships. If you really want to learn, get to know your professors and find out how they work, think, and maneuver in their discipline. Observe them in their native habitats. Find out what motivates them. Barely a month goes by that I'm not giving my undergrads a tour of our physics laboratories, with the "oh, my gosh" reaction that "I never knew professors did this."

Personal Relationships Yield
the Best Educational Environment

Think for a moment about how Jesus taught his disciples. Since Christ was the God-man, He naturally would utilize the most effective teaching methods in keeping with the culture of the first century, His learners, and His infinite wisdom. Christ's methods varied with His audience, such as when He spoke to hundreds from a boat on the Sea of Galilee; but largely, Christ taught His disciples personally. He established relationships with them, challenged their preconceived notions of God, modeled what He was trying to teach them, and used effective parables and analogies. The best pastors and teachers follow Christ's methods. He was a brilliant teacher.

Ponder how effective Jesus was as a teacher. Most of His life philosophy and message was taught over a mere three-year period of time. His students came from all walks of life and educational backgrounds. Many were fishermen, some were slaves, some were commoners, and some were tax collectors. Most had no formal education, which hardly existed at the time unless you were born to royalty. Yet, as far as we know, Christ Himself never penned a word, leaving the writing of the NT to the agent of divine revelation and largely ordinary men. The ethical ideas of Christianity changed the world and served as the template for our laws, governments, and cultures. Christ gave the world the most brilliant principles ever conceived. He taught us how to live, how to die, and how to have hope in eternal life. He dealt with all the deepest desires of human beings with unmatched simplicity. What Christ taught in a mere three years form the ethical and legal superstructure of the most enlightened cultures.

There are several messages for educators and students in Christ's teaching model. First, Christ had nothing like computers, fancy graphics, clickers, calculators, or any of the modern educational conveniences that school districts insist are needed for education today. When students tell me that they need the modern conveniences of education, I remind them that Christ wrote in the sand. Second, Christ's teaching model shows that the best education results by living and breathing with your teachers, and that means getting to know them personally. His teaching lessons were given in the heat of life experiences. Third, the best education comes not by watching but by participating. Christ told his disciples to "leave their nets" and come and follow Him. He was calling them to a collegial, close, and intimate relationship where learning was experiential and not from the pages of a book.

Simple Ways to Get to Know your Professors

How can students know their professors? Listed below are ideas that have worked for me. But first, let me first put the student-teacher relationship into a broad context. The key word is professionalism. The student-professor relationship is similar to any professional relationship. Think doctors and patients, coaches and athletes, pastors and parishioners, and attorneys and clients. A cordial professional relationship is advantageous to both parties.

Earlier, I equated teaching with coaching. If a coach is too friendly with his athletes, he will promote mediocrity and lower the standard of excellence. A coach walks a fine line between friend and mentor, hard butt and softie. It's an art and we all make mistakes on where to draw our lines, especially as rookie teachers. Worse, the lines are often fluid, depending on the culture, the students, the age of students, and their backgrounds.

Where my gray area is located, is predicated on keeping a professional distance while students are in my courses. I get to know my students during a course, but everyone knows that I'm still the teacher, and they're the students. My grading system is designed to encourage interaction with students because it's based entirely on numbers and not how I personally feel about a student. You can't go wrong when coming to see me about a problem because it's all about amassing points in the course; you only help yourself by working with me. In contrast, after a student leaves my course, the relationship can change because you're now part of my alumni association and not my immediate classroom student. I no longer have to grade you and can establish a different, more informal, relationship. Were I to get too close to students during my course, students could claim favoritism and bias, and that wouldn't benefit anyone. But I'd be lying if I said the balance was always easy; it's neither clear-cut nor easy. Here are some simple ways to get to know your professor on a personal level:

- Offer to meet for lunch at the school cafeteria. I do this regularly with my students.
- Stop by during office hours, not only to talk about the course but to talk in general about your life. This is where I usually get to know my students. Sometimes if it's nice outside, we'll walk across the street, get some ice cream, sit on a picnic table, and work on homework problems.
- Invite professors to speak to your fraternity or sorority on a subject of interest.
- If your professor is married with kids, offer to baby-sit to give him a date night with his wife.
- If you are in a singing group, a play, a baseball game, or other campus activity, invite your professor to see your performance. One of my journalism students, for example, was always asking me to comment on her editorial articles.
- Come by to talk about career advice, personal matters, or spiritual advice.
- Several of my Christian students ask me about Sunday school topics they have struggled with in their young Christian life.
- Several students come by to ask for advice on how to study, and many of the topics covered in this book.
- When students are going through a valley experience, I often get to know them personally as I help to work through their difficulty and schedule makeup tests.
- If you are a server in a local restaurant where I eat, be sure to stop by, sit with me a minute, and be friendly.
- Christian professors often serve in local churches as Sunday school teachers and associate college ministers. Get to know professors by taking their classes in churches.
- Sororities and fraternities often sponsor "invite a professor to dinner" nights a couple of times a semester. These are informal gatherings of

students and professors specifically geared toward promoting closer student-teacher relationships.

- Professors are active in club programs and athletics at universities. I was once the president of the astronomy club, faculty advisor for varsity track, and have helped the AU athletics department recruit. Such forums allow students and faculty to come together outside the classroom to focus on common goals and objectives.
- Professors often take the lead and reach out to students through informal gatherings. Professors in my cul-de-sac, for example, invite students to their homes for end-of-year celebrations and when students reach important milestones.

WHAT COLLEGE PROFESSORS DO BESIDES TEACH

College students have low appreciation for what professors do outside the classroom. When I was a student, I thought my professors were like glorified high school teachers who taught several courses during the day. In a major university, this is not close to the truth; most of us teach only one or two courses. In order to give you perspective on your college experience, it's useful to know what your professors do when they leave the classroom. This will broaden your viewpoint of professors and help answer many of the questions you have about us. Students would be less critical of professors if they walked in our shoes. University professors spend the bulk of their time in three areas—teaching, research, and service. Here are a few brief comments to show you what's involved.

TEACHING

Teaching is the obvious part of being a professor. We are experts in our fields and are uniquely positioned to teach you the principles of our disciplines. Experts are exactly who you want to teach you. That's what you pay for with your college tuition. Students often ask me why there are so many bad teachers at the university level. You would think it would be the opposite. Since universities are the primary institutions in society to transmit learning to the next generation, you would think universities would have the best teachers, not some of the worse. What's the problem?

Strange as it seems, we're not hired for our teaching skill. Universities place relatively low priority on whether or not you're a good teacher. I hate to say it but it's simple fact. There is institutional concern that professors do a good enough job in the classroom that administrators don't have to deal with complaints from students, but not enough concern to reward or hire outstanding teachers. The attitude is that universities could find any number of good teachers if that was the prime directive. It's very much an "anybody can be a teacher" attitude. When I was interviewing for my current position, nobody asked me anything about whether I had any skill at teaching, and I interviewed at five major universities. Having served on several search committees for new faculty at AU, it's clear that teaching skill is low on the totem pole of prime qualities for new hires.

RESEARCH

Sorry to say it, but money is the biggest driver of major universities. You know universities are cash hogs when they never want you to leave campus. A recent trend at colleges and universities allows alumni to hang around forever by providing a campus cemetery. I'm not joking. Duke, Notre Dame, Virginia, and the Citadel are among the universities who have recently offered to bury you under the ivy towers.[103] Crypts at Notre Dame go for about $11,000 and Duke has a memorial garden plot for about $20,000. It's not enough to take your money while you are alive but they also want it after you're dead. I can almost see the worshippers of Bear Bryant lining up to be buried near Bryant-Denny Stadium in Tuscaloosa. Talk about taking your college experience to the next level. Sorry, bad joke.

High-minded views of a university as a place of innocence where scholars and students pursue lofty goals and think great thoughts is, unfortunately, getting lost in a forest of greenbacks as administrators choose to follow a corporate model of management. More college presidents are running universities like Fortune 500 companies with accounting ledgers resembling Silicon Valley companies. The Association of Governing Boards of Universities and Colleges[104] reports that ~ 48% of public college trustees had business ties in 2004. Trustees refer to the governing group of men and women who make the large, global decisions for the university. Take the case of Harvard University. Harvard's seven-member governing board (at the date of writing) includes money manager James Rothenberg, Citigroup director Robert Rubin, and Corning Chairman James Houghton. At AU, our trustees include major players in the state banking industry, millionaire developers, business owners, and high-ranking state politicians. In 2001, the University of Kentucky hired Lee Todd, an engineer, entrepreneur, and former senior vice president of the Lotus software division at IBM, as president. Although Todd was a former faculty member at Kentucky, tell me what a vice president of a software division of IBM knows about running a university? The answer is that Todd was hired because he knows big business and had a plan for bringing big dollars into UK. His charter was to get the school into the financial big leagues. The principal contact sport for most university presidents today is to make money for the school and build the university endowment. One way to do this is to put pressure on faculty to bring in dollars. That has very little to do with teaching skill.

As a result, many professors in major universities are businessmen. The job is to run a business and make money for the university. Once a student understands that the tail wagging the university dog is profit motive, it helps to explain a whole lot of things you wonder about during your four years in college. Profit is the invisible oil that greases the university engine.

But what business? In the case of a physics professor, we are chartered to build a forefront program in physics research. Part of the job is to convince clients (government or industry) that I'm the best person to study their research problem (marketing), which hopefully results in a grant or contract (money inflow) for me to do the work, which then is used to pay graduate students, buy new physics instruments, help with the costs of supplies and services, and so on (money outflow). The university then takes a mandated share of the pot each year (45%). This is a business model. It's to a university's advantage to hire hotshot research professors who can bring in dollars since the university makes $45K for every $100K. Big money is involved.

SERVICE

The third rung of a professor's work involves service. Service comes from the Latin word servitium, meaning servant. Service is a long-established tradition for professional occupations. A lawyer offers service beyond his law practice by donating a few days of free legal advice to the most needy of our population. A physician volunteers her time in a health clinic once a month to serve those who can't afford health care. Service is giving back to society.

Professors serve outside the ivy-covered halls of academia and within the university. Service within the university is voluntary and unpaid; it's expected as part of our job and consists of serving on committees to improve and deploy educational programs within the university. Service outside the university, by contrast, can either be offered free or on a paid consultant basis; for example, I'm frequently the point person at AU to answer questions from the press on astronomy topics. Several of us serve on national committees that determine the direction of science in our nation. Professors are also called upon to assist in times of national duress, such as the physicists who served our country during World War II.

WHAT TO DO WHEN YOU GET A WEAK PROFESSOR

Now that you see what's required of many major college professors, it's easier to understand why there are so many poor teachers at the university level. Large universities are money-generating businesses and hire professors who can pull in the big bucks and establish national programs. Teaching is secondary.

So what do you do when you get a weak professor? Suffer through the class? Should you complain, suck it up, or opt to drop the course? Are there options? Here's some advice:

- In some cases, it's better to suffer through a course, especially when only one professor teaches it, and you can't afford to pick up the course later. You can't always get a great professor. Rather than viewing the situation negatively, it's best to view it as a harbinger to what you will find in the work-a-day world with good and bad bosses.

- You can drop the course without penalty if you act soon enough. The downside is that dropping too many courses slows your progress to graduation. If you truly hate a course and a professor; however, it may be better for your sanity to postpone the class and accept another year to graduate.

- Find out ahead of time who teaches the course and ask other students what they think about the professor. If the course schedule lists the course as taught by "staff," it's because teaching assignments haven't been cast before the schedule printing. Call the department offering the course and ask if the teaching assignments are decided. If yes, ask who is teaching the course. It should be public information. The more advance information you have about a professor the better. You are paying good money for your courses, and it's prudent to choose the best courses taught by the best professors.

- Student organizations compile professor evaluations. Such compilations should be viewed with caution because there are few controls or censors on the information. Many are filled with inane and critical comments by disgruntled students. You may miss a great professor because of negative comments from students with an axe to grind.

- Websites such as rateyourprofessor.com and pickaprof.com have student reviews of courses and professors, grade distributions of professors, and comparative textbook prices. Use the information with caution. The reviews are raw and uncut and students say anything they wish, including profanity. You can't believe everything. There's no attempt at scientific polling techniques or properly designed questions. Student reaction Websites attract two types of students—those who either love or hate a professor.

How Professors Grade

Some college students fail to understand grading systems used by professors. If you fail to understand the system that evaluates you, it's difficult to plan your study strategy as the semester unfolds. You waste valuable time focusing on courses that you can't improve significantly. This section seeks to get you street-smart on grading systems.

Strategies involving grades are particularly important when courses have multiple grade components. Multiple components are good for students, and you want them, but it makes it more difficult to determine how well you are doing in the course as the semester rolls out. The opposite is when you have only one or two things that determine your final grade. I remember one physics course I took where the course grade was determined by the final exam alone. The grading scheme was simple to understand, but I spent the entire semester stressing. Professors have mixed feelings about courses where the entire grade depends on a single evaluative component. Few students do well under that kind of pressure and everyone has strengths and weaknesses that affect how they perform on different aspects of a course. Some students are good at doing homework problems but perform poorly on a timed test. Other students are good at multiple-choice questions but suck at discussion questions. Some students are great at class projects, and others lack the discipline to work independently. The fairest grading scheme averages over the strengths and weaknesses of each student and includes several types of criteria.

The other side of the coin deals with circumstances in life where a single, great performance separates the mediocre from the great and the men from the boys. It may not be fair, but several things in life depend on high performance in a single, critical situation, such as a marketing pitch to a multimillion dollar client, a life-critical operation for a surgeon, a solo performance for an acting or music student, a key presidential decision, or a football quarterback's performance in the national championship. What college football fan can forget, for example, the 2006 National Championship game between USC and Texas when Vince Young took over the game. It's best for a professor to adjust the grading scheme depending on his students. For undergraduate students, I employ a multiple-criterion grading scheme consisting of tests, homework, labs, projects, and the final exam. For graduate students, my grading system relies more on evaluating high performance over a small number of critical skill tasks. In the professional world, that's where you get the big bucks.

CHANGING YOUR ATTITUDE ABOUT GRADES

Having a good attitude toward grades is nearly as important as the grades themselves. Without a positive attitude about grades, you go through college resenting what many students perceive as an unfair standard. It's funny that the students who do poorly in college are mostly the ones who believe that grades are inequitable. Students who are doing well don't seem to mind grades. Rather than continually fighting with the idea of grades during your college tenure, it's better to accept grades as a necessary part of college life that's not going to change. What I try to show here is that you really want grades.

There has been an evolution in my thinking about grades since college. When I was an undergraduate, I was always asking why I had to play the grade game. Grades seemed to get in the way of my college education. When studying for physics exams, I yearned for questions that tested whether you knew how physics really worked, rather than whether you could do some funky problem with masses and pulleys. I felt chained to learn physics in a particular way to get good grades, and I reasoned that I would have learned better without grades. Then there were all the arguments (as a sophomore) about being in classes with seniors, which to me rendered the grading system unfair because seniors were two years ahead of me, yet we were all graded using the same standards. Or the arguments that some students had more mathematics than me so they had unfair advantages. Or that it didn't seem right that so much should depend on taking timed tests. What did fast thinking have to do with whether you were a good physicist? Was there a clock on Einstein when he discovered the theory of relativity? Or should I say a clock on Einstein in his rest frame of zero acceleration. Sorry, nerd joke. And on and on it went with my list of reasons why grades should be abandoned. Here is the problem with most of these arguments.

GRADES PROVIDE INCENTIVES TO STUDY

Just about all of the thousands of college students I have taught need grades to take learning seriously. Without grades, students would be goofing off for four years. There are very few students who would work hard in college without grades. If you doubt me, poll your college friends. I once had a sociology professor who allowed us to grade ourselves by the honor code based on how hard we worked in his course. Just about everyone gave themselves an A despite the fact that most students blew off the course and used the time to work on other classes. Foreign students know that grades provide motivation. In many Asian countries, there is enormous competition and incredibly high standards. It's a matter of family honor when a child does well in school and has motivation to be successful. Getting into an American university is a high honor. Grades exist in part to force the necessary behavioral changes needed for learning and, in addition, provide the incentives to reinforce the work ethic required to study.

COLLEGE WITHOUT GRADES WOULDN'T PREPARE YOU FOR THE REAL WORLD

Occupations in the real world are based on skill and performance. Our capitalist society revolves around hard work, talent, and achievement. We are graded all the time. Any occupation you can think of is evaluated in some way to justify promotions, raises, and job classifications. Even our personal lives are evaluated. If a guy refuses to treat his girlfriend with respect and acts like a jerk, he gets dumped. Grading is a part of life in the real world and is not going away.

GRADES ENCOURAGE AND SET A STANDARD FOR EXCELLENCE

Would you want a surgeon to operate on you who received a D in biology? Would you want to take physics from me if I got consistently low grades in physics? Would you want to fly in a plane piloted by a man who flunked flight school? Of course not. If grades didn't exist and everyone was judged solely by the fact of being in college rather than what they actually did in college, our capitalistic society based on competition would quickly degenerate into socialism. Truth be told, we need surgeons who excel in biology, get good grades, and pass the mustard in terms of performance in the operating suite. The same is true of all professions. There has to be a standard to judge competence, and grades provide that standard in college courses.

GRADES IDENTIFY AND RECOGNIZE TALENT

It's a fact of life that some people are better at certain things than others. In my case, I have no talent in art. Why should a person who is truly gifted as an artist get the same grade as me in an art course? They ought to get the A's in art and I ought to get the C's and D's. I'm not good at art. A low grade tells me I should consider another vocation for my life. Parents who think that their college student son or daughter should get A's in everything are missing the point of why grades exist in the first place. It's not a realistic viewpoint.

Having discussed the importance and philosophy of grades, we now discuss specific grading systems.

STRAIGHT-SCALE GRADING SYSTEMS

Straight-scale grading systems are familiar to students because they are employed in high school. In a straight-scale system, students are guaranteed certain letter grades on a test, say, if they achieve a certain score. The range of what's considered an A, B, and so on doesn't normally change during the semester. Here is a typical straight-scale system:

A = 90-100%
B = 80-89%
C = 70-79%
D = 60-69%
F < 60%

The same scale that determines your letter grade on individual tests during the semester also determines your final course grade. This means that, if a student accrues ≥ 90% of the total points possible in a course, then that student gets an A. Students like straight-scale systems because they are familiar and easy to understand. They also tend to think they're fairer than other grading systems. In reality, however, there are a number of debatable shortcomings to straight-scale systems in certain types of college courses. Here are three of the issues.

PRODUCE A HIGH NUMBER OF LOW GRADES IN DIFFICULT COURSES

There would be few A's if I graded my freshman physics courses with a straight-scale system. Physics, chemistry, mathematics and other traditionally difficult college courses tend to have relatively low average scores on tests, homework, and exams. The class average score on a typical test in my Dave Letterman Physics course is ~ 55%. Don't freak. Were I to use a straight-scale system, most of my students would get an F in the course. One could argue that students who get a 55% should flunk, but the bar for success is high in science and engineering courses. When a science or engineering professor uses a straight-scale system, he either has to water down the tests or award few high grades. If you find that a professor is flunking a high percentage of students in his course, it's probably because he's using a straight-scale system and tests similar in difficulty to those he had as an undergraduate.

FAVOR UPPERCLASSMEN

A number of factors favor upperclassmen in college work. Straight-scale systems tend to work in favor of older students. When I look back over the grade sheets for my undergraduate courses, had I used a straight-scale system in those courses, my seniors would get the majority of A's. Part of the reason is that professors generally teach to the top of a straight-scale system. They construct tests, so their best students can get > 90%. If they make the test too easy, everyone will get an A or B and there will be little discrimination between students. In science and engineering, professors expect high proficiency in mathematics for success in the class. Who would have the best math background in a typical class? The seniors.

TEND TO LOWER COMPETENCE

As college students have fallen behind over the years, straight-scale professors are prone to dumb down their tests in order to give students higher grades. If we pitched our tests at a level similar to those we had in college, few students would do well in our courses. The situation puts a high demand on the professor who writes the tests. He has to anticipate the likely level of student performance. If a test is too hard, nobody will get an A. If a test is too easy, everyone will get an A. The trick is to write a test where a few of the top students in a course can get an A. This is difficult in a straight-scale system. Professors are not prophets and fortune-tellers.

CURVED-SCALE GRADING SYSTEMS

Undergraduate courses having a wide variety of students benefit from curved-scale grading. The downside is they are harder for students to understand. Let's take an example. Most of my undergraduate courses are graded with a hybrid curved system, so I will use my own system as the model. Here is the grading scheme of my Dave Letterman course, extracted from my syllabus:

Grading: The final grade will be determined by the following scheme.

Exams (Best 3)	45%
Final Exam	30%
Lab	15%
Homework	10%
Total	100%

PHYS 1000 is not graded on an absolute grading system (e.g., 90-100% = A etc) but rather on a relative (curved) system, where performance is compared to other students in the course based on the class average. The class average grade is assigned a C even though it may be lower than 70-79%. After each test I post a scale of scores vs letter grades, so each student knows what a score of say, 68%, on a test means in terms of a letter grade. This enables you to know how you are doing in the course. For the final course grade, I apply the weighting factors above to each grade component, drop your lowest test score, and generate a total raw score for each student that is compared to the class average raw score. The calculation is completely based on numbers, and there is no bias.

Here are some distinctives of curved grading systems.

COMPARES STUDENTS TO STUDENTS

Curved systems don't measure student performance by an absolute standard such as A > 90%. It doesn't matter what your absolute test score turns out to be in a curved system; what matters is how you compare to your peer students, based on the class average. In my system, each grade component is compared to the class average, whether it's tests, homework, labs, or the final. If the class average on the first test in my course is a 60%, the letter grade assigned is a C and not an F as it would be on a straight-scale system. This is both good and bad for students. It's good because a 60% is a C and not an F. It's bad because millennial students are used to a steady diet of 90% or better in their lives and getting a 60% is a blow to their egos.

RELIES ON EXPECTED STATISTICAL GROUPINGS OF STUDENT PERFORMANCE

Statistics is the mathematical discipline that seeks to make order out of the tendencies and/or expected behavior of a large number of test subjects. Statistics wouldn't exist if everything exhibited random behavior. In the case of my physics courses, experience has shown me that student performance on tests is roughly described by a bell curve, assuming that the test is well-constructed. If the test is too easy or too hard, then statistics have little meaning because the test itself drives the outcome rather than the tendencies of a group of students.

An ideal bell curve means that, in a pool containing a large number of students, most students will do work close to the class average (C). Fewer students will do better than the class average and get a B and fewer still will be outstanding and get an A. To the left of the average, some students will get scores below the average and get a D, while fewer students will do poorly and get an F. There is a general bell distribution of scores on a typical test in my course. I don't impose the bell shape; it just works out that way with most classes of students. The bell nature of student performance gives me a basis to determine where my grade lines should be drawn in a curved-scale system. I make a graph of student scores and see how bell-like the distribution looks. Then I determine, usually by percentages, where I should draw my grade lines between A's and B's, B's and C's, and so on.

GIVES AVERAGE STUDENTS A BETTER CHANCE FOR SUCCESS

It may be more psychological than real, but curved-scale grading systems give students who aren't naturally gifted a fighting chance to do well in the course. When students see that they don't always have to get 90-100% to assure an A in the course, the pressure is reduced and students are free to relax and enjoy learning.

Take my final exam. When I tell students I expect the average score to be ~ 60% and to get an A will require > 75%, what formerly looked impossible now seems within reach. I tell my students that they will rarely find a better deal from a professor, because it means that, on a one hundred question final exam with each question counted as one point, a student can miss twenty-five questions and still get an A on my final. That's a pretty good deal.

MINIMIZES THE INFLUENCE OF LABS AND HOMEWORK ON GRADES

Students usually love my grading system once they see that they don't have to achieve the magic ≥ 90% to get an A. But students do recognize some downsides. If you read my syllabus carefully, you find that all grade components are curved. This means that the tests are curved, the homework assignments are curved, the labs are curved, and the final exam is curved. Students don't appreciate the significance of this on their final grade. In a nutshell, students want it both ways. They want the curve to help them when they don't do well on tests but not to hurt them when they bomb tests. But it doesn't work both ways in a curved system.

Poorly performing students expect their lab grade to pick them up. Since the lab counts 20% and students have, say, a 91% lab average, they assume the A in lab will help considerably. Hate to tell you, but probably not in a curved system. Here's the situation. College labs frequently turn out to be little more than cookbook exercises. Show up at the lab, do a few things, answer the lab questions, turn in the lab, and chances are you will get a 90% or better. Nearly everyone gets above 90%. But that's the rub. Everyone gets above 90%. The net effect is near zero in a curved grading system. Do this calculation. Say everyone in a curved system gets the same score for the lab component of the course. That score is the average. Everyone gets it. But it also means it's impossible to tell who is an A student, a B student, and so on. In essence, everyone is an A student. If everyone gets an A in the lab of a curved system, that means the lab has done nothing to discriminate students. The result is that the lab turns out to have no impact on the final grade. It curves out of the grading scheme because students are compared to students in a curved system.

SIX

Managing Student Life

ENJOYING COLLEGE LIFE

If you were to ask a group of accomplished, college-educated people nearing retirement the question "What years of your life did you enjoy the most?" you would find many who answer "my college years." College life is the best. It's so good that institutions are building retirement centers near campuses because they've found that alumni want to come back to the place where life was simple, where learning opportunities were abundant, and where they had many good times.

College life is good because things are relatively uncomplicated. A college student has one primary task, to study. It never gets that simple again. When you graduate and get your job, you are pulled in all kinds of directions by forces that are mostly out of your control. You have a job, which requires you to work at least forty hours per week. Nothing like that in college with our flexible schedules and ten o'clock classes you can skip. There's nothing comparable to summer vacation, Thanksgiving, and Christmas breaks. When holding down a full-time job, you have to work all summer with only a short reprieve of two to three weeks of vacation. You feel hemmed in by the lack of freedom.

Then there are all the things that demand your hard-earned dollars, such as buying a house, with a mortgage; a new car, with monthly payments; car insurance, life insurance, medical insurance, social security, property taxes, and on and on. Solomon observed: "As goods increase, so do those who consume them" (Eccles. 5:11). It's not the cakewalk you expected and, with each step up on the ladder of success, you find yourself increasingly caught by the financial hook. If you're successful in your profession, considerable energy is required to stay on top. Working your way up the corporate ladder takes time, effort, savvy, smarts, luck, and hours of hard work. You feel that more bureaucracies have a piece of you. You long for simplicity, for the end of the endless phone calls, emails, and a cessation of having to make important decisions.

Before you get discouraged, let me tell you about my own case. While I agree that my college years were some of my best, I also feel that each segment of my life has been fruitful, enjoyable, and productive. I wouldn't want to trade any of my years. All of us who are Christians should feel that way if, along each step, we have committed our lives to the Lord. He is our shepherd, our guide, and our Father. God has a plan for each life and, if we obey Him and seek to walk in His ways, the life we live will be the very best for us. We may not see it at the time, but eventually we will see the hand of the Creator weaving the tapestry of our life. Let me illustrate.

One of my fond college memories was my first trip to the West Coast to go to seminary. The decision was difficult and life changing. Getting out of physics to study the Bible for two years made little sense to anybody. I had almost no money, a very old car, and I was moving two thousand miles away to a place I had never visited with no friends. Talk about facing the unknown. While there are many great college memories I could share, I've chosen this one in order to show that you can find always find a silver lining if you look for it. Some memories are memorable because of the hardships and what God is trying to teach you, and life is always good with the Savior in charge.

Start with the trip to the West. It was a comedy act. Picture this. Here I was with my Oldsmobile Cutlass Supreme, pulling a U-Haul trailer loaded with nothing but books and clothes. Everything was going well until I hit Colorado. If you've ever traveled I-70 through Denver, there is a steep, intimidating incline as you go into the Rocky Mountains. For a boy raised on the plains of the Midwest, where hills the size of pimples were mountains, going up, up and away for what seemed like forever was terrifying. As my Cutlass hit the slope, my hands were white-knuckled to the wheel and my eyes as large as saucers. The slope was so steep I had to downshift my automatic from D, then to D1, and then LOW as the Cutlass engine strained. I had never shifted a car into LOW. The reason? Mass and Newton's second law, up close and personal. I needed all the torque I could muster, meaning the car was in LOW, the accelerator was flat on the floor, and my rocket 350 cubes were straining to keep me going at 10 mph. When I made the near-fatal mistake of glancing over my shoulder, it looked like I was in a plane. I prayed, "Lord, get me outta here."

Praise God for the sight of a campsite. I pulled in and breathed for a minute while I considered my options. Either I would have to unload a bunch of nerdy physics books in the middle of nowhere, something I didn't think the deer would appreciate, or risk blowing the engine by going further (how far I didn't know), or Plan C. I decided on Plan C, which meant going back down the mountain to Denver and heading up to Cheyenne, Wyoming where some truckers (on a CB radio I was yelling into) had told me there was a shallower incline. They also told me to be on the lookout for those wonderful amusement park rides called "Runaway Truck Zones." The truckers are probably still laughing at rookie boy from the Midwest trying to take on the Rockies with an Oldsmobile tractor pull.

Well, I made it to about Boise, pulled into a KOA, and set up my tent for the night. I couldn't afford to stay in hotels, so I had a series of campgrounds lined up along the route. I chose them with grocery stores and swimming pools, one of my few luxuries along the way. And, did I mention, no air conditioning in my Cutlass Supreme? Think Civil War sweat box. Most of the trip, I didn't even bother checking in at the KOA desk. I just got out of the car, walked to the pool, and jumped in, sweaty clothes and all. Turns out at this particular KOA there were two biker dudes lounging at the pool with full Harley attire and beards that hadn't been trimmed in months. And there was a duck. The KOA duck. No ordinary duck and nothing like the AFLAC duck. I had noticed this thirty pounder when I pulled into the campground. The way he strutted around, I could tell he owned the place, and it wasn't going to go well if you tried to mess with him. And it wasn't wise, I found out, to be a Harley guy in his swimming pool. So, while I was enjoying a Pop Tart, what do my wondering eyes behold but the duck, doing a thirty yard dash, making a beeline to the pool, mad and honking all the way. The Harley guy was in his pool and the duck was going to kick some butt and take some names. Imagine my mouth falling open as the duck hopped over the chain link fence around the pool, jumped into the water, swam like a laser beam straight toward the offending party, ready to peck the life out of Mr. Harley. I never saw leather move that fast. He couldn't back-peddle fast enough. He started yelling for his buddy…the manager…Jesus…anyone really. He was dangerously close to conversion. The duck dived, got his toe, and started biting and pecking him. The duck went for the vitals. He got there. More screams. Water was everywhere. I laughed for hours.

That was just the start of the fun. The first time I saw Mt. Hood in Oregon, I wasn't certain if it was a real mountain or a Thomas Kinkade mural painted on the horizon. No joke. The convenience store clerk where I stopped must have thought I was on drugs as I asked him "What is that out there?" Later, when I got to Portland, there was finding a place to live and what to do with all the books. Fortunately, Western Conservative Baptist Seminary had a program to place incoming students with a local family, so I proceeded to Tom and Susan Raymond's house in East Portland. We decided that my best bet was to get a tiny apartment in an older neighborhood near the seminary. It cost $170 per month, heat included. If you were in the kitchen, you could rotate your body and touch all the appliances. The oven and the refrigerator could not open at the same time. Then there was the single neighbor lady in the paper-thin walled next-door apartment with a boyfriend who, well, let's just say, seemed to know a lot about the OT book Song of Solomon. Last, I had to buy furniture. One afternoon, Tom Raymond took me over to the Salvation Army Thrift Store in Portland where I chose a bedroom set, couch, chair, blankets, and bedding. Think about that a minute. Do you know how many creepy crawlers must have been living in that bug-infested used mattress? I wonder now what I was thinking, sleeping in a bed with a history that only God knew. But I was thankful for something to sleep on, and frankly, didn't have many options.

My point in this story is that college is full of fond memories and life lessons which are priceless and planned by God for your benefit. There I was, no money, sleeping on a Salvation Army mattress, a million bugs keeping me warm, paying $170 per month for a dive in an old part of town, riding public transit to school, in a town I had never seen, having no friends, and yet, when I look back on it all, it was one of the best parts of my life. What made it best was that it was God's plan for my life. It was exactly what I needed. The adversity turned to glory as I found I could trust God with my life, quite literally. I met the right people, lived in the right neighborhood, made lifetime friends, learned to love Portland, and couldn't have written a better script. I needed to learn how to overcome adversity with humor and patience, face the unknown, and handle the challenges. I needed the confidence. While I didn't have much, I didn't have many responsibilities either. I was there to study theology, do well in school, and that's about it.

Such is the life of a college student. Enjoy it while you can. Study hard but, at the same time, enjoy the football Saturdays, the walks across Campus, the sorority parties, dorm life, the lifetime friendships, the classes, your professors, and the freedom. There is joy in the entire college experience if you maintain a good attitude and put first things first. But keep work and play in balance. Nothing is sadder than to hear students say they can't wait to get out of college so they can "start life" and "make some money." You will be disillusioned. Start living now while you're in college and enjoy each day. Life is short, and the climb is the important thing; the voyage matters more to God than the destination.

CHOOSING A COLLEGE LIVING SITUATION

Every student has to decide where to live during their college years. Living quarters is a big decision for freshman students. It's a big decision for college parents. We talked earlier about how much money millennial students spend on their room in college. Here are the standard choices chosen by most college students:

- On-campus dormitories
- Off-campus housing
- Frat and sorority houses
- Trailer parks
- Townhouses
- Apartments
- Private residences
- Parent's home

And here are a number of creative alternatives:

- Living in a house owned by your parents. When parents plan to send several children to the same college they often buy a house near campus which is usually cheaper than paying rent or room and board for four years.
- Renting a room with an established family who have a large house and want to help a young college student; in many cases, the students live for free in exchange for doing some weekly chores such as grocery shopping, baby, pet, senior citizen, or house sitting.
- Living together with friends or partners to split the rent. Christian students often live in a Christian sorority or fraternity house where members eat, pray, and live together.

In some colleges, freshman students don't have a choice about living arrangements. They are required to live in an on-campus dormitory, fraternity, or sorority for the first year. Let me speak to this for a minute, as new students often wonder why their living choice is made for them.

My take on living in dormitories is that it's a valuable part of the college experience. Everyone needs to see what dorm life is all about. Every college student who has lived in a dorm remembers it. They remember their roommates, whether good or bad, and they remember all the late hours talking all night, studying for hours, drinking scores of cups of coffee, ordering pizzas at 4:00 a.m., the dorm functions and parties, and the warm and dedicated dorm staff. Living in a dorm shows you a small but significant slice of the real world. Talk about an education for sheltered Christian students. You see students in every imaginable situation, from struggling with grades, to dealing with alcohol and drug addictions, to turning their back on God and living in sin. You see students lie to their parents, cheat on tests, take shortcuts in jobs, and drop out of reality. You wonder why some students are in college.

WORKING DURING COLLEGE

Parents and students alike wonder whether students should work during college. There's no one-fit answer. Many millennial students accept part-time work with a consequent lower commitment to schoolwork. That's dangerous. Some majors demand concentrated effort. To work while trying to master a difficult curriculum is asking for trouble. We talked earlier about working and noted that working to maintain a commensurate standard of living to your parents is unrealistic. Here, we examine criteria to help you decide whether or not to work during college.

WORKING AT THE EXPENSE OF ACHIEVEMENT IS RISKY

Working and studying is usually a zero-sum game. A zero-sum game means that when you work more, you study less. Say before getting a job, you spent twenty hours per week studying. In a zero-sum scheme, for a ten hour per week job, you're left with only ten hours for studying. Working students must decide how many hours to work before it negatively impacts your grades. There are a large number of factors that go into the decision, and only you can decide how many work hours are appropriate. Here are some of them:

- Your weekly energy level
- Whether you can get flexible hours
- The difficulty of your courses
- How much you need the money
- How many hours you wish to spend on other aspects of college life
- Whether you think of work as an excuse not to study

A good guideline is to examine your work load during the semester and drop back on your work hours if your academic performance starts to slip. This strategy puts your studies first and your job second. A common problem is when students have an unsympathetic employer who tries to work them to death. This is particularly the case for students who are reliable and competent; a student employee who is dependable is like gold to an employer. When an employer tries to over-schedule you during the semester, you have a right to quit. You're not an indentured servant. It's not worth the small amount of money you make at student labor.

WORKING PROVIDES A GLIMPSE OF THE REAL WORLD

Students think of a college job as merely a paycheck. Nothing wrong with that but if you decide to work during college, you might as well get something out of it that will help you later in life. What should come out of a low-paying college job is to find out about life in the real world. If you're a server at a restaurant, for example, you're exposed to a broad array of people, you see their peculiarities, you learn how to balance an incredible number of plates and glasses, and you learn how to handle irate customers. You get a glimpse of how people work and live, who are not college graduates. You appreciate being in college.

Some background data on college summer jobs. The year 2007 marked the first year that most teenagers in the United States were not working during the summer. According to Labor Department studies,[105] only 48.8% of teens aged sixteen to nineteen were working or looking for work in June 2007. This compares to 51.6% in June 2006 and 60.2% in June 2000. Researchers suggest that finances, competition, and summer school are the major drivers for the trend. Net household worth has risen over the last few years due in part to stock market gains. Parents who have more disposable income are able to sock more money away for their child's college education, which takes the pressure off kids to hold a summer job. Further, there is job competition due to the influx of foreign immigrants who are willing to take many of the lower paying jobs formerly held by teenagers. This reduces the number of jobs going to American teenagers who are looking for work. The last reason for teens bypassing work is summer school. In July 2006, 37.6% of teens from six-teen to nineteen were enrolled in summer school, up from 36.5% a year earlier and more than three times the number of students in summer school two decades ago.[106] What is not mentioned in the study is how many summer school students are there for remedial reasons, such as flunking a course during the regular school year.

GETTING THROUGH COLLEGE IN FOUR YEARS

Parents and students are disappointed to find that it's difficult to get through college in four years. Parents don't like spending more money on their kid's education and students want to get on with life. It's Miller time after four years of stress, tests, assignments, and deferred rewards. On the other hand, some students get so used to the subsidized, cushy, and open-ended college life that they're in no hurry to see it end. They are the professional students. The worse case was a physics student who had been working on his master's degree for about a decade and was still not close to graduating. He attempted to live in the physics building. He told everyone he was a nighthawk who just liked to work late, but we saw him bringing in luggage, girlfriends, and sacks of groceries at all hours. He had a bed and a small stove set up in his student office to avoid paying for an apartment. After our department head kicked him out of his quarters, he moved into his car for about six months until the cold weather got to him. I lost track of him, but I imagine he is working on another degree somewhere.

College administrators are aware of the sluggish graduation rates because they see the statistics and are on the butt end of complaints from both parents and students. According to the U.S. Department of Education, only 45% of students finish college in four years.[107] At AU, the number is 37% (2005). We rank third in the SEC when it comes to getting students out in four years, behind Florida and Georgia. Schools are responding with a variety of creative solutions. The University of Minnesota allows students to take some extra classes for free in order to graduate sooner. There are several reasons why it's taking longer to graduate; the top factors are students who work part-time and transfer students whose credits fail to seamlessly transfer. My advice is to stop kicking yourself if it takes an additional semester or two to finish college. No big deal. Rather than killing yourself to finish, it's better to take another year. The price is not worth the stress.

HANDLING COLLEGE RELATIONSHIPS

When I decided to write this book, I asked my students about "must treat" topics. Near the top of every list was the subject of college relationships. The human relationships we have comprise some of the most challenging aspects of life in general, let alone college. Recently I was teaching a Sunday school class dealing with workplace relationships and one of my class members said "The hardest part of my job is the people; remove them and my job would be ideal." We all can relate on some level to that sentiment.

Given that our lives contain people the question is how to develop fulfilling relationships with them. That is the question of the ages. The Bible is filled with stories as far back as Cain and Abel who failed to find ways to get along. For college students, perhaps the biggest question is how to deal with relationships with the opposite sex. Hardly a week goes by that I don't have a student in my office who is struggling with couple relationships. Here are some of the common problems:

- Handling a breakup with a high school sweetheart
- A partner who can't seem to get the word marriage out of his lips
- Guys who would rather be hunting than with their sweetheart
- A coed who has grown beyond her boyfriend who is not in college
- News of an unwanted pregnancy
- Boredom
- Overbearing and possessive boyfriends
- Gabby and high maintenance girlfriends
- Handling drugs and sex in relationships
- Whether to get married in college or wait until graduation
- Frustration over finding life's partner

Every relationship is unique and there are few blanket solutions to relationship difficulties. Below are a few points of advice for college students, derived from years of teaching singles and college Sunday school classes.

WHEN PARENTS DON'T APPROVE OF WHOM YOU'RE DATING

Most college students eventually date someone outside the bounds of parental acceptance, particularly if you date someone from a different social or ethnic background. Society has largely blurred cultural taboos, but they still exist in many traditional families. Hardly a semester goes by that a female student doesn't tell me that her family is having a major cow with the guy she's dating. It's mainly the fathers. Mothers seem to understand dating across cultural, social, and economic lines more than fathers. Fathers hate to let go of their little girl and don't want to put their daughter in what they perceive as a dangerous situation with the wrong guy. Most parents express a healthy mixture of love and concern with dating partners, but some try to micromanage their college kids. This usually shoves college students away from their parents and the parent-child relationship suffers. Parents especially struggle with the tension between concern and control when their oldest child goes to college. The oldest child breaks the ice and is the guinea pig in most families. When parents disapprove of whom you're dating, it's best to adopt a give-and-take strategy:

- First, remember that your parents changed your dirty diapers and sacrificially gave you everything for eighteen years. They love you and want the best for you. Why would you expect that to suddenly change when you go to college? Parents are genetically programmed to protect their children. They've done it all your life. Allow them time to adjust to your new freedom. Both students and parents undergo a transition when you enter college. Letting go is a learned behavior. There's a transition during which daddy's little girl becomes an independent woman. Give the situation some patience. Your folks were patient with you growing up, and now it's your turn to return the favor.

- Second, try not to pull away from parents during times of conflict. Don't shut them out. Don't spite them by not calling for days. Don't throw a tantrum. How would you like it if someone you loved suddenly told you to get lost? Your parents were there for you long before your current boyfriend, and they will be there for you long after you dump him. It's best to respect your parents for their years of devotion, even if it's difficult some weeks.

- Third, while it's important to listen to your parents regarding the people you date because nobody knows you better and loves you more, it's also time in life for you to make your own decisions, and that includes whom you date. It's now your life. Time to make your own bed. Students need to follow the Bible's advice to respect your parents, and parents need to reread the Bible admonition to "train a child in the way he should go, and when he is old he will not turn from it" (Prov. 22:6). This passage means to give it a rest and turn the kids over to God during their college years. There is disagreement among Christians over whether college students have reached "old" but it's reasonable to think that the critical age is during college. Recognize, however, that not all parents are equally adept at making the transition from parent to adult friend. Help them during this time.

DATING BROADENS YOUR VIEW OF PEOPLE AND YOURSELF

When you date a variety of people in college you learn about yourself. You learn what you like, what you don't like, what kind of partner is good for you, what kind of partner turns you off, what kind of partner turns you on, and you see all kinds of personalities and living situations. You learn to communicate better. You learn to recognize incompatibilities. You see that people are individual and unique. Sometimes, you wonder why Christ died for mankind. As a Christian you are able to examine how people live out their faith and learn about other denominations and ways of worshipping God. A case in point. Since Alabama is at the center of the Bible Belt, some AU students have never met a Catholic, a Mormon, an Episcopalian, or a Greek Orthodox. They are familiar with Baptists,

Methodists, Presbyterians, and the Assembly of God, faiths that North-erners have less exposure to. College broadens your horizons and God uses the experience to build love and respect for others who belong to different denominations. Here is a personal illustration.

When I was a grad student, I went out with a girl who was a graduate of a Christian college. We had a lot in common at first and talked for hours. She was fun and had a great personality. One Sunday afternoon after church, she invited me home to meet her parents who lived in a small rural town in Michigan. We had a delicious home-cooked dinner and good conversation. So far so good. After lunch, however, it was tradition in her family to gather around the piano and sing church hymns. That seemed a little strange to me as a young Christian, but I went along with it. After the songfest her father said it was now time to nap. Nap? Nobody told me about nap. Did I need to leave? Was he serious? Did I need pajamas? An alarm clock? I was ready to get back to campus and study for a couple of Monday tests. Nap was messing with my schedule. But I didn't want to insult her family by begging off, and I didn't have much choice since I rode with them to their home. So, from 3–5 P.M. on Sunday afternoon, we all laid down on rugs in their rustic living room while the whole family (mom, dad, two daughters, and yours truly) "napped" for two hours. They took the verse in the Bible describing Sunday as the day of rest literally. Nothing wrong with napping, mind you, but for me, what an awkward two hours. The worse part was when I got back to the dorm and told my friends about the experience. Bad mistake. I never heard the end of it. They kidded me for months. I found pillows and rugs and notes about when nap time and milk would begin. All joking aside, the more I observed the legalistic way she was raised, it was easy to see that we would never work as a couple. So we parted on good terms and tried to remain friends. Moral of the story—you learn in college that not everyone appreciates naps.

RELATIONSHIPS ARE A MULTIPLE-CHOICE QUESTION WITH ONLY TWO ANSWERS

The single life is binary. There are only two results of the dating process––you either get married or break up. The sooner singles accept this as part of the single life, the better. It means that breaking up is part and parcel of the nonlinear, herky-jerky, and sometimes agonizing process most of us go through trying to find our soul mate. It means that singles should approach breaking-up with civility and responsibility. It means that breaking up should be viewed as a learning process and not an admission of failure. It means that breaking up should be viewed as a healthy and necessary part of learning about yourself and finding out what kind of partner is best for you.

Waiting for Your Divine Appointment

Thoughts of finding your soul mate occupy a big part of the emotional life of college students. The quest to be double is one of our deepest needs. It consumes our life when we're single. Many college students worry that they will never find the right person to share their lives. What to do? Breathe. Most of what people worry about never happens and that's especially true for finding your life's partner. Let me share a helpful observation. You've heard it before. The grass always seems greener on the other side. Married people think singles are having a blast while singles think married people are having a blast. In actual fact, neither is having a blast. Both single and married life is fraught with challenges, problems, hardships, joys, and happiness. The important thing is your attitude. Some singles are single because they can't imagine themselves tied down to one person. Some married people are married because they can't imagine living alone. My advice is to enjoy the place you're currently at. If you're single, enjoy the single life while you have it. You'll never have as much freedom and less responsibility than when you're single. If you're married, enjoy your marriage. Enjoy the person of your dreams and thank God for the privilege to share your life with a compatible partner. We spend so much time lusting for the other side of the fence that we don't enjoy our own plantation. Why pine away with discontent? Enjoy where God has planted you until He uproots you to another pasture.

Christians should find their soul mate by divine appointment. This means to let God bring your life partner to you. He knows what you need and can get the job done. Many singles spend incredible amounts of wasted time pounding the pavement, searching matchmaking Websites, manipulating circumstances to get a date, and generally taking matters into their own hands. They do what I call "spawning an Ishmael." It's better to pray specifically for what you want in a partner and then continue on with life as normal. Eventually the right one will show up.

Waiting, however, doesn't mean you're passive and do nothing. Waiting for a Christian partner is active. Get involved with life, go out with a variety of people, do things with your church group, and don't hide your light under a bushel. As my pastor says during his leadership seminars, "If you have a product and do not advertise it, it's like winking at a girl in the dark." But when dating becomes scheming and your focus becomes more on finding him than finding Him, you're not acting in faith. God is the best person to pick your partner because only He sees your future and knows who is best for you. Let Him do it.

When I suggest this to singles they usually respond by asking "What do I do in the meantime?" My answer is to get ready to meet her. Focus on God and get your life in order. Become a stimulating, interesting, and positive person who is going somewhere in life. Develop your spiritual life in the Lord. Imagine that your special someone is out there right now. Pray for her. Ask God to guide her life and protect her. Nobody wants a partner with tons of baggage. Nobody wants someone who is selfish and unable to give themselves in love and commitment. When your soul mate shows up, you want to be ready. Mature women don't want a boy, they want a man. Mature men don't want a girl, they want a woman. While you're waiting on God to bring the right circumstances together, work on yourself to give your future mate an exciting and mature partner.

Pastor Joel Osteen of Lakewood Church in Houston knows this first-hand. Joel frequently relates the story of how God brought him and his wife Victoria together. Joel needed a new watch battery and happened to stop into a jewelry store to buy a new one. It was there that he met his princess. Think of all the things that had to happen to bring them together. Joel first had to be available. I've often wondered why Joel, who's a good-looking guy and a pastor's kid, wasn't sucked up earlier in his life by one of the available women at Lakewood. It wasn't as though he was isolated and lacked opportunities to meet Christian women. The answer is that nobody else was right for him. Then Joel had to have a watch that needed a battery, just at the right time. He had to stop into the right jewelry store, just at the right time. Victoria had to be waiting the counter, just at the right time. Joel had to get up his nerve to talk to her, just at the right time. A whole series of perfectly coordinated, right time–right place circumstances had to converge to bring Joel and Victoria Osteen together. That's how God works; He delights to surprise us with far better than we can imagine. Joel would be the first to tell you that he probably outkicked his coverage when he found Victoria. It's how you know it's God because it's far too unlikely to be anything else. You can't write it off as coincidence.

A common question from Christian students concerns matchmaking services. If you look for someone on the Web, does it mean you lack faith in God? Obviously, the Bible was written before the invention of the Internet, so there's nothing specific on using Websites to meet people. There are various opinions, but personally, I don't see meeting online as being a whole lot different than other ways couples can hook up, such as set-up and blind dates. There are the same obvious dangers, such as whether the person you're talking to is really truthful, or whether someone will become a cyber stalker, but that risk exists with anyone you meet. Perhaps the biggest drawback to cyber dating is that you eventually have to meet if you want to become more than friends. You could invest a huge amount of time talking online and then, when you finally meet, find there is absolutely no chemistry. It's best to meet each other in person soon.

RESISTING NEGATIVE COLLEGE INFLUENCES

Christian students in a secular university inevitably confront difficult social issues. The college environment is filled with new freedoms to experiment with risky behaviors formerly policed by parents or teachers. While I'm talking mostly about life in a secular university, small liberal arts colleges and even Christian colleges aren't immune to bad influences brought into the school by its students and the culture. Sex, drugs, alcohol, and the culture are the four most dangerous influences that derail a successful college experience. Allow me to begin with generalities before specifics. Most bad influences can be foiled by having (1) deeply held biblical convictions and (2) the maturity and courage to make correct decisions.

FIRM CONVICTIONS TRUMP QUESTIONABLE SITUATIONS

To combat the seductions of college life, it's important to have a bedrock set of values that govern your behavior in questionable situations. Firm convictions are your armor during culture wars. When you have firm convictions, you have an ingrained value system which kicks in when a fellow student, say, offers you the latest new drug on campus; it's much easier to resist peer pressure and not participate in questionable activities. You're less prone to be knocked off your game by an on-the-spot, rash decision that tragically alters your life.

BIBLICAL AND RATIONAL ARGUMENTS

Firm convictions for Christians originate from biblical principles, but God has also given us a brain to think with when faced with moral and social dilemmas on campus. When I was in college, it was the rational arguments that carried more weight than the biblical arguments because I was just starting to learn the Bible. It's best to have both lines of reasoning operating during a values crisis. Christian leaders offer a variety of answers on how to handle sex, drugs, and the culture, much of which can be summed up by "just say no." Fine, but most college students need more than "just say no." They need reasonable arguments to "just say no." While I generally agree with the "just say no" advice, it ignores the complex sociological environment in college and the fact that students need to adopt their own moral compass instead of blindly adopting the ethical system of parents, pastors, or teachers.

When confronted by a values dilemma, it's useful to weigh the outcomes of potential actions. Christians will find that, for most cases involving sex, drugs, alcohol, and the culture, the cons outweigh the pros. Far outweigh. The sheer weight of the cons will help you stay true to your convictions during college. Here are several considerations to help with your list.

WHO'S MAKING THE DECISIONS IN YOUR LIFE?

Resisting negative influences requires wise decisions. We focus here on who **shouldn't** be making your decisions.

Parents

In college, you enter a phase of life where you begin to leave your parents' influence behind and become your own person. It's a healthy transition. Your parents will always be precious to you and desire to play a continuing role in your life. Honor them by including them in your college life. Seek them out for their advice and wisdom. On the other hand, it's your life now and some gentle leaving and cleaving are in order for you to become the person God desires.

Peer Pressure

Peer pressure is a key negative influence. When you yield to peer pressure, you allow someone else to make your decisions for you. You become their puppet. They pull your strings and you respond. Why would you do that? Why let someone who barely knows you, doesn't love you, and doesn't love God, decide your fate in life? But that's what you do when you yield to students who offer you drugs, alcohol, or encourage you to violate Christian convictions. Don't do it. Decide your own path in life rather than leave it to a loser who's trying to manipulate you.

Role Models

Refuse to allow the wrong friends and role models to influence your life. It's obvious to anyone who observes human behavior that people tend to act like the people they hang with. If you choose to hang with pushers, losers, drunks, or cheaters, your mind will be blurred about what is good and acceptable behavior. What was once aberrant will begin to look normal and enticing. It's similar to how cults work. A charismatic cult leader leads people astray by the force of their personality and an offer of prosperity and freedom. The real deal is that cult leaders enslave their people by propaganda and manipulation. If you choose the wrong group of students to associate with in college, you will be at risk of adopting their bad behaviors.

Drugs

How many people do you know whose lives have been messed up by drugs? Too many promising students go down the tubes because of drug addiction. Nobody is immune from the temptation to do drugs. If you think you are, you're fooling yourself. The National Center on Addition and Substance Abuse (CASA) at Columbia University found[108] that nearly half of all American college students abuse drugs or binge drink at least once a month; 22.9% meet the medical definition for drug or alcohol abuse; and 40% said they were binge drinkers, defined as having five drinks for male students at one "drinking occasion" during the last two weeks. The report concludes "We clearly have a drug culture in most of the country's high schools and a significant proportion of the middle schools."[109] My reaction is that you don't need a study to see what is obvious by just observing student behavior. College students know all the issues involving drugs, so I won't bore you by repeating the admonitions, but, for the purposes of this section, what is particularly dangerous about drugs is that they start to make your decisions for you. The drugs determine your life. They decide when you get up, what you spend your money on, how long you study, and how much reality you accept. Drugs create a fantasy world that puts you in bondage and takes you down with the Titanic. The drugs today are so addictive that you can't get off them without major help and upheavals to your life. Why hook yourself on something that you will have to unhook from later after you've blown away some of the best years of your life?

COLLEGE SEX

God made boys and girls and boy and girl body parts. He called it all good in Genesis. He told Adam and Eve to be fruitful and multiply. The Bible is clear that sex is one of God's gifts to humans and should be enjoyed in the right context. God made sex for a couple to renew the oneness of married life, for pleasure, for intimacy, and to bear children. The OT book of Song of

Solomon describes the joy of flirting and romance between a man and woman who are crazy in love with each other. Sex is a wonderful gift of God.

It doesn't take a rocket scientist to see how important sex is to the world. The University of Texas recently surveyed four hundred men and women about why they had sex. They got 237 different answers! The replies ranged from "I was drunk" to "Someone dared me" to "I wanted to feel warm" to "I wanted to feel closer to God" to "I wanted to give someone else a sexually-transmitted disease." Then they asked 1500 college students to rank the answers. The top three were that college students have sex because (1) they were attracted to their partner, (2) they wanted to show affection, and (3) they wanted to have physical pleasure. The study,[110]published in the August 2007 edition of *Archives of Sexual Behavior,* concluded that twenty of the top twenty-five reasons given for having sex were similar for both sexes. The number one reason was "I was attracted to that person." Physical attraction. That's the reason to have sex. My question is, whatever happened to love?

God sees it differently. God draws a sexual line in the sand and says it's wise not to violate it until marriage. That line is intercourse. When the Bible talks in the OT about, say, Abraham knowing Sarah, it means knowing her by intercourse, by having sex. In Scripture, when a couple has intercourse, in the spiritual sense, they become "one." In Genesis, when a couple leaves, cleaves, and becomes one in marriage, what God hath joined together, nobody is supposed to tear asunder. Does that sound like the casual view of sex promoted by society? The culture is saturated with sex and sends the message that it's impossible and quirky if you deny your sexual expression. The biblical mandate, however, is to a different calling and that calling is abstinence. Abstinence is not a dirty word. It's not God denying you something everyone else is doing. It's not God trying to make your life miserable. It's not God spoiling your fun. It's not God restricting your freedom.

The statistics on sexual activity among American college-age students are sobering. According to a study (2007) reported in Public Health Reports, 75% of U.S. teens have premarital sex by age twenty and 58% have it before age 18.[111] The National Center for Health Statistics (2004) reports that well over 90% of adults aged twenty to twenty-nine has had intercourse.[112] Government data shows that nearly a million births in 2004 were to unmarried women nineteen to twenty-nine.[113] It's clear to anyone who has spent time in colleges and universities that having sex is one of the favorite contact sports of college students. It's very difficult to find a virgin college student. But according to Wade Horn, assistant secretary for children and families at the Department of Health and Human Services,[114] the message is, "It's better to wait until you're married to bear or father children. The only 100% effective way of getting there is abstinence."[115]

What about hooking up? Hooking up refers to an ambiguous, no-strings physical encounter between two people, referring to anything from smooching to a euphemism for sex. Hooking up is common on college campuses. Researchers claim that hookups evolved from the free-love days of the sixties. Elizabeth Paul of the College of New Jersey has been studying hookups for years. Her latest work shows that 75% of college students surveyed have had hookups, and about half of those had sex with their hookup partner. She found that less than 25% of hookups turned into a going-together relationship.[116] One professional who sounds a warning on hookups is Merlisa Holmes, co-author of *Girlology: Hang-Ups, Hook-Ups, and Holding Out*. She says that couples in hookups "don't learn to build that emotional intimacy before they get physically intimate. In the long term, [hookups] develop bad relationship habits. They may grow up not knowing how to connect with a partner on an intimate level."[117] Other researchers believe that hooking up is innocent and should be viewed as a way for young people to find a relationship, more like hanging out. It depends on how "hookup" is defined. If you are considering a hookup relationship, there is a book *Unhooked: How Young Women Pursue Sex, Delay Love and Lose at Both*,[118] by Laura Sessions Stepp, a mother who talked to college students at George Washington University about their hookups. You should look at it.

WHY GOD INSISTS ON ABSTINENCE

Instead of thinking of abstinence as a fatal disease, it's rather some of the best advice a loving Father could give you during your college years. Let me explain. Most people presume that the Christian life is a bunch of party-pooping legalistic rules that stifle fun and freedom. It's actually just the opposite. There are in fact very few rules in the Christian life. The ones on the books are for our protection and to prevent us from imprisoning ourselves with mistakes and poor judgment. They are from a loving God looking out for His children. Remember that Christ came to set the captives free, not to put them in bondage by layers of rules. He was always calling out the Pharisees for their abundance of rules, not complimenting them for their rules. The Christian life is about freedom and not bondage. Our sins are what get us into bondage; God is trying to free us from bondage. The Apostle Paul remarks "It is for freedom that Christ has set us free. Stand firm, then, and do not let yourselves be burdened again by a yoke of slavery (Gal. 5:1)."

One creative take on this verse is given by my pastor, Dr. Bill Purvis, who always seems to have a host of terse sayings in his pocket that we've come to call "Purvisisms." "Sin takes you farther than you wanted to go, keeps you longer than you wanted to stay, and costs you more than you wanted to pay." It's hard to improve upon this characterization of sin in a Christian's life. Examine next a few practical arguments against casual sex before marriage. They buttress the biblical mandate for abstinence. The arguments kept me from messing up my life and helped me stay true to the Lord in the midst of the powerful attraction of college sex.

EVEN IN THE BEST OF CIRCUMSTANCES,
PREGNANCY IS A REAL POSSIBILITY

Say your girlfriend is religious about birth control or insists you use a condom. Do you really want to trust your future to a 75¢ piece of rubber that you can buy in a gas station? Not me. And, despite the > 90% success rate of birth control pills, we all know couples who have been on birth control but still got pregnant. It's not foolproof. Do you want to chance those odds with your future? Not me.

COLLEGE COEDS DON'T ALWAYS USE BIRTH CONTROL RESPONSIBLY

Many female college students use birth control casually, either by forgetting to take it, not taking it as prescribed, or not being mature enough to think of the ramifications of being careless with it. Pregnancy is something that happens to someone else. If I ask my female students if they would trust a man to take birth control if a male pill existed, the answer is universally no. But yet we men should trust you? Not me. There's too much at stake.

STDs are Rampant on College Campuses

Beginning in middle school, students are warned about the dangers of sexually transmitted diseases (STD), which are epidemic in our society. Listed here are some STD facts, from the Center for Disease Control:[119]

There are 15.3 million new cases of STDs each year. Human papilloma virus (HPV), which affects twenty million men and women, is the most common STD. Approximately 6.2 million Americans will contract a genital form of HPV every year.

At least 50% of sexually active people will contract HPV at some point in their lives. By age fifty, approximately 80% of sexually active women will have contracted it.

Almost half of all new STD cases occur in men and women ages fifteen to twenty-four.

One out of four sexually active teenagers will contract an STD.

College life is so unsupervised that the opportunity to have sex with multiple partners is a very real option. Why risk exposure to a suite of diseases that can dog you for life? It's not worth the few minutes of sexual pleasure.

Sexual Activity is Hazardous to your Academic Health

College life is stressful enough without adding the stress that comes with college sex. The emotional issues that come with being sexually active, particularly for a Christian, can ruin your academic performance. Most Christian students can't have sex and be peaceful with God simultaneously. The Holy Spirit will convict you, and your conscience will sound a warning bell.

AVOIDING ENCUMBRANCES AND ENTANGLEMENTS

The enemy would like nothing better than to entangle us in his web of lies. You don't have to read very far into the OT to see the entanglements when Christians fail to take God seriously. Adam and Eve would be the first to tell you about consequences. So would Abraham, Sarah, Jacob, Moses, David and Bathsheba, Sampson, Job, Joseph, Jonah, and the children of Israel. All had dire and long-lasting consequences of disobeying God and doing it their way. They were trapped and encumbered. Consider some of the worse-case scenarios involved with having sex in college. Let me speak from the male perspective. Imagine your Christian girlfriend gets pregnant. What happens then? Count the number of bad things in the list, and ask yourself if anything with that many bad consequences is worth the risk:

- First, your girlfriend will be torn about what to do. Does she continue to go to school? Move back home with her parents? Give up her academic and career dreams? She will worry herself sick over the effect of her pregnancy on your relationship. Will you accept it? Reject her? Tell her to get lost? How will she break the news to her parents and church? Her entire world spins out of control.

- Second, if she is like most Christian women, abortion is not an option, which means you, as the guy in the relationship, lose control of the situation because she will have the baby regardless of what you think or how you feel. If she is pro-choice and you are pro-life, she may decide to terminate the pregnancy but still, the decision is out of your hands. Are you ready to live with her decision?

- Third, there are financial concerns. Who's going to pay the medical bills? The hospital stay? The care and nurture of the baby? Do you quit school to find a job? Do you get married? Are you ready to be a father? Are you prepared to support a family for the next twenty years? Are you prepared to leave college because you have to get a job? Are you prepared to give up your dream of being a college graduate? Are you ready to give up your promising career?

These are only some of the hundreds of questions that couples face in exchange for those few minutes of sexual pleasure. Your life is changed in an instant, and you watch helplessly as your future passes before you. Don't short-circuit your college career. Don't settle for less than God's best for your life. Wait until God leads you to the right partner. God will bless your decision, and you will thank Him for the rest of your life. The price of playing sexual dice is too high, and the benefits of waiting are too glorious.

HOW TO HANDLE THE GRAY AREAS

So what do you do as a Christian? If abstinence is on the table and causal sex is off the table, what do you do with a girlfriend or boyfriend? How do you handle the tension about how far to go and when to put on the brakes? What do you need to watch out for when dating?

Many of my Christian students would agree with the abstinence line, meaning no intercourse before marriage. But what about the other lines during dating? Is it okay to smooch on the first date? Okay to spending the night but not have sex? How about getting close to intercourse but stopping? What about traveling with your boyfriend to another city to watch your team play football and staying in a hotel afterward because it's too far to drive back after a night game? How about studying late at your girlfriend's house and falling asleep on her couch? What about parallel dating, going out with several people at once? Are there guidelines which govern the difficult grey relationship areas not explicitly handled in the Scriptures?

As you would expect, there are varying viewpoints on the grey areas. Let me offer a few words of advice from years of living in a college environment. The basic difficulty for Christians is that the Bible offers principles to guide us rather than treating the specifics of every imaginable situation of human behavior. This used to frustrate me, as I prefer more black and white answers, but as I have matured in my Christian life, I see the wisdom of the Bible offering guidelines rather than specifics. Specifics tend to legalism and insult our God-given intelligence by offering oversimplified solutions codified by laws. Legalism shuts off our thinking. When God fails to treat a specific point in Scripture, it's usually because He allows us some leeway to use our best judgment and common sense. We have a brain, and He wants us to use it. Here are some guidelines that have worked for me.

THE STRICTER VIEWPOINT ON DEBATABLE ISSUES WINS

Christian college couples frequently draw their relationship lines at different locations, such as whether it's okay to smooch on the first date. There were a couple of Christian girls in my college youth group, for example, who were very strict, not allowing so much as hand-holding during dating. They wanted to reserve physical contact until they were certain they had met the right one and an engagement ring or marriage certificate was in place. Other devoted Christian young people consider physical contact an essential part of the dating process and would never date anyone who you couldn't kiss or hug until marriage. Who is right? Who is wrong? What do you do when each party has different viewpoints?

A sensible course of action is for the person with the more liberal line to defer to the person with the more conservative line. Say you are okay with getting a hotel room with your girlfriend after a late Saturday night football game in a distant city. Late night football games are common in SEC country since we love our football and frequently go to games in places ranging from Florida to Kentucky. Nothing sinister is involved. You're an honorable Christian male and aren't going to compromise your relationship and sleep together, but it makes more sense not to drive home late at night when you're tired after a long day of tailgating. Besides that, you will be with four to six other friends and roommates in the same room so it's not as if there's no accountability. Your girlfriend, however, who has the stricter line, is not okay with spending the night, even on a platonic basis. It would prick her conscience, cause emotional turmoil, and she believes the Bible advises to avoid the appearance of evil. What should you do?

Defer to her wishes. There's really no other reasonable alternative. She wouldn't be able to live with her conscience, and it would put a strain on your relationship if you forced the issue. If you begin to think that her positions over a variety of relationship issues are ridiculous and unworkable over weeks and months together, those positions may be the basis for deciding she's not the girl for you. But to force your more liberal code of conduct on her will lead to conflicts that neither party needs.

GUYS SHOULD TAKE THE LEAD

Christian women complain that they usually have to be the stronger one in relationships when it comes to sexual issues. They would like the guy to say "no" for a change and assume leadership in the physical part of the relationship. It's difficult to always play the spoiler and watch Christian men abdicate their role as leader. The call is for Christian males to "man up."

Is this biblical? I think so. Men should be the first line for protection and leadership in a Christian relationship. This is not to say that Christian women are totally off the hook, as there is strength in numbers, and both parties should be working to uphold Christian values and help each other when the hormones are raging. But too many guys are missing in action. AWOL.

There are rewards if a Christian guy steps up and takes the lead in the physical part of a relationship. First, it's the biblical model and you are honoring the Lord. Second, it shows your sweetheart you have discipline and will make her life easier. Third, it shows you care about her welfare and not just in satisfying your own fleshly desires. Fourth, it shows her that you value God in your life together. She wants to see you struggle with the issue and undercut your own desires because, when you struggle, you place God in the lead role in your life and show strength of character. Black and white is easy; it's the gray areas that show what kind of Christian man you are.

TALKING SHOULD PRECEDE DOING

Issues between Christian couples are best handled by honest communication. College students and everyone else is thinking about sex, so why not talk about it and figure out how your partner feels about it? How many problems could be avoided if people would just be honest and talk? Talking before doing is recommended by all Christian counselors.

A useful approach is to talk to your partner in "off-line" conversations. These are conversations about situations, events, and hypotheticals that keep things in the third person and away from being taken personally. By talking off-line, you learn how the other person feels in an unthreatening manner because you're not talking about your own relationship. You don't take it personally. You find out what is important to your partner, what she expects, and where she is in her Christian life. An example. After a college party, I saw that my date was upset by the way her roommate's boyfriend had treated her. He was spending a lot of time with his guy friends, leaving her to sit alone. She was a freshman and didn't know many people, so she felt awkward and uncomfortable. Later, we learned that he had been pressuring her to be intimate, and that was the thing that was making my date upset—that He wanted her in the bedroom but neglected her when his guy friends were around. For me and my date, this incident led to a discussion of how a Christian woman should be treated, what she thought about sexual pressure, and what level of disrespect was unacceptable to her. The conversation was about someone else, so we could freely air our feelings and learn about each other without personalizing it to our relationship.

Everyone Struggles with Drawing Lines

Only the most black-and-white Christians who define physical contact of any kind out of their life can claim they don't struggle with physical lines in relationships. In most cases of the Christian life, it's best to avoid the extremes of conduct when few explicit directives are offered in Scripture. Better to fall somewhere in the middle.

Realizing that everyone struggles with intimacy boundaries gives you courage to talk about the subject with mature Christians. You're not the first person who has struggled with youthful hormones and strong sexual feelings. Useful accountability results if you seek the perspective of Christians who are older in the Lord and let them pray for you and become your unconditional friend. Churches are full of wise Christian veterans who would love to share their wisdom with a young college student to avoid messing up their life. Seek them out. They wait for your questions.

Ask your local pastor to identify them, and let your church place you with a wonderful family who will serve as your home away from home.

Drugs, Booze, Cigarettes

AU is located in the heart of the Bible belt and you wouldn't think the unholy trinity of drugs, booze, and cigarettes would show up in our college students. Yet it's amazing as I drive around town to see a large number of our students smoking in their cars.

You've heard the admonishments against drugs, booze, and cigarettes, so I won't bore you by repeating the prohibitions. But know there is another side to the story transmitted by the media, Hollywood, movies, and magazines. The message is that, if celebrities such as Brittany Spears and Paris Hilton can party, smoke, drink, do drugs, and still be successful, then it can't be that bad. They are young, beautiful, rich, and famous. What's the problem? You get the sense that your parents and teachers are fuddy-duddies trying to spoil your fun. Isn't part of the college experience to try the time-honored taboos of campus life?

No, it isn't. In fact, the more thoughtfully you ponder the downsides of drugs, booze, and cigarettes, the more you realize just how stupid and expensive it is to get hooked on them early in life. There are several reasons to steer away from them, particularly if you value a high quality of life.

Addictions Put You in Bondage

Drugs, booze, and cigarettes are enticing at first because everyone seems to be using them at parties. It's like you can't have fun unless you shoot up, sniff, smoke, or get drunk. But it's all hype and peer pressure. Consider the long-term effects of addiction. First, when you are addicted, the vice is driving your decisions. When you can't get going in the morning without a hit of alcohol, the alcohol starts to control your life. It decides when you need to skip class, skip doing homework, and skip life. Drugs work similarly in that they dull your reality, create a false sense of power, and, due to the laws of nature, you can't stay high forever. Crashes from drugs and booze invariably show up. You are a slave to your addiction and spend most of your day thinking about your next fix. You begin orienting your life around buying more. It's a slippery slope.

Studies by the Harvard School of Public Health[120] have shown that 44% of all college students binge drink, defined as five drinks at a sitting for men and four for women. Fraternity and sorority members are the heaviest drinkers. A study by Outside the Classroom[121] (Needham, Massachusetts) showed that college students begin heavy drinking in their first semester at school. Drinking reaches its lowest point when underage drinkers drive and wind up killing someone. Annual alcohol-related deaths among drivers ages sixteen to twenty increased by ~ 12% in 2004 according to James Copple, director of the International Institute for Alcohol Awareness. Steve Schmidt, vice president with the National Alcohol Beverage Control Association remarks that "Underage drinking wasn't always considered a public health crisis as it is today."[122] Legislators around the country have passed 129 bills in 2007 and 166 bills in 2006 to combat underage drinking, according to research by the National Conference of State Legislatures (NCSL). The consensus is that traditional intervention programs to lower teenage drinking are not working. Do you really want a substance to make your decisions? One of the advantages of college life is that, for the first time, you are truly free to determine your path. Why relinquish the very freedom you crave by putting yourself in bondage?

ADDICTIONS ARE EXPENSIVE

Do this calculation. Add up the total costs over a lifetime of doing drugs, booze, or cigarettes. Take the case of cigarettes. Currently, a carton of cheap cigarettes at a convenience store costs ~ $25. Say you are a pack-a-day smoker. Quiz question. How much do you spend on cigarettes over twenty years? Answer: The number is so big you need scientific notation. Then think of all the other, more productive, things you could have bought with the money and how far ahead you would be with your health. What Hollywood is not telling you is that Brad Pitt is going to be old someday and, after a lifetime of vices, is not going to look very handsome. Ever see a lifetime smoker before? They are wrinkled, haggard, cough most of the day, and couldn't run a block. Ever seen pictures of a lung of a lifetime smoker?

It looks like a charred piece of flesh. Is that what you want for yourself? If you think it won't happen to you, you're kidding yourself. Father Time catches up with everybody.

ADDICTIONS SUCK YOU DRY

What starts out as youthful experimentation with drugs and booze can end up to be an existence that sucks you dry and leaves you bewildered as you wonder what happened to your lofty goals. Even prescription drugs are becoming a problem. Using prescription drugs to enhance academic performance is considered widespread by many experts, including Mike Bradley, an adolescent psychologist and author of *The Heart and Soul of the Next Generation*.[123] A trend called "pharm parties" is common in many areas of the country. Pharm parties are where youths gather to chug fistfuls of pharmaceutical drugs.

The Partnership for a Drug-Free America (2005) found that 19% of teens reported taking prescription drugs to boost memory and concentration during tests.[124] The most common drugs are stimulants such as Ritalin or Adderall. Researchers at Kansas State University found that the number of college-age students suffering from depression has nearly doubled from 1989–2001.[125] The Depression Center at the University of Michigan estimates that roughly 15% of college students are depressed.[126] There have been way too many promising students that I've met over the years who dropped out of school due to drugs and booze. What a waste. I can almost spot them in a lecture room. They are hardly ever in class. When they do show up, they are mentally fried and look like a deer in the headlights. The ability to concentrate is out the window.

The sad part is when parents find out their Little Johnny has wasted months of time and money on partying and sleeping in with hangovers. The psychological effects of drugs and booze become easy excuses for avoiding the harsh realities of growing up and having to work for your future. They rob you of your goals and substitute a golden calf of indulgence for reality. It's easier for students to deceive themselves by drugs than to put in the work required for a successful life. Resist it. Reality is too good to miss, especially for Christian students who have the Lord as their

Shepherd. I don't know about you, but I want to be fully aware of all the good things He plans in my life and not be fogged out in an alcohol- or drug-induced stupor.

WHOSE BODY IS IT?

Scripture describes the body of a Christian as a tabernacle of the Holy Spirit. This is an awesome and mysterious biblical fact. During conversion, a number of theological transactions occur; we are saved, justified, reconciled, sanctified, sealed, and adopted. The sealing ministry of the Holy Spirit means that the third person of the Trinity comes to live inside of you in a way that nobody understands but accepts by faith through biblical affirmations. The Spirit seals you as a precious vessel and adopts you into the family of God. Now reason with me. If you are a child of God and your body is shared by the Holy Spirit, doesn't that make it precious? Would you want to grieve the Holy Spirit by taking harmful substances into your body? Our biological machinery is stupendous. Why would you want to tear it down prematurely by abusing yourself with things that harm the most amazing mechanism to come from the hand of the Creator?

SEVEN

Living the Christian Life as a College Student

THE IMPORTANCE OF QUIET TIME

It's easy to neglect God in college. This is a mistake for a Christian student. So much is riding on your college years that you need God more than ever during college. You need daily wisdom, guidance, and strength. You need help in studying for tests, doing assignments, finding good friends, finding a college job, finding a church, and a host of other college-related experiences. You need God's protection from cultural forces that seek to derail your life. It makes no sense, when you are part of God's family, to leave God out of your college life, especially since He is the primary reason you're in college. The adage "Leave with the one who brought you to the dance" applies to your quiet time with God.

The problem with devotions is doing them. All of us in college struggle with the time restrictions in our cluttered lives. We can have the best intentions to guard our quiet time but fail to follow through because school assignments and projects have drop-dead timelines. Devotions can slide right off the end of the day and never get done. What's a student to do? The answer is to develop spiritual discipline and put your quiet time on the same level as other critical tasks in your day, such as work or attending class. If you were a server at Appleby's and were scheduled to work on a given night, you would show up for work because of its importance in your life. You need the money. Why then would you skip out on time with the Lord?

It comes down, as so many things do, to a question of values. What do you consider valuable in your life? If money is important, you won't consider missing work. If your boyfriend is important, you won't go days without seeing him. If your parents are important, you will call them regularly. If learning is important, you will get yourself in the library. Your passions define your path. When we find that our quiet time with God is slipping, we are forced to admit that something has usurped His rightful place. An idol has moved in and is sleeping in our beds. Our quiet time is a measurement of how important we consider God. There are three things that helped me to remain consistent with quiet time in college.

GIVE QUIET TIME THE SAME IMPORTANCE AS OTHER CRITICAL AREAS OF YOUR LIFE

Until you put your quiet time on the same par as other important parts of your life, it will slide right off the end of your day and not get done. Trust me, it's inevitable. In my case, it took a few months of fits and starts before I determined to use force when doing my devotions. By using force, I mean making a commitment with myself that, no matter how long my day was, no matter how many physics problems were due, no matter how tired I was, no matter how many excuses I could conjure up, I would do my devotions before hitting the pillow. It was often at 2:00 A.M. in the morning but, by first making an inviolable rule, I was able to jump-start a regular pattern with my devotional life. Later, the more you spend time with Him, the easier it gets. You end up developing a love for your quiet time, and it becomes an instinctive and vital part of your Christian life. It recharges your emotional and spiritual energy and renews your life. It's a great way to end or start your day. But I had to the start the process by imposing a rigid, disciplined rule in my life until it became habit.

QUIET TIME SHOULD BE CREATIVE

We err in our devotional time by repeating the same things time and again. For many Christians, devotions consist of a daily reading from one of the many fine devotional guides (see Appendix). Problem is, after a steady diet of five-minute readings when you're half-asleep, your devotional life becomes stale, boring, and lifeless. It becomes routine instead of invigorating; a chore rather than a joy. To combat the sameness, be creative with your quiet time. Ask why you are doing devotions in the first place. What's the goal of quiet time?

I'll give you the answer to this one. The major reason for having a quiet time is to maintain and nurture your relationship with the Lord. As you get older in the Lord, you find that the Christian life is more about relationship and less about knowledge. Yes, you want to grow in knowledge of the Lord by reading the Bible and studying books about Christ. Devoted Christians read several Christian books each year and have a schedule of Scripture readings in order to learn more about the Savior. I'm a college professor, so I would never diminish the value of education. But quiet time is also for the personal and relational aspects of your Christian life. It's to grow closer to the Lord and is like spending time with the people you love. If you love someone, you spend time talking, sharing, doing things together, and just hanging out. What precisely you do is secondary; the important thing is that you are together. Most of the times with your boyfriend, for example, it doesn't matter whether you go to a movie or study together, whether you have a Coke at McDonalds or walk through the park. You just enjoy each other's company. You want to be creative in your important relationships because you want to please the other person, see them in different environments, and prevent boredom.

In your quiet time, talk to God, listen to Him, ask for His advice, and seek His will for your life. You'll find that the process renews you and cements your relationship to Him. You don't always have to read something. You don't always have to pray in the strict sense of the word. You don't always have to do it at a specified time. Some of the best quiet times for me in college were simply walking in the woods around my dorm, thinking of God and His Creation. There's always been a special place where I can go to be alone with the Lord; sometimes it was as literal as my clothes closet. The important thing is not what you do, but that you do something to keep it creative and not bored down with legalism. Allow God the time to speak to you in your quiet time in college and the process will become an integral part of your entire life.

BUILDING ACCOUNTABILITY INTO QUIET TIME

One of the best things I did in college was to share my quiet time with my girlfriend or have a trusted friend get on my case if I started to let my devotions slide. When you share your quiet time with a close friend, you build relationships and affirm the importance of spending time with God. It can be as easy as leaving a friendly note on the mirror of your suite mate in the dorm, asking if he did his quiet time that day, or text messaging a new friend in your church group to tell him what you are learning about God. As society becomes more spectator driven and regular church attendance drops, we need the support and help of our Christian brothers and sisters to do the right things for our spiritual growth.

CHOOSING A COLLEGE CHURCH

It's a fear of mine for millennials that you'll miss the important role of a college church in your life. The fear originates from the current trend toward getting all your information from television, computers, and cell phones. You miss something valuable if you depend only on media to get your spiritual food. The value of personal contact, interacting with real people, and benefiting from college ministries will be missed if you only watch church. It's ironic today that, while we're the most connected society ever, we are also the most isolated and alone. God made us for interaction with other Christians in personal, physically close ways. We need the touch of other people, the warmth, the hugs, and the accountability.

My college church set the tone for my entire Christian life. It taught me what was expected from a Christian. A young life in Christ needs mentors to show you the ropes. You find that the Christian life is more about transformation and less about information. Not only did I need to know cognitively about God, but I needed to learn how to live the Christian life after years of nary a thought about the Lord. The favorite event at my college church was the Wednesday night prayer meeting. It was held in the chapel of our church, which was a smaller, more intimate setting than the Sunday morning service. The core Christians of the church attended and Dr. Howard Sudgen, our minister, always gave a biblically relevant message to buoy our spirits in the middle of the week. It was easy to meet people. You felt like you belonged somewhere. It was like a walk in the fresh air. Don't miss being involved in a local church during your college years. Here are some of the things you should look for in a college church.

SOUND BIBLE TEACHING

Students should continue to build their knowledge of God in college. Without a sound background in the Scriptures you are susceptible to being knocked off by your liberal professors and their world of secular ideas. The onslaught of secularism in college requires an effective counterweight to help you keep perspective. It's important to find a church whose pastor and staff emphasizes the primacy of the Scriptures and a love for the Savior. Look for a church with a strong emphasis on Bible teaching. You should be learning something new each week about the Bible, Christ, and how to live the Christian life. If you aren't, that should raise a red flag. We either advance in Christian maturity or fall backward. Nobody stays in neutral.

PASSION BEFORE PROGRAMS

Churches today use polished marketing to attract college students. By offering a free tee shirt to college students in exchange for at a church visit, they try to buy you off with cheap goodies. Resist this when looking for a church. There's nothing wrong with programs that appeal to college students, but when the attraction is free food, free entertainment, a rock band at every function, and a college minister who is more interested in padding his attendance numbers than in serving the Lord, you should be suspicious. Look for a church with passionate, dedicated ministers who serve the Lord with gladness and humility. The best churches sometimes come in small packages. The best pastors are like tough-love teachers who are less interested in entertaining you and more interested in getting you ready for life. Go beyond seeking the most popular programs and largest college groups unless they are grounded in the Word and have great people at the helm.

BALANCED APPROACH TO MINISTRY

The best college churches offer opportunities for students to get involved with the larger community of Christians rather than segregating students to a corner of the church in an isolated college group. True, college students prefer their own brand of music and worship, but you shouldn't feel like a temporary appendage to a church. Churches which are alive need people of all ages to make an effective body of believers. They err when they emphasize one group of believers over another, say, youth and high school over senior citizens. It never works well. All people are God's children, and everybody is special in God's eyes. Churches that promote programs only for college students insult other segments of the church who eventually leave and take their tithes and offerings with them. This leaves the church in financial peril because it's difficult to build a church financially off the backpacks of starving college students. Look for a church that has a diversity of people and programs that encourage interaction throughout the Body.

ESTABLISHED COMMUNITY REPUTATION

You are wise to ask around when looking for a church. You don't have the time to visit every church in your college community. Narrow your choices by allowing informed locals to guide you; for example, ask classmates and friends who have lived in the area. The problem with asking friends, however, is that you often get directed to the largest, most popular college churches, which may not be the best choice for everyone. Many students search for a church by visiting Websites. Nothing wrong with that but, like college catalogues, everything looks good on a Website. It's best to ask a wide variety of people about churches and don't forget your professors who are Christians. It's always a privilege for me to recommend churches in the Auburn community to my freshman students. I am able to assess where they are spiritually and point out the pros and cons of particular churches in order to save them time and frustration. Gather advice and allow the Holy Spirit to lead you to the right church.

FLEXIBILITY REGARDING DENOMINATIONS

Church labels are blurring with time, and it's useful to consider a range of denominations when you're in college. This means that, say, if you were raised in a Methodist church, you might consider trying both Methodist and Baptist churches in your college town to see what fits your style. Take the case of my current church, Cascade Hills Church in Columbus, Georgia. It used to be called Cascade Hills Baptist Church, but our pastor, whose passion is saving souls, dropped the Baptist label a few years ago because he thought it turned off people who would never otherwise darken the doors of a church.

Teaching elective Sunday school classes for years at a wide variety of Atlanta churches taught me to highlight the similarities, rather than the differences, between conservative protestant congregations in the South. Yes, there are some doctrinal differences, but a warm Christian spirit pervades many Baptist, Methodist, Presbyterian, and Assembly of God churches in this part of the country. The major difference is the style of the worship service. It's difficult to generalize, but Presbyterians tend toward traditional services at one end of the spectrum. Assembly of God churches, at the other end, emphasize celebration of the Christian life with music and an emphasis on the Holy Spirit. Baptist and Methodist services are in the middle with a variety of contemporary and traditional choices. It's worth keeping your options open, and let God lead you. While I look with respect at my Catholic background and enjoy the serenity and beauty of a large Catholic cathedral, I am no longer comfortable in a Catholic service because of the doctrinal differences. But I love my Catholic friends and still watch EWTN occasionally.

Community churches are especially in vogue today. Community churches are Christian churches that choose not to formally affiliate with a denomination. A good example is North Point Community Church in North Atlanta, pastored by Andy Stanley. Andy started out as a pastor at First Baptist Atlanta with his father, Dr. Charles Stanley, but then left to start his own church. North Point Community is now one of the largest churches in the South. It's thoroughly evangelical in doctrine but claims no denominational label. The point is to broaden your church choices in college. Just because your daddy went to a Baptist church doesn't mean you have to go to a Baptist church. It's your life, and you should begin to take control of your own Christian experience. The other side of the equation is to be respectful and grateful to your parent's church if you happen to choose a different denomination (or none) in college. The reason it's now important to you to find a local body of believers is because your parents loved you enough to take you to their local church.

RESIST CHURCH HOPPING

When I was teaching a large singles class at First Baptist Atlanta, it always amazed me how many singles would hop from church to church, spending a few weeks at one church, then going to another church for a few weeks, and so on. This was due primarily to singles wanting to be double. Revolving door visits to several churches exposed them to a bigger number of potential partners. But consider what you lose by uprooting your church allegiance every few weeks. It all comes down to what's a higher priority to you—finding a mate or building spiritual maturity. Here are some of the downsides to church hopping:

- First, you never feel connected to anything.
- Second, there is minimal accountability to other believers.
- Third, what does church hopping say about your faith in God to bring you the right partner?
- Fourth, church hopping is selfish because it says that "I don't really care about the church or its members. I just want to meet someone."
- Fifth, say the bottom drops out of your life. You don't have a support group to help you if you constantly switch churches.

My advice is to develop a short list of church possibilities, visit them, and then choose one. Refuse to church hop. It's a principle of Scripture that if you put God at the head of your life, He will give you the desires of your heart, and that includes your soul mate. God needs you to serve in a local body and not just suck off the hospitality of churches and hard-working pastors. Your lowly college or singles Sunday school teacher needs your support too because, when one-third of your class rotates in and out of church every few weeks, it's difficult to build a class that nurtures your Christian life. Help your Sunday school teacher to help you by sticking with a church once you have made the rounds.

Being a Christian Witness on the Secular Campus

No two Christians are made the same, and not all Christian students are made for a Christian college. It depends on where God leads you. Since this book is focused on Christian students who are led to study on large university campuses, it's helpful to discuss effective ways to live the Christian life in the midst of the secular world.

There's Hardly a Better Mission Field

People often ask me whether I prefer secular over Christian colleges. The answer is easy. For me, there's nothing like being a Christian on a secular campus. Nothing wrong with Christian colleges, but they weren't for me on a permanent basis. I was made to be a Christian in a secular university. But don't read too much into my particular case. All God's children are different. One person's plum is another person's prune. You have to live out your own dream and not adopt someone else's.

One of the challenges of being a Christian on a secular campus is that you're right where the need is great and people are searching for truth. You feel a bit like Jesus who would rather spend His time with the people who needed Him most than with the professional Jewish religious establishment. You get to rub noses with some of the best minds on the planet and mentor young minds that need role models. You feel like you're making a difference.

Being Street-Smart about Secular Culture

One of the challenges of being a Christian on a secular campus is that not all is rosy in the secular academic environment. You're surrounded by liberal and power hungry educators who wield politically-correct dogma. You have to tread lightly, exercise caution, and watch your back. You have to work hard as well as smart. Christian professors are particularly vulnerable before tenure. You have to choose your battles wisely and have a balanced picture of what is kosher in a public institution. Because many Christian college students will end up working in the secular world, it's useful to share some observations on how to maneuver outside of the Body of Christ.

Take the issue of tenure. Tenure is the highest professional achievement in a professor's career. It refers to lifetime job security in an academic organization, meaning the university has bought into your performance as a professor and intends to secure your services for life. To navigate the choppy waters of tenure as a Christian in a secular culture, my strategy was to employ a goal-oriented approach, modeled after the Powell Doctrine. The Powell Doctrine was the strategy followed by Colin Powell when he was our army general during Gulf War I. It says that the best way to defeat an enemy is to apply overwhelming force. Give adversaries no reason to doubt the outcome of a battle with the United States. Overwhelm them with such firepower that they are finished before the fighting starts.

The Powell Doctrine in my situation meant to attack the issue of tenure with performance. It meant not only being better than my peer professors around the country, but much better—to present a case for tenure so overwhelming that my faculty colleagues would have no reason to vote against my package. It meant to make their decision easy by being an outstanding professor and valued colleague who happened to be a Christian. The Powell Doctrine is what women had to employ to break through the glass ceiling in businesses that were historically dominated by men. They had to work harder, longer, and smarter than their male counterparts. It may not have been fair, but it was the deck you were dealt. Don't choose to tap on the glass ceiling if you're not up to the task. The Powell Doctrine meant for me first, to publish more research papers in leading journals than comparable faculty members, and second to be the one of the top teaching professors at AU. Turns out that I probably didn't need to invoke the Powell Doctrine since my faculty colleagues at AU are reasoned and professional colleagues who themselves hail from a wide variety of religious backgrounds, but you don't know that about secular organizations up front. You may also opt to apply the Powell Doctrine when you get your job in the secular world, at least until you get into a stronger political situation within your organization.

COMMITTING TO HIGH PROFESSIONAL STANDARDS

For Christians who work in the secular world, it's imperative to be professional in your occupation. Few work colleagues will buy your Christianity unless they first see you as a hard-working, talented, and valued employee. In my case, to get my faculty friends to objectively embrace the gospel, I first had to be an outstanding physicist. Few of my scientist friends will listen to my life of faith unless I first get their respect, and I get their respect by being outstanding in my field and by living an ethical life before them. The world is convinced more by our lives than our arguments and that also applies to highly educated people who face the same maladies common to everyone. It's rare that I lead anybody to the Lord by my best teleological arguments for the existence of God. It's more likely that I lead them to the Lord by the quality of my life. This is why, earlier in the book, I reported my surprise that more Christian students aren't better college students. Christian students should be our most outstanding college students. They should be taking the bulk of the world's summa cum laude honors and moving on to be the movers and shakers in society. The Body of Christ needs our Christian students to step up to the plate and take your place in our world; without this, the slide toward secularism and humanism hastens. It's often been said that the world is one generation away from losing Christianity. You begin to believe it when you see Christians giving away the store in our nation due to our lack of excellence.

PLAYING BY THE WORLD'S STANDARDS

When Christians make their home in the world, it often brings conflict as we seek to balance our Christian values with the demands of secular society. The world does not strum to the same Christian guitar as we do. They have different standards; often, higher standards; often, much higher standards than many Christians are willing to pay. The standards may deal with power, money, fame, and fortune, rather than truth, integrity, and honesty, but to say that the world has no standards or low standards is wrong. There are phenomenally accomplished people in the secular world. When you take a job, say, at a Fortune 500 company such as Hewlett-Packard or Smith Barney or Northrup Grumman, it's often the case that, unless you commit to the pace of that world, you will be left in the dust professionally. This means you have to decide what sacrifices you are willing to make to be successful in the secular world. You have to ask "at what price?"

To provide balance, it has helped me to choose outstanding Christians who work in the secular world and adopt them as role models. Some of us will choose athletes, politicians, presidents, civil rights leaders, pastors, celebrities, authors, surgeons, professors, writers, singers, or movie stars. One of my role models is Condoleeza Rice, Secretary of State in the Bush II administration. Dr. Rice was required to sacrifice many things due to the incredibly high standards of the job and the compromises required to be effective. A Secretary of State who is also a Christian won't be able to get to church twice on Sunday and for prayer meeting on Wednesday; she probably won't be able to lead a Sunday school group; she won't be allowed the freedom to pray in public; and she won't be able to push her denominational beliefs onto a pluralistic and multicultural society. She has to represent Joe Q. Public and watch out for all American citizens, whether they are Christian, Muslim, Catholic, Jewish, or atheists. Her Christian convictions must be tempered by wisdom and experience in the public square. A persistent fine line is walked when a Christian serves in the secular world.

It's similar when a Christian college student moves and breathes in a secular university community. To succeed in the world of college academics, you have to adopt the standards set by that world, which often collide with the priorities of your Christian worldview. Let's take a specific. Say you have a goal to get straight A's in a demanding major such as architecture. Then say you also want to get to church three times per week. It's doubtful you can do both successfully; translated, it means you're forced to choose what's more important. We're back to the priority question. Many Christian students had it drilled into them that you have to put God first by pounding the church pavement whenever the doors are open. I'm not so sure. That is more legalism than I'm comfortable with and ignores the reasons God led you to college in the first place. Christian students too often tend to make it an either/or proposition rather than opting for the middle ground. To me, it's better to have the best of both worlds rather than choosing one over another. This means that, if you're going to college to get an education, God will understand it when you can't get to every church service. He will understand when you can't attend two Bible studies during the week. He will understand it when you have to postpone an outreach ministry activity to study for an important test. If leading people to Christ depends in part on being an outstanding leader in your field, then He won't object too strongly when you choose to be that outstanding leader by doing well in your college studies.

The trick, of course, is to balance all your balls in the air. The balancing act is accomplished by doing the best you can in a given week with the range of responsibilities on your plate. Then let it go. Don't allow others or yourself to give you a guilt trip when you're merely trying to walk the path God has chosen for you. If you believe God led you to college, it's doubtful He led you there to second guess every decision that involves getting good grades and being successful. Christ didn't spend His earthly ministry operating in only one sphere of activity, say praying to the Father. He diversified his ministry by successfully moving in several, diverse directions. Christ had lots of balls in the air; He worked in parallel. Take your Bible and start to list the number of activities Christ was involved with in his short three-year ministry:

- He spent time resisting Satan.
- He spent time teaching the apostles.
- He had an incredibly busy itinerary with travel throughout the Middle East.
- He took on the Roman and Jewish religious authorities.

- He did considerable one-on-one ministry to individuals.
- He performed miracles.
- He continually prayed to the Father.

The list quickly gets large. We are not Christ, but the division of labor in His life shows that you can effectively operate in the secular world as a Christian and still hold your Christianity near and dear. Doing poorly or flunking out of college because you think you have to be in church all the time only shoots yourself in the foot of the fantastic future God has planned for you. You can be an effective witness on the college campus by first being an effective student who happens to also be a Christian. The secular world needs to see that Christians can be outstanding and highly successful in their chosen fields.

RENDERING TO CAESAR WHAT IS CAESAR'S

The secular world requires that you play by their rules. Jesus talked about playing by society's rules in His famous "render unto Caesar" answer in Matthew 22:21 when asked by the Pharisees about paying taxes. Paul also played by secular rules when he quoted Roman legal precedent to save himself from being roughed up by the Roman authorities (Acts 16:37). He asked why he was in jail when he was a Roman citizen. The actions of Christ and the Apostle Paul admit there are times when it's prudent to work within the world system.

Christians err when they act as though everything in the secular world is terrible and godless. Although Christ refers to Satan as the ruler of this world, much of the world's democratic legal and ethical principles are based on Judeo-Christian values of equality and justice. Not all secular rules are thoroughly secular. It's possible for Christians to avoid falling in love with the world system and yet be an effective citizen and contributing member of society. Many of the great figures of the Bible such as Joseph and Moses were educated in the laws and ethics of secular society yet were stellar men of God. Most of the great leaders in our history did not attend a Christian college. There is a difference between playing by the rules of society and getting sucked into the world's cesspools.

Here is an illustration of a college situation where you have to cooperate with society's standards to achieve your goals. It's about one of my former grad students. I will call him Brian. Brian failed our Ph.D. comprehensive exams in physics and ended up having to terminate his physics career at the M.S. level. He subsequently transferred to engineering and received his Ph.D. in mechanical engineering, so the story ends on a high note, but his first love was physics and it was unfortunate for him to miss his ultimate goal. Let me tell you more about his story. Brian was a committed Christian. He was older than the average grad student since he had been a secondary science teacher for a couple of years before returning to college. He was married, and he and his wife decided that they didn't want to wait until after college to start their family. So they decided to move forward and had three kids over a six-year span while he was a graduate student. Brian strongly believed in setting the right tone for his young family by leaving work at 5:00 P.M. and spending the night with his family. He hardly ever missed prayer meeting or church and taught a weekly Bible study at his house. Brian was the ideal family man and husband who put his family and faith first in life. I admired him for being so steadfast.

Problem is, to become a professional physicist, you can't be successful by leaving work at 5:00 P.M. and then spending the night with your family. Physics is not even close to a forty hour per week occupation. Secular standards of performance demand that physics professionals put in at least sixty hours a week. You work a forty hour week in the lab doing experiments and then spend your nights writing up your results, preparing talks, writing papers, working on new courses, and preparing research proposals. A physics career consumes most of your life. Professional careers generally consume most of your life. Don't go there unless you are prepared to make the sacrifice. While you have to admire Brian for his devotion to faith and family, things which truly matter, you have to fault him for thinking that he could become a Ph.D. level physicist by not putting in the hours. The moral is to avoid choosing demanding professional careers if you aren't willing to accept the prevailing secular standards.

Rendering to Caesar reduces to a Romans 14 issue. Romans 14:4 says not to judge each other. Each person has different motivations, drives, and priorities. Each individual decides what is important and walks in different shoes. Each person is at a different place in life. Each person treads a unique path through life. No one Christian can point his finger at another and say his priorities are wrong. There are no dogmatic judgments except by God Himself. That being said, it's important for Christians who serve in the secular world to walk with their eyes wide open and understand the sacrifices necessary to compete with secular counterparts who are willing to work the sixty hours a week needed for high achievement in their fields. The same is true for college students. Each Christian student needs to weigh what sacrifices they are willing to make against the Christian priorities in their life. This is done through time on your knees in prayer. One person can remain close to God throughout the week by simply pondering the Lord and praying between classes and during devotions. Another person needs a more regimented schedule of Wednesday night and Sunday church services. The question of how much to render to Caesar is a highly individual decision and never an easy one. You will have trouble with it throughout your life.

VALUABLE CHRISTIAN COLLEGE MINISTRIES

There is a buffet of Christian ministries available during your college years. The problem is not that there aren't ministries; it's carving out the time to participate. Most of my Christian students get involved at the local church level or hook up with one or more of the on-campus college life groups. Virtually every denomination has a college ministry near universities. At AU, there is the Baptist Student Union, the Neumann Center for Catholic students, and even a local chapter of Athletes-in-Action (AIA) that sponsors teams of Christian jocks who travel around at the start of the basketball season and scrimmage NCAA level teams. The AIA athletes come back out onto the court during halftime and offer testimonies of their Christian faith to the crowd. Even our football team has its own minister who leads prayers after the game at the fifty yard line and works with college-level athletes. One of our AU students, Shaemun Webster, started the group GANG, which stands for God's Anointed Next Generation, which seeks to provide students with encouragement through Facebook in God's Word during college. GANG members post prayer requests and testimonies on the group's cyberspace. They get together in worship services on Sunday night at the AU Chapel. At a large university, you can find what you want.

DOING VOLUNTEER WORK IN COLLEGE

Just about every year I'm asked to evaluate the admission packages of college students as they apply for graduate, medical, dental, law, or nursing school. Most students have a list of community service activities as long as your arm. My first reaction is "oh, really?" When you ask why so many activities, after hemming and hawing for a few minutes, students' straight answer is that "It looks good to admissions committees." Then you find that "volunteer work at a child cancer ward at East Alabama Medical Center" translates to a half-hour tour as part of a class project in sociology. You begin to wonder if students do anything divorced from self-promotion. Many students are visiting senior centers or helping in hospital rehab clinics not out of love of service, but rather to pad a resume. It's like the purpose of community service is to get a material reward such as admission to a top-of-the-line graduate school.

But true service is selfless. You look first to help others and not to get something for yourself. If you can get past the payoff viewpoint of service, one of the most rewarding things you can do during your college years is to help others through volunteer work. Volunteer service is good for college students because college life is largely selfish and you need some balance. Being selfish is not necessarily your fault but comes with the territory. Student life is busy with many overlapping demands. You have to learn to say no to a lot of tertiary things while bearing down on getting a degree. To be single-minded on your academic goals is, by nature, selfish since you have to focus on your goals, your grades, your life, and your challenges. As Christians, we feel conflicted about this, but self-interest is a fact of college life.

The problem with a busy college schedule is that you can become too selfish, which makes you one-dimensional and causes you to lose perspective on what is important. You focus on the trees but miss the forest. You get so caught-up in busy activities that you forget that God has given you your college years as a vital preparatory period in which to serve Him.

Volunteer work is a wonderful way to get out of yourself, to do something different, to serve someone, and to serve the Lord. In the process, you are the one who gets a reward.

There is good news. According to the Corporation for National and Community Service,[127] about 3.3 million college students volunteered in 2005, up more than 20% from 2002. That's 30% of students. College students have a long history of performing volunteer work. There are several creative ways you can volunteer. Your church is a direct route. Every local church has tasks that need people. The old saying is true that, in a typical church, 10% of the people do 90% of the work. Churches always need volunteer help. In my current church, the staff is desperate for people to step up and help in kid's church and the nursery. The sports ministry needs umpires and coaches for church league baseball. The TV ministry at Cascade Hills needs cameramen, people to work the sound board, and volunteers to use software to create presentations and brochures for the *Real Time* Ministry. Rather than merely coming to church on Sunday morning, college students can get involved and, in the process, feel that you have a home away from home.

Most college ministries run events that are ideal for volunteer work. One of my favorite college group activities was to travel to Chicago once a year to serve at Pacific Garden Mission,[128] a ministry for street people and home of the long-running radio program *Unshackled*. We usually helped the Mission in the soup kitchen, worked to stock the pantry, answered phones, sorted clothes donations, and ministered to street people. We were rewarded by seeing how the other half lived and returned home thanking the Lord for a clean bed, a shower, and air conditioning. College groups at AU traveled to Louisiana after Hurricane Katrina to help clean up communities and rebuild housing. A number of student organizations volunteer for Camp Smile-a-Mile, a nearby camp that serves children who have cancer. You can't take the little hand of one of the precious and brave bald kids who are fighting cancer there and come away the same. The list is endless. There is more to life than the next test, the next assignment, and the final exam. Remember this proverb: If you hold back, you lack; but if you give, you live.

WHAT TO DO WHEN THE BOTTOM FALLS OUT

Last week Alabama experienced a series of violent storm cells. Deadly tornados ripped through several southern counties and Enterprise High School, a large school in Enterprise, Alabama, absorbed a direct hit. The school was reduced to rubble and several high school students were killed. One of the victims was the girlfriend of one of our AU baseball players who was a student in my PHYS 1150 Astronomy class. Words cannot express the grief he feels. In one tragic brushstroke of nature, gone are the hopes, dreams, and aspirations of a promising young couple. Gone is the joy of their courtship, gone is the promise of an upcoming marriage, gone is the blissful future of sharing their lives together. Not only her life, but the lives of all who loved her were forever changed in one moment of time. Those of us who have lost a loved one in a tragic accident know how difficult it is to deal with the empty spot in our hearts that can never be filled short of heaven. We struggle to cope with the loss and are left wondering where God was and why He allowed the tragedy. We question God's integrity. We ask whether God is a good God. It's a test of our faith and trust in God's wisdom.

A few years ago one of my best student friends got a call out of nowhere with the news that her boyfriend had committed suicide. There were no precursors, no hints of a problem, no signs he was going to kill himself. No way to get ready for the tragic news. They were like Ken and Barbie. She was beautiful, intelligent, supportive, the perfect partner. He came from a stable, God-fearing home and was the son of a pastor. Yet he checked out in a tragic moment of desperation. Suddenly and without warning he was gone. Think of the shock, bewilderment, and guilt she felt as she rehearsed every minute of her life with him, searching for answers and wondering if it had anything to do with her.

Life is full of tragedies and hard knocks. College is when you start to see this with clarity. During high school you are insulated by your youth and your parents from seeing the seamier sides of real life. But college life is different. There's a reality check as you begin to experience life's inevitable appointments with hardships. You begin to notice the aging of your family, you see your grandparents' failing health, you read about people you know found dead in their apartment after a drug overdose, and you see some of your high school friends settling for mediocrity and abandoning their goals. The first time I saw a dead body was when I was in college during the funeral of my grandmother. The realization of life outside the safe bubble of your parent's home offers a strange dichotomy to college students because most students think of themselves as ageless. That's why college life is filled with dangerous and reckless behaviors. College students don't see themselves as mortal. Life is all ahead of you, and what you do now doesn't seem to have much effect on your life. I don't think I seriously realized that life is short until I was about thirty. That's when you start to think "Oh my gosh, one-third of my life is over; I better get on with doing the things I truly want to do while I can."

What do you do as a college student when the bottom falls out of your life? If you were my friend whose boyfriend committed suicide, or the baseball player who lost his soul mate in a storm, what would you do? How do you cope? What do you do about school? Can you continue to maintain your focus when dealing with a tragic, unforeseen event that occurs during your college years? It's that question I hope to answer in this section by offering advice and encouragement to college students when they hit a large speed bump in the road of life. The answers are both practical and spiritual. Two of the hats you wear as a Christian college professor are those of counselor and pastor. After a few years, if you love your students, you hear nearly every story, experience nearly every tragedy, and hold the hand of countless students as they go through their valley experience. Every good teacher realizes the high calling and privilege to help guide our students through the difficult areas of life. First, the spiritual advice.

CLING TO YOUR FAITH THAT GOD IS GOOD

As a Christian, we have a shelter to run to during the storms of life. That shelter is the Lord Jesus Christ. When you find yourself facing tragedy, run to Him. Get alone and cry out to Him. He is our strength and our shepherd when the storms of life rage against our boat. It's difficult for me to imagine facing life's tragedies without Him. When I hypothetically ponder the absence of Christ in my life, I sink to my knees in grateful thanks that God brought people into my life who led me to Christ. Running to God when our valley is deep is exactly what a relationship in Christ is all about—to let your loving Father take you in His arms and tell you that everything will be all right because He is in control. We may not understand all the whys of the tragedies in life; those are questions that greater thinkers that us have pondered, but when we can't trace His hand, we trust His heart.

It helps to view God as a good God during a valley experience. A good God has our best interests at heart. He tailors the experiences of our life to suit the path He has prescribed for us. If you truly believe that God is good, then when He chooses to take a loved one before we think He should, or when our friends get a debilitating disease, or when we find out our dad is an alcoholic, or when our reputation is ruined by vicious rumors, or when we get that call in the middle of the night that says an accident has occurred, then it's because He sees things in His infinite vision that we can't see with our finite eyes. I often think back to one of my astronomy lectures where I talk about the electromagnetic spectrum. The electromagnetic spectrum refers to all the radiation that exists in the physical universe. It includes radio and infrared wavelengths, the visible spectrum of colors we see with our naked eye, and the high energy, short wavelength radiation such as ultraviolet, X-, and gamma rays. Radiation is how God transmits information in the universe. The point is, if you lay out the entire electromagnetic spectrum on a linear scale of, say, a mile, the portion we see with our naked eye only amounts to a few inches. Most of the universe is cloaked and invisible to the rods and cones in our human eyes and impossible for us to see. There's a lot happening in the universe we cannot see and are unaware of because we lack the correct eyes to see it. Astronomers are very familiar with the experience of looking up into the heavens, thinking that they see nothing in particular, but when they put an ultraviolet detector in their telescopes, entire galaxies are suddenly visible because most of the radiation they emit is in the ultraviolet portion of the spectrum.

The same is true for the God we serve. He sees the entire spectrum of our lives. We see only the visible part of the spectrum, the few inches. He sees the full mile. God is able to see all of our life and is the perfect one to providentially care for us. We couldn't have it better. The One who loves us and created us is the same One who carefully crafts our life. When I find that I'm struggling with the whys of life, I look up at the stars and remember that He is Lord and only He sees the full picture. When my friend dies in a tragic car accident that seems to make no sense, I consider that God saw something ahead for him that I didn't, that perhaps he needed to be spared from by taking him home early. When I see one of my Sunday school members getting canned unfairly by an uncaring company after twenty years of faithful service, I consider that God has a better job for him with a Christian employer who has been praying for God to send him someone. I think of all the possibilities, all the different ways that God can use someone or some tragic incident to glorify Him, and know I have considered only the few inches of light God allows us to see with our human eyes. That helps to comfort me.

Some Questions in Life Will Never be Answered

God never says He will answer all our questions in life. He rather asks us to trust His heart. The pages of the Bible are filled with stories of people who went through unspeakable horrors and trials with little explanation. The early Christian martyrs were impaled alive on poles and then set on fire to make human streetlights approaching the Emperor's castle. They did nothing to deserve their fate other than to loyally worship the one true God. Think of Job, who went through hell to prove that one man could be faithful to God when everything near and dear was taken from him, all without knowledge of the prior conversation between God and Satan (Job 1:6–12). Joseph was unfairly left to die in a well and then sold into slavery in Egypt (Gen. 37:19–28). It took most of his life to figure out why God allowed the tragedy and hardship in his life. He was one of the lucky ones. Many people never receive an adequate explanation or are permitted a broad perspective about why things happen in life. Virtually everyone has something that they are frustrated about involving the actions or inactions of God.

But He understands. He understands when we lash out at Him when we're frustrated and lack perspective. He understands when we think we have to forgive Him. He understands when the pitiful clay cannot comprehend the potter's master plan. He knows when we're in anguish and crying ourselves to sleep on our pillow. We can never hide anything from Him. In my Sunday school classes, I'm frequently asked how I visualize the omniscience of God. Omniscience means that it's impossible to conceive a question He can't answer. Think of the most subtle mystery of nature, the most difficult mathematical equation, or the most puzzling quagmire men find themselves facing, and God always has an answer. I often walk through the campus at AU and try to think of a question that could stump God. I think, "Okay, God, can you tell me what the 1,389,539,201th atom in my brain is doing at the moment? He says, "no problem." Or I say, "Can you tell me where all the insects in the earth are located at a given time?" He says, "no problem." Or I ask if He can explain to me how a thought in my brain gets to my vocal cords and then how the vocal cords know how to form the complex series of vibrations needed to form the sound wave that goes out of my mouth as an intelligible sentence. Or I ask if He knows where all the animals around the world sleep at night. Or I ask if he knows what I was thinking on January 17, 2003 at 2:07 P.M.? The answer is always yes for our omniscient God. There is nothing God does not know. He knows every atom in our frame and knew us before we were a twinkle in our parent's minds. He can answer every question about us. Nothing is beyond His control or scrutiny.

But while God knows everything, He doesn't choose to tell us everything. This used to bring me grief as a young Christian. It was like God was playing an irresponsible and not-so-funny game of cat and mouse with mankind. Why not just tell us what we want to know? Why all the guessing games? Why all the hiding? If you really love us, why keep things from us? Do you really love us?

Part of the answer why God doesn't bear His soul to us is that He is infinitely wise as well as omniscient. It's the difference between knowledge and wisdom. While God knows everything it's often not the loving and wise thing to answer all the questions of His children. Think of your earthly parents, who often withheld good and perfectly normal things from you because you weren't ready to handle them yet. There is a right and best time for certain pieces of knowledge. Consider, for example, the barrage of questions that small children ask their parents about how babies are born. Would it be prudent for parents to get out the Anatomy Coloring Book that details the male and female reproductive system? But yet that's what we expect God to do when our life questions arise. We expect Him to get out a flowchart and demand to know what is happening. Then we follow up by demanding an explanation of why we think He failed to act.

Only in rare cases do God's children get such detailed explanations. God's higher priority is that we grow in faith, and faith is not built on detailed explanations. In fact, faith has very little to do with explanations at all. Do you need to know all the details involving the cohesive inter-molecular forces between the atoms in wood to believe that a wooden chair will hold you up when you sit down? If you do, you may be waiting forever, because physicists struggle with the interactions between **two** atoms, let alone the billions and billions in a chair seat. When you think about it, explanations require little or no faith.

Further, it's often true that the most loving thing God can do is to not tell us everything. Would you want to know your future if the curtains of time could be lifted by a time machine, prophet, or fortune-teller? My answer is no. That would be cheating, like sneaking into your parent's closet before Christmas to find what they bought you. It takes all the fun and anticipation out of Christmas. Would you really want to know how you will die or who you will marry or what trials you will experience in life? That's asking for trouble. Think of the untold hours of worry and alternate planning if you knew your future. God wants to spare us such unending concerns by concealing some of His plan for us. He delights in surprising us with good things. So rather than questioning His motives for allowing hardship, it's better that we don't know what He chooses in His wisdom to keep to Himself. Put another way, I often wonder whether the tree of knowledge of good and evil chosen by Adam and Eve in Genesis was worth plunging mankind into sin and separation from God. It was not. We should learn from our first parents and not let our curiosity become a stumbling block to our happiness. It's best to leave some things with God. He will answer our questions when He thinks we are ready to hear the answer. Until then, we should thank Him for remaining silent when we desperately seek answers. It's the most loving course of action He can take.

DON'T WASTE YOUR VALLEY EXPERIENCE

The Bible says that it's not the hardships themselves that make the difference in life, but rather how you respond to the hardships. Ask any pastor and he will tell you that there are a common set of maladies men experience in their brief lives on the planet. I have problems, you have problems, and all God's people have problems. Two women lose their husbands after a half century of marriage. One woman reacts by cursing God for taking her loved one. The other woman recognizes that few people are lucky enough to find a good husband and thanks God for fifty years of marital bliss. One man responds with ire and wrath after losing his job with the same company after decades of faithful service. Another man sees the loss of his job as an open door to try something new that he was thinking about anyway. One student thinks that he is stuck with a dull, ineffective calculus professor who would just as soon flunk him as look at him, while another student sees it as an opportunity to learn calculus on his own and, in the process, gain confidence in his ability to learn.

Attitude is everything when dealing with hardships. We all have a choice to make when our valley experience shows up. We can kick and scream or try to see something positive in it. The valley is there either way. Why not choose to learn something about yourself and about God as you work through the valley? Consider a general principle, observed in both the spiritual and natural worlds. Nature rarely wastes anything. Everything is used for some part of the Creation. The bird that falls to the earth in death becomes the food a vulture needs for life. The water we regularly flush down the toilet ends up back in the atmosphere to be used again. God wastes nothing in our life. He uses every circumstance to accomplish His goals, which is to grow us up to Christian maturity. He uses our trials to break us into obedience and motivate us to a higher plane of relationship with Him. It's best, but not always easy, to cooperate with His plan for your life and not waste the lessons He is trying to teach.

LIFE ON EARTH IS ONLY A BLIP ON THE SCALE OF ETERNITY

When you face tragedy for the first time, cushion the blow with a renewed view of eternity. Most college students are too young to have seriously considered questions of time and eternity. Heaven is still too far into the future. But that's the point. Heaven is closer than you think and, when you lose someone, the reality suddenly crashes into your life. Mortality is just around the corner for all of us. Solomon was precisely correct when he likened our lives on earth to a vapor which is here for one instant and then gone the next.

There is comforting and inescapable logic to follow when you lose a loved one during your college years. They just beat you to heaven by a few years. You will see each other again soon and the reunion will be indescribably sweet. In the meantime, they would want you to get on with your life and live each day to the hilt. They of all people realize that life is short—that each day is a precious gift from the Lord that you never get back. Time is a commodity you can't store up or conserve. You use it or you lose it. All we can do is to make wise choices on how we spend it. The choices you make with your time hold the key to successful living.

Allow me one final analogy from science, this one involving time. The goal is to show you how long eternity will be compared to our brief span on earth. Physicists of all people know time. We deal daily with incredibly short and incredibly long times. When an electron interacts with another electron in an atom, the interaction takes place over a unit of time called a picosecond (one millionth millionth of a second). Light radiated from distant galaxies can travel for billions of years before reaching Earth.

Start with the speed of light. It's incredibly fast, 186,000 miles per second or 3×10^8 meters/sec. Light travels faster than anything. The fastest rocket in our space arsenal (the space shuttle) tops out at a measly 18,000 miles/hour, slightly greater than the escape velocity needed to attain low earth orbit. The space shuttle is traveling at turtle speed compared to the speed of light. If a commercial jet was able to travel at the speed of light, it would go around the Earth ~ seven times in a second. At the speed of light, it would take you 1.2 seconds to get to the Moon and 8.3 minutes to travel to the Sun. When we see the Sun, we are seeing it as it was in history, 8.3 minutes ago; if it blew up during the next second, we would have 8.3 minutes to evacuate Earth. Good luck.

The nearest star is Alpha Centauri. Instead of saying that the Sun is ninety-three million miles away it's easier to call this an astronomical unit, written 1 A.U. To get about one-fourth of the way to Alpha Centauri you would have to travel 95,300 A.U. That will get you to **one** light-year. Going the entire 4.3 light-years to Alpha Centauri takes four times as much time, and that's the distance to the **nearest** star. In our home galaxy, called the Milky Way, the average distance between stars is ~ five light-years. There are two hundred billion stars in our galaxy, and the distance across the Milky Way is a hundred thousand light-years. This means that a spacecraft going at the fastest possible speed would take a hundred thousand years to travel across the Galaxy. And we are only one galaxy. Astronomers barely have large enough calculators to estimate the number of galaxies in the observable universe. Pick the largest number you can think of and the number of galaxies is larger. Added to that, the average distance between galaxies is ~ two million light-years. This scale analysis is what the Psalmist meant when he said "We serve an awesome God." The grandeur of our universe is barely fathomable to even the brightest human minds. The scales of time and distance are so incredible that it's beyond reason to think that a Creator wasn't behind it all.

The point is this. Amidst all this time and space, the time scale of a human lifetime pales by comparison. The few years of separation when a loved one is taken early is **nothing** when set against eternity. True, the pain we feel is real when a loved one dies. Nobody can deny that. Nobody wants to be separated for even a few years. We struggle against the separation and miss our loved one every day. That's how love works. The relatively brief separation, however, is rewarded by billions and billions of years that we will share in eternity. Short of the second coming, any sane person would rather have it this way than the other way around. God gets it in the right order. He shows His love for His children by rescuing us for eternity at the Cross.

Now for the main practical thing to do when tragedy strikes.

TELL SOMEONE IN AUTHORITY AT YOUR COLLEGE WHAT HAPPENED

The biggest mistake students make when the bottom falls out of their life during college is not to tell someone. Students who try to deal with bigger-than-life problems by themselves usually end up making everything worse. They fall behind in classes, neglect homework, and skip tests while trying to deal with the crisis. Unless you are an unusually stable student, or are having a cakewalk of a semester, or have a large support system, dealing with serious emotional valleys while simultaneously trying to survive a hectic college semester is nearly impossible.

Nearly every month a student comes to me with gushing excuses and apologies for doing poorly in my class due to personal issues. I've kept a record over the last year of the things students have dealt with:

- A heart-wrenching breakup with a high school sweetheart
- A divorce in the family
- A girlfriend entering rehab for drug abuse
- The student himself entering rehab for drug abuse
- An unplanned pregnancy
- Deaths of family members and significant others
- A sick parent who requires help at home with the family business
- Depression
- Rejection from a highly-sought graduate or professional school
- Worries over contracting a STD
- Worries over flunking out or going on academic probation
- Students who absolutely can't stand college and want to get a job

Each person has a threshold when emotionally-charged situations become debilitating roadblocks that negatively affect your college performance. One person needs a few days to deal with an emotional crisis and other people need weeks or months. There are no rules. My point is that, if you are having a semester from hell and the emotional issues are so overpowering that you simply cannot focus on your schoolwork, talk to someone. Don't keep it to yourself.

Try this. Walk over to Student Services on your campus and ask to talk to a counselor. Tell them what happened and how it has affected your school performance. If you have supportive parents, have them call your college and talk to Student Services. You will be surprised at the empathetic and supportive reaction. The professional counselors at AU are happy to come to your aid, either by offering creative suggestions, by letting your professors know about your mishap, or by cutting you some slack. Depending on the severity of your situation, they may suggest that you cut back on your credit load temporarily by dropping your most demanding course. Sometimes they suggest talking to a counselor who can guide you through your difficult situation. Even if your crisis occurs deep into the semester after the official course drop date, most rules can be bent or broken in a university during a crisis. It makes no sense to take an F in your courses when you can talk to someone and at least drop out of courses. In case you're wondering, there's nothing wrong with withdrawing for a semester; it's smart if the issues are serious and unavoidable.

If you're in a fraternity or sorority, your fellow pledges will offer a supportive helping hand during a crisis. Our AU sororities send care packages, cards, notes, and food to grieving students. They lend practical assistance by helping you keep up with homework assignments during absences, doing your laundry, and stopping by to check on you. Counseling staffs at colleges frequently use local pastors to take care of grieving students. It may be best for you to drop out of college for a semester in order to preserve your sanity, regain your emotional balance, and conserve your GPA. There are a host of gifted and trained caregivers around colleges who are ready to deal with your emergency with experience and professionalism. Use them. Take the case of the student I mentioned who lost his girlfriend in Enterprise. The day after the tornado, an academic counselor in our Athletics Department sent me an email letting me know what happened and whether I could show some leniency as far as assignments and tests while he spent time at home. I was glad to help.

Being honest about personal problems goes a long way. College officials are so used to students trying to scam us that when a student comes to us with an honest issue we are happy to help. It's not a sign of weakness, and we don't think you're trying to make excuses if you honestly let us know what you're going through. We appreciate the forthrightness and courage. If you are shy about seeing a counselor, at least encourage your parents to phone us and describe the events. You will be pleasantly surprised that your professors are human and empathetic.

Postscript

EVERYONE BELIEVES IN SOMETHING. The wealthy man believes in his money. The athlete believes in his muscles. The actor believes in his training. The professor believes in his intellect. The gambler believes in the odds. Suicide bombers believe in martyrdom. Since everyone believes in something, you might as well make it something that will produce good in your life. Follow this argument. If you don't believe in God, and you're wrong, you make the worse mistake of your life because there are eternal ramifications that the Bible clearly teaches. If you believe in God, on the other hand, and you're wrong, the worse that can happen is that you're wrong. In the meantime, you've lived life abundantly, with peace, joy, contentment, and excitement. You have a destiny. The Christian life is high adventure and you don't want to miss it. I'd rather be wrong than eternally mistaken.

Say I gave you the assignment of trying to come up with a philosophy of life better than living the Christian life. You won't succeed. Living life as God suggests is genius. Consider what God does for you when you accept Him by faith as Savior. You are adopted into His family. You become one of His children. He becomes your shepherd, guide, advocate, and best friend. He carries you through every step of your life. He sends His Holy Spirit to indwell, seal, protect, and teach you. He is always available, always ready to provide wisdom, always ready to lend a shoulder to cry on, with strong arms to carry you. He loves you unconditionally and gives you eternal life in heaven. He took a bullet for you on the Cross. He is omniscient, omnipotent, and omnipresent and is precisely the Being you want to play these roles in your life. You can't imagine a better plan or a better God.

The Christian life is the best way to live even if we are all wrong about it. And the chances that we are wrong about it is slim due to the sheer weight of historical evidence for Christ and the persistent impact of Jesus in the lives of millions of people over centuries of human history. There are too many instances of sincere and intelligent people whose lives Christ has changed to chalk off as mere coincidence, wishful thinking, or the weak-minded delusions of needy people.

In case some of you in the millennial generation haven't heard it, I can think of no better way to end this book than to leave you with the thoughts of Phillips Brooks, a nineteenth century preacher, who gave us these dramatic reflections on Christ and His impact on world history.[129] Read reflectively.

He was born in an obscure village, the child of a peasant woman. He grew up in another obscure village. He worked in a carpenter's shop until he was thirty, and then for three years He was an itinerant preacher. He never wrote a book. He never held an office. He never owned a home. He never had a family. He never went to college. He never traveled two hundred miles from the place where He was born. He never did one of the things that usually accompany greatness. He had no credentials but Himself. He had nothing to do with the world except the power of His divine manhood. While still a young man, the tide of popular opinion turned against Him. He was turned over to His enemies. He was nailed on a cross between two thieves. His executioners gambled for the only piece of property He had on earth while He was dying—His coat. When He was dead, He was taken down and laid in a borrowed grave through the pity of a friend. And on the third day He arose from the dead. Nineteen centuries have come and gone, and today He is the centerpiece of the human race and the leader of the column of progress. I am far within the mark when I say that all the armies that ever marched, and all the navies that ever were built, and all the parliaments that ever sat, and all the kings that ever reigned put together have not affected the life of man on earth as powerfully as has that one solitary life. The explanation? He is the Son of God, the risen Savior.

History is littered with people who put their faith in money, power, position, friends, intellect, and themselves. The Bible says that all objects of faith short of Christ fall flat, not only in this life, but the life to come. Solomon, in the OT book of Ecclesiastes, asks whether you've ever seen a hearse towing a U-Haul trailer. Do the golden artifacts found in King Tut's tomb look like they've been used in the afterlife? Are all the billions amassed by Bill Gates going to be taken with him? Does all the fame and fortune of Hollywood actors really matter after they're gone?

Secular students ask me what you give up to become a Christian. Only things like bitterness, resentment, sin, jealously, anxiety, worry, concern, and allegiance to a world system that's finite and perishing. What you get is so much more. Jesus came to our planet to offer restoration for your life, hope for your future, and a reason to live. In your college studies, if you are on the fence of faith, reconsider the claims of Christianity and realize during your investigation, as I did, that Christianity is the most scrutinized, studied, verified, and vindicated faith system ever conceived, largely because it was invented by a God who loves you and has a wonderful plan for your life.

APPENDIX I

CHRISTIAN COLLEGES

There are over four thousand degree-granting higher education institutions in the United States About 1,600 of them are private, nonprofit schools and about nine hundred describe themselves as "religiously affiliated." The Council for Christian Colleges and Universities (CCCU) has qualified 105 as "intentionally Christ-centered institutions" according to specific criteria listed in their Website (www.cccu.org). Use this Website if you're interested in small Christian colleges.

Appendix II

Building a Collegiate Christian Library

Christian college students should start a small library of biblical resources during your undergraduate years. You don't need many. My college library had three core areas—devotionals, references, and books on practical Christian living. Christian Book Distributors (www.christianbook.com) is an excellent source for Christian books, although I support my local Christian book store for purchases of easy-to-find titles. Here's a few recommendations to get you started:

Devotional Guides

- *Our Daily Bread,* Radio Bible Class, Grand Rapids, MI 49555
- *In Touch Magazine,* P.O. Box 7900, Atlanta, GA 30357

Commentaries and Theologies

- Warren Wiersbe, *The Bible Exposition Commentary* (Colorado Springs: Cook, 2003)
- Josh McDowell, *Evidence that Demands a Verdict* (Nashville: Thomas Nelson, 1972)
- C. C. Ryrie, *Basic Theology* (Wheaton: Victor Books, 1986)

Practical Christian Living

- Charles Swindoll, *Growing Deep in the Christian Life* (Colorado Springs: Multnomah Press, 1986)
- Charles F. Stanley, *In Step with God: Understanding His Ways and Plans for Your Life* (Nashville: Thomas Nelson, 2008)

REFERENCES

1. Patrick Welsh, "For Once, Blame the Students," *USA Today,* Mar. 8, 2006, A-11.
2. Interview in *USA Today,* Apr. 28, 2004, A-13.
3. Brian Gallagher, "Teach, Study, Experiment," *USA Today,* Oct. 14, 2005, A-22.
4. G. Toppo and A. DeBarros, "Reality Weighs Down Dreams of College," *USA Today,* Feb. 8, 2005, A-1.
5. Gallagher, "Teach, Study, Experiment," A-22.
6. Brian Gallagher, "Not Ready for College," *USA Today,* Mar. 2, 2006, A-10.
7. J. D. Baer, A. L. Cook, and S. Baldi, "The Literacy of America's College Students," *American Institutes for Research,* Jan. 2006, (www.air.org).
8. "Rising Above the Gathering Storm: Energizing and Employing America for a Brighter Economic Future," *National Academy of Sciences,* Washington, D.C., 2007 (http://www.nap.edu).
9. Dan Vergano, "U.S. Could Fall Behind in Global 'Brain Race,'" *USA Today,* Feb. 9, 2006, D-2.
10. National Geographic-Roper Public Affairs 2006 Geographic Literacy Study.
11. Stephen Prothero, Religious Literacy: *What Every American Needs to Know— And Doesn't* (New York: Harper Collins, 2007).
12. Stephen Ohlemacher (AP), "College Degree Worth Extra $23,000 a Year," *MSN Encarta,* Nov. 27, 2006, http://encarta.msn.com. Data from U.S. Census Bureau.
13. Olivia Crosby and Roger Moncarz, "The Job Outlook for People who Don't Have a Bachelor's Degree," *MSN Encarta,* Nov. 27, 2006, http://encarta.msn.com. Data from U.S. Census Bureau.
14. Colleen Maxwell, "Community College," *The State News,* Michigan State University, June 11, 2007, 1.
15. Richard Florida, "A Search for Jobs in Some of the Wrong Places," *USA Today,* Feb. 13, 2006, A-11.
16. Liz Szabo, "Rage of the Green-Eyed Monster," *USA Today,* Feb. 7, 2007, D-7.
17. Mary Beth Marklein, "A Detour for College Fast Track?" *USA Today,* Mar. 21, 2006, D-1.
18. Ibid., D-2.
19. Ibid., D-1.
20. Ibid., D-1.
21. Patrick Welsh, "Watering Down 'Advanced Classes,'" *USA Today,* Mar. 8, 2005, A-21.
22. Rick Garlick and Kyle Langley, "Reaching Gen Y on Both Sides of the Cash

Register," Mays Business School, Texas A&M University, Center for Retailing Studies, Vol. 18, No. 2, 2007, 1.

23. Neil Howe and William Strauss, *Millennials Rising* (New York: Vintage Books, 2000).

24. C. H. Sommers, "Enough Already with Kid Gloves," *USA Today,* June 1, 2005, A-11.

25. Laura E. Berk, *Awakening Children's Minds: How Parents and Teachers Can Make a Difference* (New York: Oxford University Press, 2001).

26. Chip Jones, "Dear Job Applicant, No Parents Please," *Opelika-Auburn News,* May 14, 2007, 6B.

27. Sharon Jayson, "The 'Millennials' Come of Age," *USA Today,* June 29, 2006, D-2.

28. S. G. Niederhaus and J. L. Graham, "Back to the Nest," *USA Today,* Feb. 7, 2007 and L. Gordon and S. Shaffer, *Mom, Can I Move Back in With You: A Survival Guide for Parents of Twentysomethings* (New York: Tarcher, 2004).

29. Sharon Jayson, "Generation Y's Goal? Wealth and Fame," *USA Today,* Jan. 10, 2007, D-1 and "Gen Nexters Say Getting Rich is Their Generation's Top Goal," *Pew Research Center* (http://pewreseach.org/databank/dailynumber/?NumberID=239).

30. Allan Bloom, *The Closing of the American Mind: How Higher Education Has Failed Democracy and Impoverished the Souls of Today's Students* (New York: Simon & Schuster, 1987).

31. Victor B. Saenz and Douglas S. Barrera, "Findings from the 2005 College Student Survey (CSS): National Aggregates," (Los Angeles: Higher Education Research Institute, 2007). Also Sharon Jayson, "The Goal: Wealth and Fame," *USA Today,* Jan. 10, 2007, D-2.

32. News Release, "Spending on Back to College Shoots Past $34 Billion," National Retail Federation, 325 7st Street, NW, Suite 1100, Washington, DC 20004 (www.nrf.com/content/press/release2005/btc0805.htm) and Mindy Fetterman, "Costly College Prerequisite: Decorator Dorm," *USA Today,* Aug. 4, 2006, B-1.

33. Jayson, "The 'Millennials' Come of Age," D-2.

34. Teenage Research Unlimited, 707 Skokie Blvd., Northbrook, IL 60062 (www.teenresearch.com).

35. Jean M. Twenge, Generation Me (New York: Free Press, 2006). See also Sharon Jayson, "Are Social Norms Steadily Unraveling?" *USA Today,* Apr. 13, 2006, D-4.

36. Ibid., D-4.

37. Ibid., D-4.

38. Ibid., D-4.
39. Brian Gallagher, "As Boys Slip Behind, Some Feminists Reject Helping Them," *USA Today*, Apr. 24, 2006, A-17.
40. Ibid., A-17.
41. Brian Gallagher, "When it Comes to Your Sons, Schools Miss the Mark," *USA Today*, June 15, 2007, A-24.
42. Mary Beth Marklein, "College Gender Gap Widens: 57% are Women," *USA Today*, Oct. 20, 2005, A-2.
43. Mike Snider, "iPods Knock Over Beer Mugs," *USA Today*, June 8, 2006, D-9.
44. Sharon Jayson, "Totally Wireless on Campus," *USA Today*, Oct. 3, 2006, D-2.
45. Ibid., D-2.
46. Ibid., D-2.
47. Ibid., D-2.
48. Ibid., D-2.
49. Rachel Abramowitz, "Media Options Swamp Nation; 2 Months a Year Spent Watching TV," *Chicago Tribune*, Jan. 1, 2007, 1.
50. Heather Powell, "New Study Shows Students Addicted to TV," *Auburn Plainsman*, Mar. 23, 2006, B6.
51. Vicki Courtney, *Logged On and Tuned Out: A Non-Techie's Guide to Parenting a Tech-Savvy Generation* (Nashville: B&H Publishing Group, 2007).
52. Justin Pope (AP), "Grades Creep Up, Challenging Colleges to Tell Applicants Apart," *Opelika-Auburn News*, Nov. 19, 2006, D-8.
53. Ibid., D-8.
54. Ibid., D-8.
55. Brian Gallagher, "The Graduate, 2005," *USA Today*, June 3, 2005, A-14.
56. Justin Pope (AP), "Grades Creep Up, Challenging Colleges to Tell Applicants Apart," D-8.
57. Brian Gallagher, "What High Schoolers Need: Cheat Sheet on Universities," *USA Today*, Feb. 22, 2006, A-10.
58. Across the USA, *USA Today*, Sept. 20, 2006, A-11.
59. Brian Gallagher, "Wanted: College Counselors," *USA Today*, May 2, 2006, A-12.
60. G. Jeffrey MacDonald, "Christian Colleges Rebound," *USA Today*, Dec. 14, 2005, D-1.
61. Ibid., D-1.
62. Naomi Schaefer Riley, *God on the Quad: How Religious Colleges and the Missionary Generation are Changing America* (New York: St. Martin's Press, 2005).

63. Pat Ordovensky, "A Visit May Avert Mismatch—Tour the Campus Before You Commit, Experts Say," *USA Today*, Oct. 29, 1998, D-10.

64. Ibid., D-10.

65. MacDonald, "Christian Colleges Rebound," D-1.

66. Mead Gruver, "Districts Giving Students Cars, Trucks for Going to School," *USA Today*, Dec. 1, 2006, A-2.

67. Greg Toppo, "Kid's Good Grades Pay Off—Literally," *USA Today*, Jan. 28, 2008, A-3.

68. Gruver, "Districts Giving Students Cars, Trucks for Going to School," A-2.

69. Mary Beth Marklein, "Schoolteachers, Professors Differ on What's Important," *USA Today*, Apr. 10, 2007, D-11.

70. Michael D. Lemonick, "The Flavor of Memories," *Time,* Jan. 29, 2007, 102.

71. P. Steel, "The Nature of Procrastination: A Meta-Analytic and Theoretical Review of Quintessential Self-Regulatory Failure," *Psychological Bulletin,* Vol. 133(1), Jan. 2007, 65.

72. Seth Borenstein (AP), "Study is a Put Off: Scientists Research Why Procrastination is Getting Worse," *USA Today*, Jan. 12, 2007, A-8. See also W. J. Knaus and J. W. Edgerly, *Do It Now! Break the Procrastination Habit* (New York: Wiley & Sons, 1997).

73. Charles R. Swindoll, "So You Want to Be Like Christ" (W Publishing Group, 2005).

74. Tom Weir, "Time to Tango for Manning," *USA Today*, Feb. 2, 2007, C-2.

75. *Schaum's Outline Series* (New York: McGraw-Hill Book Company).

76. Tali Yahalom, "Time for Students to Go to Bed," *USA Today*, Sept. 17, 2007, D-7.

77. Weir, "Time to Tango for Manning," C-2.

78. Press Release, "U.S. Job Satisfaction Declines," *The Conference Board,* Feb. 23, 2007 (www.conference-board.org).

79. Laura Vanderkam, "You Don't Have to Hate Your First Job," *USA Today*, May 29, 2007, A-11.

80. Ibid., A-11.

81. Ibid., A-11.

82. Mike Szvetitz, "AU's Marsh to Step Down After '07 Season," *Opelika-Auburn News*, Oct. 19, 2006, 2B.

83. Brian Gallagher, "Too Much, Too Soon," USA Today, May 18, 2007, A-17.

84. Pam Belluck, "And For Perfect Attendance, Johnny Gets …a Car," *The New York Times,* Feb. 5, 2006.

85. Brian Gallagher, "Outdated Attendance Laws Hinder Anti-Dropout Efforts,"

86. Greg Toppo, "Big City Schools Struggle," *USA Today*, June 21, 2006, A-1.

87. Nancy Zuckerbrod, "1 in 10 Schools are 'Dropout Factories,'" from Yahoo News, Oct. 29, 2007 (http://news.yahoo.com/s/ap/2007/ap_on_re_us/dropout_factories).

88. National Center for Educational Statistics, "Dropout Rates in the United States: 2005," NCES 2007-059, June 2007.

89. Brian Gallagher, "When it Comes to Your Sons, Schools Miss the Mark,"A-24.

90. Policy Brief, "Are Boys Making the Grade? Gender Gaps in Achievement and Attainment," Rennie Center for Educational Research and Policy, October 2006 (www.renniecenter.org), 2.

91. Laura Venderkam, "The Tuition Game," USA Today, March 26, 2008, A-11.

92. Sharon Jayson, "Totally Wireless on Campus; Today's Young 'Digital Natives' Can't Live, or Study, Without Technology," USA Today, Oct. 3, 2006, D-1.

93. Across the USA, USA Today, Sept. 25, 2006, A-15.

94. National Association of Colleges and Employers, 62 Highland Ave., Bethlehem, PA 18017; NACEWeb (www.naceweb.org/).

95. Mary Beth Marklein, "Panel Urges Collegians to Focus on the Liberal Arts," USA Today, Jan. 11, 2007, D-9.

96. Barbara Hagenbaugh, "More Employers Recruit the Military Work Ethic," USA Today, Feb. 16, 2007, B-1.

97. Across the USA, USA Today, Apr. 20, 2007, A-8.

98. Alan M. Webber, "Business with a Higher Purpose," USA Today, Oct. 10, 2006, A-13.

99. Across the USA, USA Today, June 28, 2007, A-7.

100. Lori Higgins, "Michigan School District Cracks Down on Cellphones, iPods," USA Today, July 25, 2007, D-7.

101. Nancy Cole, Letters to the Editor, USA Today, Nov. 9, 1998, A-24.

102. John Bacon, "Is Cheating by Students Prevalent in Texas?" USA Today, June 4, 2007, A-3.

103. Craig Wilson, "Colleges Offer Choice of Major—and Headstone," USA Today, May 30, 2007, D-1.

104. Jim Hopkins, "Are Campuses Becoming Battlegrounds?" USA Today, Mar. 22, 2006, B-2.

105. Barbara Hagenbaugh, "Most Teenagers Forgo Summer Jobs," USA Today, July 9, 2007, A-1.

106. Ibid., A-1.

107. Jack Stripling, "Out in 4 Years?" Opelika-Auburn News, May 13, 2005, 1A.

108. Donna Leinwand, "College Drug Use, Binge Drinking Rise," USA Today, Mar. 15, 2007, A-3.

109. Sharon Jayson, "Schools 'Infested' with Drugs? It Depends," *USA Today*, Aug. 16, 2007, D-7.
110. C. M. Meston and D. M. Buss, "Why Humans Have Sex," *Archives of Sexual Behavior* 36(4), Aug. 2007, 477.
111. A. Jones and M. Miley, "Abstinence Approach Not the Only Sex-Ed Option," *USA Today*, Oct. 31, 2007, A-11.
112. Sharon Jayson, "Abstinence Message Goes Beyond Teens," *USA Today*, Oct. 31, 2006, A-1.
113. Ibid., A-1.
114. Jayson, "Abstinence Message Goes Beyond Teens," A-1.
115. Ibid., A-1.
116. Sharon Jayson, "What's Up with Hookups?" *USA Today*, Feb. 15, 2007, D-10.
117. M. Holmes and T. Hutchinson, *Girlology Hang-Ups, Hook-Ups, and Holding Out: Stuff You Need to Know About Your Body, Sex, and Dating* (Deerfield Beach: Health Communications, 2007).
118. L. Stepp, *Unhooked: How Young Women Pursue Sex, Delay Love and Lose at Both* (New York: Riverhead Books, 2007).
119. Reported in Center for Disease Control publication, "Our Voices, Our Lives, Our Futures: Youth and STD."
120. Norval Stephens, Letters to the Editor, *USA Today*, Jan. 31, 2006, A-10.
121. Ibid., A-10.
122. Marissa DeCuir, "States Get Creative in Fight Against Underage Drinking," *USA Today*, July 19, 2007, A-1.
123. Michael J. Bradley, "The Heart and Soul of the Next Generation" (Gig Harbor: Harbor Press, 2007).
124. Sharon Jayson, "Gen Nexters Have Their Hands Full," *USA Today*, Aug. 21, 2006, D-2.
125. Ibid., D-2.
126. Ibid., D-2.
127. Michelle Healy, "College Students Take Lead in Volunteering," *USA Today*, Oct. 17, 2006, D-9.
128. Pacific Garden Mission, 1458 N. Canal Street, Chicago, IL 60607 (www.pgm.org).
129. Source unknown.